London Street

London Street

A Memoir

Jane E. Griffioen

RESOURCE *Publications* · Eugene, Oregon

LONDON STREET

Resource Publications
An Imprint of Wipf and Stock Publishers
199 W. 8th Ave., Suite 3
Eugene, OR 97401

www.wipfandstock.com

PAPERBACK ISBN: 978-1-7252-6755-8
HARDCOVER ISBN: 978-1-7252-6756-5
EBOOK ISBN: 978-1-7252-6757-2

Manufactured in the U.S.A.   05/21/20

For Mom

My father said a line called the antithesis separated some of us from others. The line often included five or six houses on our street before it changed direction. Sometimes it curved in front of only one or two houses before turning, like a snake slithers over one certain rock, yet other times coils around three or four. Except a snake is often concealed, whereas the antithesis was obvious. If you knew your theology well. Or so my father would say.

Een

T he last time something like this happened, my father pointed his finger at us and said, "Get upstairs and stay there."

We did as we were told. We watched from the top of the stairway as the stranger with a black satchel entered my parents' bedroom. Only minutes later we disobeyed and chased down the steps to follow the two men in white uniforms. They carried my mother on a stretcher outdoors and into a station wagon with red flashing lights. Father jumped in the back as the attendants slammed the double doors. We could still hear the siren even after the speeding ambulance turned the corner.

My mother returned seven days later. By then, the memory of the vivid red liquid all over her bed was fading and I had a new baby brother who came home with her.

I was four then. This time, a year later, no doctor came to the house. No stretcher or ambulance or hideous sheets. But I counted six days since my mother went away.

In the kitchen of our house on London Street, a furnace register was located in the floor between the refrigerator and the basement door. Mother often stood there on the register, leaning against the corner where the vine-printed wallpapers met. Quiet, arms crossed, cardigan sweater over her housedress, slippers on her feet. When I came in from sledding or ice-skating, sometimes she would share the grilled square so I could thaw my toes. Or sometimes I would pretend a chill in the late afternoon and Mother would make room for me to stand and share the warmth.

Eleven days since my mother was gone, a heaviness followed me around like I was homesick in our own house. Father said she was in the hospital. I walked into Mother's bedroom and helped myself to her variegated-knit slippers. I took the old cardigan down from the peg in the basement-way and slipped it on. I stood on the kitchen register, arms crossed.

I kept counting the days.

Day fifteen. We finished our supper and waited around the table while my father ate a second helping. He cleaned his plate, opened the King James Version of the Bible and read a chapter.

Before he began the prayer, I piped up. "Will Mom bring a baby home again?"

"No, Janie," he answered in a low voice, hands folded on the Bible in his lap.

"How long will Mom be gone?" my brother Bobo asked, now that I had mentioned it.

"I don't know." Father crossed his legs and rubbed his forehead with thick, stubby fingers.

"I'm sick of Campbell's soup," Bobo said. Mother always served casserole on Wednesday.

"Fold your hands," Father told us, cutting any other complaints short. "Gracious God and heavenly Father, we come unto Thee in this evening hour . . ." He swallowed. A big noisy swallow. ". . . Be merciful unto us and forgive us our many sins. In Jesus' name. Amen." He said the word "Amen" with a broad "a." "Aah-men."

There was no more discussion about Mother. My older sisters—eleven-year-old Babe, twelve-year-old Deannie, and Gracia, already fifteen—wouldn't talk about it.

If I needed to know more, someone would tell me.

My father worked at the grocery store six days a week. A butcher. Short and stocky and solid. He kept fit carrying around sides of beef. He had a second job at another grocery store on Tuesday and Friday nights. Every Monday night was Sunday School Teachers' Meeting, which he never missed, even while Mother was gone. He visited Mother three or four times a week. When he came home those nights, I wished I dared to climb out of bed and ask about her. But I didn't.

No one else spoke to me about my mother. Not my kindergarten teacher, not the kids in my class, not the neighbors, not people from our church.

Another week went by.

On Saturday, we ate pancakes for lunch. My brother, Bobo, is two years older and a head taller than me. "Your pancakes are so good," he told Father, and sopped up the remaining syrup on his plate with his last bite.

My father did not reply. He read aloud from the Bible and when finished, folded his hands and laid them over the closed book. "We're going to see your mother tomorrow." He pursed his lips and told us, "Fold your hands now." In other words, end of subject.

I squirmed and peeked at my sisters, their eyes closed, their hands folded on the table. Arie J sat in his highchair, content with a sipper-tumbler of milk and a messy graham cracker. I squeezed my eyes shut and put my folded hands on the sticky table in front of me, wondering what a hospital looked like inside. I peeked again. Bobo saw me. I pinched my eyes closed.

". . . Guide us by Thy Word and Spirit. Be merciful unto us and forgive us our many sins. In Jesus' name. Aah-men."

We arrived late for church the next day, something that never happened when my mother was home. We were unable to sit in the third row from the front like we usually did. The ushers set up folding chairs in the side aisle and we sat at the edge of the congregation. When the minister prayed for the "sick and shut-in," he omitted Mother's name again. I wished he would remember.

Sunday dinner tasted like most of our Sunday dinners since Father gave instructions how to cook the beef roast every week anyway. At the end of our meal, he read Galatians 6. After we prayed, he went outside to back the car out of the garage while I was allowed to help dry the dishes. Father let me sit in the front, but Bobo got the window seat because he was a boy. Gracia, Deannie, and Babe sat in the middle seat with Arie J. The rear seat of the station wagon was empty this time.

Although the air was cold, the sun was out and I saw traces of water around the edges of the snow banks.

"How many miles is it?" Bobo asked.

"Not too many," Father said.

The top of my rubber boots pressed between my legs and the edge of the seat. When we stopped at a red light, I recognized a hardware store on the corner. "This is the way we take to Jackie's. Are we going there, too?"

"No. We don't have to go that far," he explained.

I was glad about that. Jackie was my oldest sister. Her husband would have the television on and Father would be upset they watched a ballgame on Sunday like they belonged on the other side of the antithesis he always talked about.

Father turned the station wagon into a drive off 68th Street. Through the pine trees, I saw a rectangular building four windows tall. Father parked the wagon in a large parking lot that was bordered with pine trees on three sides.

We scuffled across the parking area, our rubber boots dragging on the pavement. Arie J walked slowly, assisted by the older girls. My father, in his Sunday overcoat and brimmed hat, walked between Bobo and me, holding our mittened hands. We climbed six concrete steps at the front of the building and went through the first set of doors. There were three more steps, not as steep and with a silver finish on the edges. Another set of doors, this time heavy and wooden, opened into a lobby.

Shiny little marble-like stones covered the cemented floor inside. The lobby looked huge, with a high ceiling like church. When Father put his index finger to his mouth with a "shhhh," I could hear our rubber boots echo as we walked. Two other doors inside the lobby had big brass doorknobs with large keyholes underneath. Each door had a window with thick wire screen in the glass. A single green vinyl chair sat in the back corner next to a counter. The rest of the lobby was empty except for a bench in the center.

Removing his hat, Father ran a hand over his crew cut and pointed to the bench. "Wait here," he commanded.

He spoke quietly for a minute with a lady in a white uniform and nurse's hat behind the counter. When he followed her across the room, her white thick-soled shoes were silent. But her jangling keys rattled loudly.

We watched without making a peep. The lady unlocked a door and held it open. Father passed through without us. As the heavy wooden door closed, the nurse checked the lock. She gave us a quick smile and returned to her station. We could only see the top of her cap when she sat down.

The bench was long enough for all of us. Arie J blabbered, his sounds somewhat comforting to me. After what seemed a long while, my sisters had a hard time keeping Arie J settled. Gracia let him practice walking along the length of the bench where we waited.

My curiosity was shrinking. I wanted to see my mother, but felt a hesitation I couldn't identify. I only knew I didn't like it.

My wool coat pricked my skin. I lifted one side and scratched the top of my leg.

Bobo whispered loudly to me, "Don't itch your butt here."

I wished Father would return.

Each of us took a turn entertaining Arie J. At last Father's face appeared at the window. He knocked lightly and the nurse behind the station walked over with the keys and unlocked the door. He followed her to the counter while Deannie held my arm and kept me back.

"Come with me," Father told us. He carried Arie J and grasped my hand while Gracia, Deannie, Babe and Bobo walked behind. I wished those keys weren't so noisy. The nurse unlocked the door once more. "We won't be long," Father said to her as we passed through.

We climbed more steps until we came to a double door. I saw a doorbell. The buzzer startled me when Father pushed it.

I heard more keys.

The doors opened. There was better lighting here than in the lobby where we waited so long. This area looked much smaller, but had a familiar looking counter in the corner. Besides the lady who unlocked the door, two more nurses stood behind the station. One smiled at our procession.

We continued follow-the-leader as my father proceeded down one of the halls. Our rubber boots shuffled along the floor. Each door had numbers. I counted five before Father stopped, turning to check if we were all there, and went in.

The small room looked dark compared to the hallway. My eyes adjusted and I could see two beds pushed into the corners along opposite walls. I lingered in the door with Father as my sisters and older brother went ahead. I noticed a woman in the bed on one side of the room, not my mother. When I looked to the other side, I saw Mother lying on the sterile bleached-white sheets. She had lost weight, her pale face looked worn out. She had her glasses on. The way her hair stuck up between her head and her pillow scared me.

Babe got closer and Deannie followed behind Gracia. Bobo hesitated. My father stepped forward and led him toward the bed. They lined up along the side while Father held the baby and I stood at the foot of the bed.

It seemed to take a lot of effort for my mother to reach out her long, bare arm. The bed was raised enough so her head and shoulders were elevated, but she strained to kiss us as, one by one, we took a turn near her.

"Hi, Honey," she said when it was my turn. I could feel trembling when we touched to kiss.

An awkward hush in the room lasted until a soft, raspy voice came from the opposite bed. "Your children are beautiful."

"Thank you," Mother said quietly.

No one had ever called us beautiful before. We were not unfamiliar with kindness, but the stranger's comment seemed exaggerated. I crouched closer to my father.

Father lifted Arie J from my mother's hug and brought the baby to Gracia. He returned and gave Mother a long kiss on the forehead, picked up her hand and squeezed it.

I wished my mother wouldn't cry.

"Good-bye, Honey," he said to her. He rose from the bed and motioned for us to follow him into the hall where he blew his nose loudly.

Our rubber boots shuffled down the hall, through the doors unlocked with jangling keys, out onto the sidewalk and into the parking lot.

On the way home, Arie J sat in the front seat and fell asleep after a drink from his bottle. Bobo asked if we could listen to the car radio. Deannie wondered out loud if it might be too late to go to church that night.

I wished the window of my mother's room didn't look like jail.

Twee

My mother came home in early spring. I didn't know what made her sick and I didn't know why nobody talked about it. I didn't know what made her better, but one evening as we were eating our supper, Father announced, "Your mother's coming home tomorrow," and that was that.

Summer brought warm weather, hopscotch in the backyard, Wiffle ball in the street and Popsicles from Sid's grocery on Wednesday afternoons.

Our green, two-story house at 711 London stood halfway down the north side of the street. Most houses on the block were two-story, each set apart by a single, concrete driveway. There were no attached garages. Houses with attached garages were for big shots, my mother would say.

"Don't lock the gate!" I called, chasing Bobo up the driveway.

He was inside before I could unhook the latch. "Mom! What time is it?" I heard him yell over the noisy window fan. "Can we go get Popsicles now?"

The screen door slammed behind me.

"Shhh! Arie J's sleeping." Mother's voice sounded sharp. "You have to wait for Babe." My sister Babe's real name is Aleda. But no one called her that except maybe her teachers.

"She's in the back yard," Bobo said. "I'll give her the money."

"I can carry my own money." I followed Mother into the bedroom.

She took a purse out of the closet and sat down on the bed. Because of the hot weather, her eyeglasses slid down on her nose. She wore her sleeveless housedress and the freckles that spotted her arms showed. Her brunette hair, bobbed in a home permanent wave, didn't match our blond hair. By the brown blotches on the towels in the basement, I knew Mother colored it.

She pulled out a red vinyl billfold and took three nickels from the coin section. "Don't lose it," she said, putting a nickel in my hand.

"I'll take Babe's money," Bobo repeated.

We ran out the back door, the coins already sweaty in our hands.

"Babe! Make sure you're back before 3:30," Mother called.

Our cemented backyard was wrapped in white picket fence, a foot and a half of garden in between. The gate hooks and latches, giving my mother peace of mind when Arie J was playing outside. Father made a small ice pond one winter in the backyard where I learned to skate behind an old dining room chair. The cement cracked in several places that year.

Along the fence, crocus poked out in late March, perennials flowered all summer. Chrysanthemum took over in the fall. In two corners of the backyard, lilac trees grew, one purple, the other white, and around Mother's Day, we could smell them from the house.

My mother also grew rose bushes. On Saturdays in the summer, she would cut a bud, just one, barely opened, and place it in a vase on the coffee table in the living room, in case *bizonder* company came on Sunday. Special company or not, my sisters and I were required to help in a thorough cleaning ritual on Saturdays that rarely included any dust or dirt since Mother cleaned every day except Sunday anyway. Where we lived, a clean house was a Godly house.

"Where's my money?" Babe wanted to know.

"I have it," Bobo told her.

"Gimme it," Babe said.

He took off down the driveway, but she caught up before he reached the sidewalk.

"Gimme it," my sister demanded as she grabbed his arm, skinny as a chicken bone, and started to slowly twist it.

Bobo opened his hand and let the nickel drop. When the coin hit the cement, Babe stomped her foot on it. I placed my nickel safely in the deep pocket of my shorts, wiping a sweaty hand on the side of my shirt.

"I'm getting grape," I said, starting down the sidewalk.

Babe caught up. "You always get grape."

Bobo walked next to me, but in the curb. His sweaty face flushed. "I'm getting orange," he told us.

"You always get orange," Babe said.

At one time, London Street was just an alley between two wider streets so now there wasn't any lawn between the sidewalk and the curb as the other blocks had. But all the concrete was swept tidy, like in the old country. In The Netherlands, *straat klompen danseren* push a broom while dancing in wooden shoes to the folk songs.

My maternal grandmother, *Grootmoe*, and my Aunt Dienke moved to London Street two years ago, in 1955, and lived across the narrow street from us. Grootmoe had more tulips and lilacs than we did. And roses. Mother used to pull Bobo and me in the red wagon every Tuesday to visit when they lived up the hill not quite a mile away. Up the hill the neighborhood was rougher than London Street. Up the hill were more *sortjes*. *Sortjes* are something like transients and slum people combined. *Sortjes* are on the wrong side of the antithesis.

Anticipating our Popsicles, we hurried down the sidewalk and passed the VanderGoots next door. Their lawn was the greenest on the block. Mr. VanderGoot never used a sprinkler. He hand-sprayed the lawn, walking back and forth with a garden hose, wearing his wooden shoes. One never walked on VanderGoots' grass. If any of us kids forgot the rule, we'd hear a loud rap at the window, followed by harsh words Mr. VanderGoot hollered in Dutch.

Richters were the next house. Definitely *sortje*.

I knew the names of all the people between home and the corner. DeBoers, Posts, Hoekstras. Most went to our church. Not the Hoogeveens, though. They went to the Reformed Church, the church our church broke off from. The Reformed Church allowed lodge membership, Father said, and sent their kids to the public school where people wanted to be part of the world and didn't understand the antithesis. That might be, but Mr. Hoogeveen was a nice man who always waved when we passed.

"Hey! Wait up!" I called to my sister.

"You need to learn to get it in gear if you're going to first grade," Babe said.

Bobo waited at the corner.

Sid's grocery was two blocks up, which seemed extra far today. I reached way down in my pocket to check the nickel. The entire month had been so hot and dry that a sprinkling ban was in effect in Grand Rapids. Large trees shaded London Street but now, walking along Clyde Park, we were in the direct sun.

When we passed the stone parking lot, Bobo kicked as many stones as he could with one swipe, spilling them over onto the sidewalk. We came to Lynch Street and the paved parking lot. I copied Babe and balanced on the cement bumpers at the side of the blacktop.

Across the street was Kelvinator, a factory four stories high and five blocks long counting the warehouse and yard. Once a year the factory held an open house. Mother took us one afternoon to watch the assembly line where they made refrigerators. They served us free Kool-Aid and cookies.

At least a dozen men from London Street worked at Kelvinator. If I happened to be on the corner when the 3:30 whistle blew, I could also see women leaving the factory. Women with short black greasy hair and cigarettes in their mouths. They wore tight pants with zippers in the front. I could tell what side of the antithesis they were on.

Crossing the side street, Babe and I caught up to Bobo who sat on the front steps, wiping the sweat off his face with his shirt. He jumped up and opened the wooden screen door.

Sid VanderPloeg, a fat, long-faced man, looked up from the cash register but said nothing. The freezer was in the last aisle to the left, but we went the other way. Our ritual required that we walk through all three aisles to check everything out like we did at the grocery where our father worked. Except where Father worked, the store had six aisles twice as long.

At Sid's, customers could get to the butcher shop through the double swinging doors next to the ice cream freezer. We were familiar with the smell of raw meat, so even on this simmering afternoon, the odor from the adjacent shop hardly fazed us.

Babe lifted the chrome knob on the glass door, opening a third of the top of the chest. Four cardboard boxes held different flavored Popsicles, push-ups, paddle-pops and fudgesicles.

"Hurry up and close that freezer case," Mr. VanderPloeg barked at us. "This heat and my electric bill." He wiped his large forehead with the bottom of his white butcher apron.

Babe took cherry, Bobo took orange, I took grape. We brought out our nickels and set them on the black counter-top, taking a minute to eye the candy displayed behind the counter. We listened for the little bell to ding as Mr. VanderPloeg opened the till.

The noisy ceiling fan ran full blast. Mr. VanderPloeg never said another word. He belonged to our church but we didn't like him. In fact, we were afraid of him. We went out, letting the door slam behind us.

Cement steps along the front of the butcher shop and grocery didn't have shade, but the three of us sat on the steps anyway, like we always did to enjoy our treat. We were soon slicking and slurping hard and fast. I worried the sun would beat me to the last delicious lick. The bottom of my short-shorts gapped and the purple drips ran freely up my leg.

According to Mother, we had to get home by 3:30, before the Kelvinator traffic. I licked my fingers on the way. Reaching London Street, we saw water fanning back and forth from DeLeeuws' lawn sprinkler. Bobo ran right through it. I put my hands in and rubbed them together to remove the stickiness.

"Chicken," Bobo teased.

"Am not," I answered.

"Are too."

I ran through and screamed.

"Get out of there!" Babe warned. "You're gonna get it!"

Bobo stopped and raised his eyebrows. Over the summer, they had bleached almost invisible. "How come?"

"Not supposed to sprinkle, remember?" Babe used her know-it-all big sister tone.

We took off running.

"DeLeeuws are sprinkling!" Bobo called when he saw our mother on the screened front porch. "Mom! Should we call the police or something?"

She held Arie J on her lap with one hand and with the other, tilted a glass of iced tea on the chair's aluminum arm. "The ban is for every other day," Mother explained. "People with even house numbers sprinkle on the even days and people with odd numbers sprinkle on the odd days."

"Whew," I said. That was my best friend, Barbie DeLeeuw's house.

Sometimes Mother let me run through the sprinkler in my bathing suit. Though the lawn was yellow and prickly, it would have been fun to cool off today. There would be a complete ban on all sprinkling if it didn't rain by week's end. Then it wouldn't matter if one were even or odd.

It was Thursday, so we had pork chops for supper. When we finished eating, Father read the Bible aloud and prayed. We were reading the book of Hebrews. He read chapter 3. He always read the entire chapter.

That evening, we heard distant thunder. Before bed, Father washed my face, hands and arms at the bathroom sink. He sat me on the edge of the tub to wipe down my sticky legs with the washcloth.

The thunder came louder.

By the time I knelt in the bedroom next to my father to recite, "Now I lay me down to sleep," I saw lightning. Soon, after my father left the bedroom, it was sprinkling on the window. Before I fell asleep, the drops fell hard and long.

And it rained on both sides of the antithesis.

Drie

E very day but Sunday, my father got up at five in the morning to make a fresh pot of coffee and a bowl of oatmeal. Butchers had to be to work by 6 to put up meat before the grocery store opened. Sometimes Father let me watch him make his breakfast before sending me back to bed. When he finished the oatmeal, he would mix two raw eggs and a teaspoon of sugar in a plastic cup. He beat the egg with a spoon in the cup and drank the thick foamy mixture in a few swallows.

But today was Sunday, the day we ate breakfast together. There wouldn't be oatmeal or the clatter of raw eggs beaten in a plastic cup. Instead, we would have raisin bread with frosting for breakfast. There would be no meat cutting, no going to the store. The store wasn't open. Not on Sunday. People on the right side of the antithesis went to church on Sunday. Twice.

Mother came into the kitchen carrying Arie J, the quilting thread on her housecoat undone and one of the flat white buttons down the front missing. She put Arie J in the highchair. Still in our pajamas, each of us found a place at the table.

We needed to look our Sunday best today. Just like Mother, Gracia wore dozens of bobby pins in her hair. Deannie had brush rollers held in place with plastic picks. Babe's were sponge curlers. I wore the rags Mother twisted my hair around and tied at the top of my head every Saturday night. When the white strips were taken out on Sunday morning, my long blond hair would be set in tight, perfect pipe curls.

Only I didn't like pipe curls.

Father came to the table in his T-shirt and trousers and we all hushed up.

"Gracious God and Heavenly Father . . ."

I kept an eye on the raisin bread while my father prayed.

Usually after Sunday breakfast, Deannie prepared the beef roast for dinner. Mother gave basic instructions, though Father, the meat man, always added a comment like "Put a little nutmeg on there" or "Be sure the oven's not too hot, *hoor*?" Father liked to end his sentences with the Dutch word for "hear."

But today a beef roast was not prepared because it was the second Sunday of the month and on the second Sunday of the month we ate our dinner at Dienke's house.

Father backed the 1955 Mercury wagon out of the one-stall garage and left it running in the driveway to warm up. To keep the chill off, I wore a white cardigan over my Sunday dress, but those little white anklets of mine didn't keep my legs warm. My sisters and I scrambled into the middle seat, squishing down our starched petticoats. Bobo climbed in the bench facing backward, where I often sat with him—but not on Sunday. Not with my best dress on.

Our church, at the end of Van Raalte Drive on Roosevelt Park Hill, was a structure my father said either loomed over the neighborhood or lent a visible solace, depending on what side of the antithesis you were. The school building where I attended second grade was next to the church. All that separated the church from the school was a sidewalk, and all that separated the church and the school from London Street was four blocks.

Father dropped us off at the steeple-side of the large brick church, and then drove around the one-way block to park on the hill.

The purpose of the worship service wasn't social, Father said, so no greeters met us at the door. But we always arrived early enough to shake hands with Mr. Kamps, the janitor.

"*Hoe ist te mae*?" Mother said as we waited for my father.

"Pearl! *Hoe ist*?" Mr. Kamps answered. My mother's name is *Peiterke*, the feminine of Peter in the Netherlands. Somehow, it translated to "Pearl" in America.

Close to four hundred families belonged to our church. My parents only visited with a few of them. The Kamps were one. In the summer, we went to Gun Lake for picnics with them. Sometimes they came over on Sunday night, and though I was already put to bed, I could smell the coffee and pig-in-the-blanket Mother would serve.

Mr. Kamps smiled at me this morning, shook my hand and went up the stairs to ring the church bell.

As the first bells sounded, my father came through the door. Exactly nine o'clock. He removed his hat and placed it above the coat rack in the back vestibule. If a woman wore a coat to church, she kept it on. Women always kept their hats on.

Every Sunday we arrived earlier than the ushers. Father preferred leading his own procession into the sanctuary. When he stopped at the pew on the right, third from the front, he turned and indicated for us to go ahead—first Gracia, Deannie, Babe, and me. Next came my mother, Arie J, my father, and then Bobo. Being the oldest boy, he was allowed the end seat.

The front of the church stretched wide and immeasurably tall. In the center, a stained-glass window portraying Jesus as The Good Shepherd reached almost to the ceiling. I had to stretch my neck and tip my head back to see the entire picture. The Good Shepherd, in a pale blue robe and sandals, grasped a staff in one hand while holding a small lamb in the other.

Organ pipes were mounted on each side of the Good Shepherd window. I spent many long sermons occupied with those pipes, counting them, pretending the shiny forms were kings and queens or soldiers. Once I imagined the stiff rows of vertical pipes were brassy, mechanical men and women with gaping mouths, which scared me. I didn't want to think about that again.

The choir loft was a recent addition to the front of the church. Father wasn't happy about it. Every time the choir sang, we heard his disapproval in the station wagon on the way home. "The people of the congregation should sing response to God directly, not through a small group of other voices," he would say. "And what will it lead to?"

"You're right," Mother would answer each time.

The Good Shepherd in the center of the church was my favorite, but there were other beautiful windows—five stained-glass works along each side of the sanctuary and another on the back wall, each telling a piece of the biblical story. Adam and Eve walking with lions in the Garden of Eden. A large ugly snake and Adam and Eve wearing fig leaves. Noah, the rainbow, and all the pairs of animals. A Christmas star and the baby Jesus. The last window of the east wall showed three crosses that stuck out on the hill of Golgotha.

Directly across the sanctuary from the crosses was the stained-glass window with angels sitting in front of a tomb on a large rolled-away stone. "He is not here, for He is risen," the inscription read. Then, the window called The Ascension, picturing Jesus floating into the air with his hands up, like when Bobo and I played cowboys. The next window showed the inside of a church with rows of benches, a pulpit, and an open Bible. There was a window with Jesus coming down in the clouds, and finally a window of the New Jerusalem with streaks of light and streets of gold. I wasn't allowed to turn around in church and, because it was the window farthest back, I seldom saw the New Jerusalem.

While the elders came through the side door of the sanctuary and filed into a pew reserved for them, Mr. Kamps rang the church bell again. The minister approached the pulpit, wearing a black flowing robe over his dark suit. He sat down in an upholstered chair and bowed his head in prayer. He waited for the organist to finish the prelude before rising to the pulpit.

"The Lord is in His holy temple. Let all the earth keep silence before Him."

A moment of silent prayer.

"Beloved congregation of our Lord Jesus Christ; grace, mercy, and peace be unto you from God the Father, and from our Lord Jesus Christ, through the operation of the Holy Spirit. Amen." He pronounced the "Amen" with the same broad "a" as my father.

The congregation stood and sang Psalm 122, a song of the Israelites, God's ancient chosen people and on the right side of the antithesis. They were glad to go up to God's house and worship Him there. Their care for God's house would never cease.

After the minister read the Law of Moses to "mirror our sins," he always said, the congregation sang a penitential Psalm. I recognized Psalm 51. Father and Mother often sang it at home. They sang a lot of Psalms at home. I knew a lot of them by heart.

The long congregational prayer gave me plenty of time to peek and look around, but risked a pinch from my mother. A black and blue spot on my upper left arm still showed from last week, under my sweater.

The sermon began. Now we could have our peppermints.

Forty minutes passed. When the minister gave the Benediction, I paid attention. "The Lord bless thee and keep thee. The Lord lift up His countenance upon thee. The Lord be gracious unto thee and give thee peace. Aah-men."

With an extra peppermint in my purse and coins for Uncle Bob's kids in Africa, I headed eagerly to Sunday School, along with Bobo and my father, who was the Sunday School superintendent.

We never called my Grandmother's house "Grootmoe's house," but instead, we said "Dienke's." Aunt Dienke already had ten place settings spread on the crisp lace tablecloth when we got there. At our house, we ate in the dining room only on Thanksgiving, Christmas and Easter. At Dienke's, we ate in the dining room every time and we visited in the living room, a place in our house reserved for grown-ups.

Dienke nodded a greeting, took our coats and sweaters and laid them carefully on Grootmoe's bed. We had changed out of our best clothes as soon as we got home from church. I wore one of my school dresses that used to be Babe's that used to be Deannie's. We weren't allowed to wear play clothes and girls were not allowed to wear pants. Because it was Sunday.

"*Komest hier te zitten,*" Grootmoe softly called, pointing to the couch. I could see freckles and age spots on her wrinkled arm.

I never heard Grootmoe speak any English, although she had been in America for more than twenty years. She sat in her chair next to the living room window where she could see our house. She wore thin wire glasses with round lenses, the same shape as her face. Her grayish-white hair was pulled neatly, but not tight, into a bun fastened invisibly with hairpins. Her dark navy print dress was almost long enough to reach her black, thick-heeled shoes.

I walked over to my grandmother while holding Father's hand and waited for his cue. Bobo held Father's other hand.

"*Hoe ist?*" Father dropped Bobo's hand and extended his to my grandmother. Grootmoe took it warmly in both her hands, pursing her lips while nodding her head in reply.

"Say hello to Grootmoe," he reminded Bobo.

"Hello," Bobo managed quietly, half extending his hand to her. She took it between her hands and held it there, pursing her lips while nodding her head.

"Say hello to Grootmoe," Father cued me.

"Hello," I squeaked shyly, not extending my hand. But Grootmoe reached and gently took it in both her hands, pursed her lips and nodded in reply.

We went to the couch where I sat on Father's lap while my three older sisters greeted our grandmother. When Babe and Deannie each extended their hand, Grootmoe repeated her response.

Gracia was last in line. "Hello," she said and offered her hand. Grootmoe took it warmly in both her hands, pursed her lips and nodded her head. "*Arme kind.*" She reached up and brushed Gracia's cheek slowly with two fingers. "*Arme kind,*" Grootmoe repeated quietly, inhaling the words in short gasps as if afraid to speak either Dutch or English.

I knew the phrase meant "poor child," but didn't understand why Grootmoe called my sister that.

With the ritual of good manners and respect finished, I sat quietly with my hands folded. The room had a certain smell. "Old," my nose said. A delicately crocheted doily rested on the back of Grootmoe's rocking chair. A matching doily was spread out on the chair in the archway that divided the living room from the dining room. On Grootmoe's left, a small bookcase with glass doors held a-half-dozen books in Dutch and a Delft tobacco jar with a silver lid. Above the bookcase hung the dark brown cuckoo clock, always accurate. When the bird popped out, Father let me stand close, next to Grootmoe, to watch and listen to the cuckoo call.

Dienke entered the archway. "*Eten,*" was all she said.

We knew where to sit. When we were in our places, Dienke took Grootmoe's arm and helped her walk from the living room to the table. Grootmoe bent and slowly lowered herself onto the cushioned chair.

"Orie will pray," Dienke said, giving my father's name, Arie, the informal pronunciation.

Orie always prayed.

"Gracious God and Heavenly Father, we draw nigh unto Thee in this noon hour . . ."

Keeping my head bowed but one eye open, I could see to the end of the table. Both Mother's and Dienke's hands were folded on their printed, crispy half-aprons. During the week, butcher aprons Father had taken home from work served the purpose. But this was Sunday.

One by one, we each said our prayer. "Lord bless this food forJesussakeamen."

Sunday dinners were always *bejzonderis* but when we ate our dinner at Dienke's, an even bigger occasion took place. In addition to the lace tablecloth, pretty starched aprons, and fine china, Dienke served two vegetables, whipped potatoes and gravy, a platter of meat full enough for second helpings, bread-end bakery rolls. And Dienke always served dessert.

"Orie will read," Dienke announced when we had finished.

Orie always read.

He read Hebrews eleven, about the faith of our fathers. It was a long chapter—forty verses—and I fidgeted once too often. He stopped in the middle of a verse and with his head still down, raised his hand in my direction. "Janie Ellen. You sit still and listen, *hoor*?" he commanded, shaking his index finger.

After he prayed, my father helped his sister-in-law bring Grootmoe to her chair in the living room and sat with her until the ladies finished the dishes. Then we walked across the street back home.

On Sunday afternoons, Dienke and Grootmoe attended the Dutch Service at our church. My mother and father took a nap. Gracia's boyfriend, John, came over every Sunday afternoon and they kissed on the couch and talked about getting married.

Sundays at 2:30 was candy bar time. Every week Father brought home a six pack of Mars Bars and we each got to have our own. As we ate our prized chocolate, Bobo and I listened to "The Children's Bible Hour" on the radio. I think Father let us listen to what he called "those Arminian songs," so we didn't interrupt his Sunday nap. Sometimes we sang along.

In the evening on Sundays, Mother walked to church if the weather permitted. My older sisters went with her, but Bobo and I got to stay home with Father and Arie J. We watched "The 20th Century" with Walter Cronkite, and "Lassie" on the television. Those two programs were the exception, the only time we were allowed to watch the television.

After all, it was Sunday.

Vier

With our squeals in lawn sprinklers, shouts of Hide and Seek, whacks of Wiffle ball and the rhythm of double-dutch jump rope slapping the sidewalk, summer again echoed along London Street. Summer seemed somehow infinite to me at eight years old. I could not imagine its end.

My father said he worked two jobs so he could pay our school tuition, so he could go fishing on Drummond Island for three days every fall, and so we could rent a cottage for a week each summer. When my best friend Barbie DeLeeuw showed me her new striped pedal pushers, I looked down at my red, hand-me-down shorts, embarrassed. Barbie's mother kept soda pop, not Kool-Aid, in their refrigerator all summer. When Barbie's father bought a new car, it meant, "never been used before." Barbie's father was a semi-truck driver. He made a lot of money Mother said. But he didn't take his family to a cottage every year.

The cottage we rented that summer had a long dock from the shore over the shallow water and ended with a platform like a "T" over the deeper water. I was learning to poke my own slimy, squirmy worms onto a fishhook. Cream-colored guts oozed out of the twisted worm like custard from the first bite of Dutch pastry. Bluegill and small perch nibbled the bait and emptied the hook as soon as I dropped it into the water.

Mother came out of the cottage with a cup of coffee.

"What time is it?" I yelled from the edge of the dock. My bare feet dangled in the water.

"You have twenty minutes to go yet," she said.

Bobo was lying in the grass near her lawn chair. "Can I at least put my bathing suit on?"

"Me too!" I said.

She ticked her tongue and sighed before finishing her coffee with one more swallow. "Okay. But hang your clothes up nice."

When Mother announced the end of the waiting period, Babe called, "I got the inner tube!" She ran with all her might and splashed Arie J playing in the sand on the shore.

Bobo followed her. "I get the air mattress!"

That left me with the Charlie the Tuna blow-up my father got free at work. I had taken swimming lessons at Garfield Park earlier in the summer and wasn't afraid to get dunked, but the fat blue tuna was slippery. On the other hand, once in the water I could get a better hold on Bobo's mattress and flip it. Which I did right away.

He came up through the water's surface, spitting and wiping his face with his hands. "Rugged," he said.

"Don't flip me. Don't flip me!" Babe shouted while both of us lunged toward the black inner tube. "Maaaaam!" she screamed just before going under.

We swam and flipped and yelled until our fingers and toes were soft and wrinkled as raisins. The next day we did it again at least three times.

Father spent a couple of hours fishing out in the rowboat in the mornings and again in the evenings but joined us in the water during the late afternoons. He would slip under the water and glide along, popping up under the mattress, tube, or tuna. Sometimes he'd help me climb on his shoulders and let me jump off.

Bobo and I made up adventures when we took the rowboat across the lake on our own. Lost in open waters, we dodged horned sea monsters. Or we rowed like madmen, oars splashing, escaping pirates. We took our adventure stories home, play-acting them over and over until the next summer.

It seemed to me that when rich people went on vacation, they traveled. I was glad we couldn't afford to make trips.

∽

Painted white bricks that my father painstakingly set on top of each other outlined the edge of our driveway, making a rickrack trim in the dirt. I practiced walking on top of them when I thought no one was looking. Yet when the bricks were tilted, my father admonished me, not Bobo or my sisters.

In the small space of grass between our driveway and the VanderGoots, a decorative wooden windmill about my height stood exactly like the one in Grootmoe's grassy backyard. Uncle Gerritt built them. Every spring, glossy red and yellow tulips from the old country surrounded the windmills.

At the end of our driveway, a large maple tree grew. A squirrel lived there. Bobo and I put a peppermint near the end of the trunk where a dent in an old root stuck up in the grass. We spied from the garage until the squirrel swiped the candy and ran back into the top of the tree. We made a daily thing of it. Before the end of the summer, the squirrel dared to nibble on the peppermint in his paws before climbing to stash it somewhere in the branches.

The large maple grew on our property, but most of the afternoon shade fell on the VanderGoots' lawn, a problem if Mr. VanderGoot was home. One very hot sticky day in late July, I stretched out on my stomach in the shade, bare feet in the air. Theresa VanderGoot, a year older than Babe and a year younger than Deannie, came and sat down in the grass.

"Want to make necklace chains?" Theresa asked.

A chance to hang out with the older girls didn't happen often. "Sure," I said.

We gathered dandelions. After picking off the yellow flower, we stuck the hollow ends of the stems into each other and formed chains large enough to put our heads through.

"Do you like butter?" I asked her.

"Oh, yes." Theresa lifted her chin. When I put a flower to her neck, it reflected yellow on her skin.

My mother came outside and moved the sprinkler further along the lawn. Mrs. VanderGoot knocked on the glass window of her porch and called into the side yard. "*Peitje? Hoe ist?*"

"*Ik ben het benaauwd*," Mother answered, emphasizing the closeness in the thick, humid air.

Mrs. VanderGoot, older and often housebound, gestured to come by waving her arm. My mother stepped onto the grass. After crossing the lawn, she came up the neighbor's cement stoop and entered the porch for a visit and a lemonade.

Other days that summer, I made a clothesline tent with an old bedspread and bricks. Inside the tent, I read books from the church library. *Rebecca of Sunnybrook Farm, The Five Little Peppers and How They Grew, Beautiful Joe.* Later in the afternoon, I would strap on my roller skates and twist the square screws with a key my mother had laced onto a string. When I accidentally dropped it, the key rang like a mechanic's small pliers on the cement. Finally on my way, the steel wheels would sing along the concrete, punctuated with the regular rhythm of cracks in the sidewalk.

Now and then on Wednesdays, Mother gave us a dime rather than a nickel. On those days, instead of our trip for Popsicles we hiked past the park, beyond the Pepsi bottling plant, and down to George's Drive-in where we bought soft ice cream piled in swirls on fresh cones.

Every summer, one of the neighborhood churches offered Daily Vacation Bible School. Each year I asked my father if I could attend Bible school and each year he would answer, "No. Of course not."

Except this year, when my mother convinced him otherwise.

"*Aach, laat haar mag geworden,*" she said, which meant something like just let me go ahead and do it. "It's no worse than 'Children's Bible Hour.' They hear that every week," Mother pointed out.

"But what will it lead to?" Father asked.

It led to ten mornings of singing, Bible stories, coloring, cutting, gluing, punch and cookies with the Arminians. Father said Jacob Arminius, a minister in Amsterdam long ago, stood against John Calvin. Jacob Arminius believed in freewill. "If you believe in freewill," Father told us, "you deny God's Sovereignty. That's all there's to it."

Barbie DeLeeuw and I rode our bikes to Bible school those mornings that summer. We pedaled by Treat's Drugs and the barbershop where Bill the barber always cut my bangs too short. We passed the Dutch store where tea, chocolates, metworst, cheese, and rubbery black licorice shared the shelves with Delft, wooden shoes, imported lace.

Jürgen's and Holtvluwer's Department Store stood at the top of Roosevelt Street hill along the way. The wooden floors in the store echoed the heels of clerks who assisted my mother when she came to buy hosiery or a handkerchief. Ceiling fans on the main and upper level rotated in a lazy silence.

Next came Haan's grocery and across the street just before Grandville Avenue made a sharp curve north, a bakery and a shoe repair shared the block. Father told me that years ago, his father owned a bookstore on this corner. One year, on Sunday, December 23rd, Father was called out of the morning worship service. The store was burning and all their customers' books laid-away for Christmas were ruined by either fire or water. Grandpa did not have insurance. He didn't believe in insurance.

Bible school was held at Bethel Christian Reformed Church. Two blocks past Bethel was the public school. The public school was my boundary. I was not permitted to walk or bike further. Nor did Father want me playing at the public school. "People who use that school are from the other side of the antithesis," he explained. "They're from the world."

People from the world had playgrounds that seemed like amusement parks compared to playgrounds at the Christian school. I pedaled my Rollfast bike there now and then anyway. I just didn't tell anybody.

A few days after Bible school finished, Barbie and I decided to ride to the public school playground together. We parked our bikes and grabbed hold of the monkey bars so we could hang upside down. As I twisted back up straight and set my feet on the ground, I noticed the boy.

Barbie stopped climbing, turned and looked. "Uh-oh. Let's get out of here."

Although a little shorter than us, he looked older. Eleven, maybe twelve. He wore dingy beige shorts and had bare feet. Both his brown striped T-shirt and his olive brown face were streaked with dirt. His wavy hair was dark, nearly black. So were his eyes.

The boy had tied one end of a kite string to his wrist. At the other end of the string, he had tied a dead mouse. He began shouting, chasing us as he whirled the string around and around, closer and closer.

"Hey, sweet blondies. Don't run away! Don't run away, I wanna touch your hair!"

I ran hard while his mouth gushed out words I hadn't heard before, words that sounded like bad words. I kept on running in the direction of our bikes.

"Hey little blondie. Com'ere. You should see what else I have. Here in my pants. Com'ere!" He caught up to me, swinging the string around like a lasso. The putrid mouse circled above my head. He stopped swinging and the rotten thing hit me in the face.

I screamed one long scream. He laughed and reeled in the string. I ran, grabbed my bike and pushed it down the sidewalk toward Barbie. The boy ran after us for a moment before turning away still laughing.

I didn't tell Mother or Father about the boy on the playground. Bible school with the Arminians was one thing, playing at the public school another. And the boy with his mouse made me fear all the more what my father said about the other side of the antithesis.

~

The morning was sunny. I skipped along the sidewalk and stopped to check the contents of my brown paper bag. Bobo carried his bag upright, walking slower than usual. I pranced past and waited for him to catch up. Reaching the tunnel, we went through its arch into the dimness. The cement walls were spray-painted with words we were not allowed to mention or repeat. The other end of the tunnel came out in front of the church.

We reached the school next and crossed over Van Raalte Drive. Roosevelt Park ran adjacent to the Christian school playground, separated by a chain-linked fence. Plaster Creek ran along the opposite side of the park.

During the wintertime, Bobo and I would ask for an empty refrigerator box at Jelsema's Hardware and drag it over to the hills in the park. After we slid down inside the cardboard box a hundred times, it would fall apart. We sat on the largest pieces and skimmed over the snow some more, our hands with double mittens clinging to the sides of the cardboard. Once last winter, some rough kids pushed us around and swiped our cardboard box. Bobo and I never told anybody. We just went home and took turns on the kitchen register.

The only equipment on our school's playground happened to be a set of monkey bars. On this particular summer day, they served as a jail for our cowboy and Indian game. We ran like wild horses around the border of the entire playground. When we returned to the grass, we decided it was lunchtime.

Roosevelt Park itself was off limits during school hours, making it that much more appealing to us during summer vacation. Instead of choosing the hills we use for sliding, we decided to relax on the side of the park where the incline was less steep, under the crabapple tree alongside Plaster Creek. At least once a week the color of the creek changed, depending on what Kelvinator was dumping. It could be green like pea soup. It could be brown like chocolate milk. Today the creek looked clear. In contrast to the dusty playground, the grass here grew long, soft, and comforting like pastures I imagined in the land of Goshen.

Packed lunches were a treat for us because during the school year, we were required to return home for lunch hour. Opening my brown paper bag, I lifted my sandwich. White bread with butter and brown sugar. I removed the wax paper wrap and laid it exactly on the center of my paper towel. Carefully, I pulled out a glass peanut butter jar, unscrewed the lid, and took a large gulp of milk.

"Aaaaaahhh!" I exhaled and looked at Bobo. He copied me, adding a loud belch.

We ate our sandwiches and potato chips, then chocolate-covered marshmallow cookies, now rather softened, and the rest of our milk.

"Aaaaaahhh!" Bobo exhaled and wiped his mouth on his shirt. "This is the life of Riley!"

I lay back in the grass, looking at the cloudless sky. Neither of us talked.

There were just two of them. At first they appeared to be enjoying the day as we were, walking along the fence in the thick grass, laughing and joking with each other. Junior high age, no older. Spotting Bobo and me, they pointed and then walked on a ways.

I stashed my glass jar in the brown paper bag. "Let's go."

"They won't hurt us," Bobo said in a ridiculing tone.

I felt ashamed for being afraid, but watched until they were out of sight beyond the top of the hill.

With my daydream scattered, I lay on my stomach watching the Chicago Drive traffic. A few pedestrians passed. A man from the gas station, another wearing a Roadway Truck uniform.

I didn't notice that the boys came back and I startled when they laughed. Grabbing the bag with the glass jar, I stood up. One of them pushed me on the chest. I lost my balance and fell in the grass. The other climbed on top of me.

I screamed.

He slapped me.

I wondered where Bobo was. Then heard him yell, "Get off me! Get off me!"

Slapping or no slapping, I started to yell too. "Get off me! Get off me!" I twisted and pushed my stomach as high as I could under his weight.

He slapped me again. I stopped shouting, but continued to wrestle while I felt my tears sting my eyes. He flashed his white teeth and called me a name I didn't recognize. He was breathing on my face. He put his hand on my chest and pinched. It hurt and I squirmed and pushed harder. He said something that sounded like "cheek-o" and reached his hand up through the leg of my red cotton shorts. I screamed again.

He spit.

I winced. The drizzle lay on my face. I screamed some more.

He spit again and I stopped screaming.

I heard my brother yelling as the boy touched my panties.

I heard someone else yelling. "Hey you kids!" the grownup voice said. "Hey! What are you doing down there? You better get on out of there!"

The boys ran away.

I rolled to my stomach, wiped my face with my cotton blouse. The voice belonged to a man in a Pepsi plant uniform. He was standing on the bridge over the creek. Bobo waved to him and the man went on his way. Without a word, we snatched up our paper bags with the glass jars and didn't stop running until we were through the tunnel.

We never spoke of the incident again. But I stayed on the lookout.

Vijf

My mother was sympathetic to kids on our street like Billy Bosch. Even if their family was on the wrong side of the antithesis. Billy's mother would go downtown for the afternoon and lock Billy out of the house. Mother let Billy Bosch use our bathroom.

"Poor kid," she would say.

David lived on London Street but wasn't "our kind" either. He wore blue jeans with holes at the knees, even to school. He went to a special school called Lincoln, a public school, far enough away that he had to take a bus. When he walked home from the bus stop, his lanky frame bounced in a steady, easy-going rhythm. I often heard him whistling.

"Poor kid," Mother would say. "Retarded."

VanderGoots next door were so very Dutch they rarely spoke English. According to my mother, they were our kind. The family went to our church and Theresa and her brother Henry went to our school. Hankie, we called him, knew a lot about the Church. He knew a lot about a lot.

"Too smart for his own good," Mother would say.

Once when maneuvering my wagon down Vandenbergs' driveway while they were gone on vacation, I lost control and crashed into their basement window. Most of the glass fell inside the house. I considered keeping the incident my secret.

It was Thursday, so we were having pork chops for supper. There was a knock at the back door and Mother answered.

"Hello, Mrs. Griffioen," Henry said. "I thought you might want to know your daughter broke a window today. Were you aware of that?"

"No. I was not. Thank you, Hankie. We are eating supper right now. Good-bye."

I'd had enough of Henry. I was eight years old and even though Henry was at least thirteen, he was always tripping me in the yard. Laughing. Sitting on me and sticking his wide tongue in my face. And now tattling.

A few weeks after the broken window, Barbie and I hung out on the steps to the front porch when we all finished playing Kick-the-Can and Stone School. Babe and Theresa started a game of jacks on one end of the steps. Bobo and Billy Bosch plopped down on the cement step nearest the sidewalk, a few feet ahead of us. Our shorts and sleeveless scarecrow shirts were grimy from our street games. We sat resting with elbows on our knees and heads in our hands. My mother came out on the front porch. Henry, standing in our grass since the games ended, came and sat down next to Bobo.

We were starting to learn about Total Depravity in our catechism class—a doctrine that claims we are all born in sin and prone to evil. As if confirming the doctrine, an idea popped in my head that day in the front yard. I dismissed the idea, but the thought came right back. "Better not," I told myself before I changed my mind again.

I got up and whispered to Babe, my hand cupped around her ear. "Watch this."

I went to Theresa. "I have a secret to tell you," I said purposely aloud, then whispered in her ear. "Watch this."

"I have a secret," I said out loud. Stepping between Bobo and Henry, I whispered in my brother's ear, "I'm going to get Hankie."

"Hankie!" I said. "I have a secret to tell you."

I could tell he was pleased to be included. I bent down and cupped my hand loosely on the side of his face, opened my mouth and chomped his ear. Hard. Hearing the crunch, I spit over and over because I saw blood. Henry left for home hooting and crying.

I was a hero that day. Even Mother said that's what he gets.

~

"The Lord is in His Holy Temple; let all the earth keep silence before Him."

We sat with our heads bowed in silent prayer, then rose to sing Psalm 146.

Hallelujah, praise Jehovah, O my soul Jehovah praise;
I will sing the glorious praises Of my God through all my days . . .

Reverend Piersma wore his black robe. He lifted his arms and gave the salutation, the same exact words as last week, the week before, the month before, the year before. "Grace, mercy, and peace be unto you from God the Father, and from our Lord Jesus Christ, through the operation of the Holy Spirit. Aaa-men."

We sang Psalm 48, how we are in God's Holy temple, that we abide in Zion, and that Israel's God will be our God forever. The minister read the Law, the mirror in which we could "behold our trespasses." Then we sang Psalm 51, David's penitential one.

God, be merciful to me,
On Thy grace I rest my plea;
. . . .
Broken hearts are in Thy sight
More than sacrificial rite;
. . . .
Prosper Zion in Thy grace
And her broken walls replace . . .

The minister assured the people of pardon and proclaimed, "Though your sins be as scarlet, they shall be as white as snow; though they be red as crimson, they shall be as wool."

The long prayer started and I folded my hands, covered with little white cotton gloves.

After Scripture and the Catechism reading, the sermon began. I tried to listen closely. The sermon was about God's Providence. My father always told us that Providence is primary and sustains the world. It nearly holds position with The Sovereignty of God, but not quite. Providence is included in Sovereignty. My father said all theology is included under Sovereignty. He says God's Sovereignty is the starting point from where all theology needs to be understood. He said this at the dinner table. He told us these things every week.

The sermon had three points, and each point was worth a peppermint. That was important to me. One sermon equals three peppermints.

Mother and Father liked to talk about the catechism. They liked to talk about God's Providence. They liked to talk about Reverend Piersma. They did it all the time. I knew they liked Reverend Piersma.

"Dominee had a good sermon this morning," Father summarized for everyone on the ride home.

"Yes. Dominee had a good sermon." Mother verified. That was her place. The husband is the spiritual leader, the head of the house. To be obeyed. But my mother wasn't agreeing just for that reason— she knew a good minister when she heard one.

We ate our Sunday dinner, juicy beef roast with whipped potatoes and gravy, vegetable and applesauce. Plus a rehash of the morning's sermon.

While my parents took their Sunday afternoon nap, Deannie, Babe, Bobo and I studied our catechism lessons. Then I played paper dolls until 2:30 when we had our candy bars and listened to "The Children's Bible Hour."

The entire family returned to church in the evening for the seven o'clock worship, which started with a song service. George Vander Woude led the singing, beginning with his favorite selection "Jesus Saves." It ranked high in the list of most Arminian songs in the Hymnal, Father said, right along with "Come to the Savior Now."

After my father tucked me into bed that night, I recognized the brewing coffee sound from the electric percolator used only for *bizonder* company. I recognized the smell of pig-in-the-blanket baking in the oven. Before falling asleep, I heard Mr. and Mrs. Kamps visiting with my mother and father in the living room. From time to time I could hear them raise their voices. I knew what they were discussing. Providence.

Providence and pig-in-the-blanket. I nestled comfortably into the night.

∽

One day that fall when I came home from school, I could tell my mother had been crying. Leaning against the kitchen counter, she grasped a flower-printed handkerchief in her hand, staring at nothing but the pot of potatoes on the stove, waiting for them to boil. I had seen her this way before, just last week.

A few nights ago after everyone was in bed, I had heard her sobbing, "I can't do it. I can't."

My father asked, "What do you mean?"

Mother spoke louder, like she was angry. "You know what I mean. I can't be like her."

"What are you talking about?" Father asked. "You're being silly."

"You know very well what I'm talking about," Mother said.

Father dismissed her. "It's all your imagination, Mom," he said.

It wasn't the first time I heard my mother talk that way. Usually my father answered, "No, Mom." Or, "Don't be ridiculous." Or, "Baloney."

Once I heard Father say, "That's crazy."

◌

If my mother packed a suitcase, I didn't see it. I'm sure she would have said good-bye and kissed me if I was home. But I was at school when she left for the place we visited that one Sunday afternoon four years ago. The place with the beds and the windows like jail and the jangling keys.

Two months this time. A long time for a nine-year old. A long time when colorful, crisp days of October turn cold and drag into November days chilly and damp with drizzle. If anyone had said to me, "Your mother will be gone for two months," it wouldn't have helped me.

I sought consolation on the register, though without my mother's slippers, without my mother's warm, worn housecoat—without Mama, the forced furnace air didn't help.

To keep a secret when I wasn't even sure of its ingredients wasn't easy. Eight weeks is a long time to stay hushed. When I did ask Father, he didn't answer except by shaking his head.

My father didn't talk about my mother, but sometimes I caught him with a sudden wet streak on his face, or a need to swallow hard as he prayed at our evening meals. When I asked details from my sisters, they told me "I don't know."

Eight Sundays is a long time in a community that supposedly ignores these kinds of unpleasant things. It's a long time when it seemed that everyone was keeping the secret so well that I must too.

So I did. And with pretty good perseverance for a Calvinist of nine.

But it was a long time, crying into my pillow every night, adding to my prayers, "Heavenly Father, please send Mama home tomorrow then, since it couldn't be today after all."

Then the eight weeks were over and my mama came home. As far as I knew, the secret everyone knew stayed a secret, and I decided keeping quiet about the matter was what Mother wanted.

Thanksgiving arrived and the darkening drizzle turned to white snow. We all went to church together. Reverend Piersma led the congregation in a prayer of thanksgiving for crops, health, work, the Word and Sacrament. John and Gracia came for dinner. My sisters and I were happy to wear pants after church—it wasn't Sunday. Deannie was glad she didn't have to prepare beef roast. Father helped Mother cook a turkey. Babe was thankful to get out of dishes, Bobo was happy to do them. Arie J was glad to have his first turn with the wishbone. The entire family went bowling.

And silently, I gave thanks that my mama was home.

Christmas season came and Christmas Day passed. Then the New Year holiday. We sang, "Our God, Our Help in Ages Past, Our Hope for Years to Come." We hollered and shot caps off the front porch at midnight.

Orie kissed Pearl a long time in front of us.

Zes

M ichigan springs could be tricky. Sometimes most of spring would consist of winter. Sometimes most of spring would consist of summer. This year, spring was spring.

I took my time on the way home from school that afternoon, noticing crocuses along the edge of Kingmas' driveway, the concrete a quarter-circle with one side ending at Clyde Park Avenue and the other on London Street. Their large weeping willow made the yard messy, my mother said. I thought the tree swept the sidewalk in a dreamy way, as if Kingmas' double lot was a southern plantation where girls wore dresses, even for play.

"Don't Kingmas go to church?" Babe had asked once at supper.

"There's only Mrs. Kingma now," Father explained, chewing his potatoes. "Someone usually picks her up."

"Do Slatterys go to church?" Bobo asked while we were on the subject.

"No," Father answered.

Mother corrected him. "I have seen her take the car out alone once in awhile on Sunday morning."

"How come they don't go to church?" I asked.

Bobo shrugged. "Beats me." He set down his milk glass, wiping his mouth with his bare arm.

"They're just not our kind," Mother had explained. "Eat your supper."

At the end of Kingmas' driveway, on the sidewalk again, I waved to Mr. Hoogeveen. He stood wearing his railroad overalls, waiting and watching for his grandson at the corner of London Street like he did every afternoon after school.

As I reached the VanderGoots next door, I could see a man leave our house through the front door, climb into a car, and drive off. He was dressed in a suit and tie. A suit and tie on Wednesday.

"Who was here?" I greeted my mother and wondered why she stood on the kitchen register during such a mild afternoon in March.

"What do you mean, who was here?" I could tell she didn't want to answer.

"I saw somebody leaving in a dark green car."

She hesitated. "Reverend Piersma was here."

"Oh, he was? Somebody sick or something? No wonder he had a suit on."

Bobo barged in the door. "Hello! What can I have to eat?" He opened the refrigerator. "Can I have this apple?" He took a bite before Mother could answer.

"The minister was here," I said, proud to tell him.

"He was? Here? Somebody sick or something?" He took another bite and slurped the juice around the peeling. "The sixth-graders have to make a rock collection for school," he said. "Guess I'm going outside and start looking."

"Can I help?" I asked. "I got a real good piece of gypsum you can borrow."

"If you hurry up." He ran out the door.

Upstairs in my room, I scrambled out of my dress into my play clothes. Alex, a stuffed cat, sat propped on my bed. Alex was made of heavy black cotton and had an embroidered face. Deannie had given me the cat last Sunday, one of the few days she'd been around lately. "Homemade, just for you," she said and I beamed with her attention.

I tucked the cat under my arm, grabbed my piece of gypsum and dashed downstairs just as Mother put Wednesday's casserole in the oven. "I'll be with Bobo," I called.

On the next Wednesday, the green car was leaving again when I came up London Street.

"Reverend Piersma was here again today," I said while Bobo and I ate our apples. "I saw his car."

My mother said nothing, warmed up the oven and put in a casserole.

Bobo and I went outside to ride our bikes.

The third Wednesday, I splashed through puddles left on the sidewalk from the afternoon shower and again, I watched the green car leave. Bobo and I each had an apple. We played in the basement. I heard Mother put a casserole in the oven.

No green car in front of the house the next Wednesday. A gray one instead. As I came up the driveway, a lady in a navy blue suit left through our front door. Her hair was twisted and tied into a tight bun. She carried a briefcase and marched to the gray car. I stood on the sidewalk and stared after her as she drove off.

"Who was here?" I greeted my mother.

"What do you mean, 'Who was here?'"

"That lady with the suit on. That lady with the mean face."

"That is an old maid who thinks she knows it all," Mother explained from the kitchen register.

I didn't understand. I took an apple. My mother hadn't put the casserole in yet. She stayed on the register. I went outside to play by myself.

A week went by. When I came home from school on Wednesday, Gracia was drinking tea at the kitchen table with Mother.

"May I have tea?" I asked.

Mother answered exactly as I thought she would. "On Sunday you can."

"What can I have?"

"There's cookies. Save a couple for Bobo."

Arie J was up from his nap. Although he would start kindergarten in the fall, my mother still made him take a nap every day. I gave him one of the windmill cookies and went and stood at the sink.

"Janie, you have a new baby brother," Mother announced.

"What?"

"You have a new baby brother," Mother repeated. "Ronald Lee. Born yesterday."

"I do? Yesterday?" I put my cookie down on the counter. "Holy smokes. Ronald Lee." I took the red plastic cup that we all shared from corner of the sink, filled it and gulped the water down. "I have to call Barbie."

"No, don't call Barbie," Gracia said.

"*Aach! Laat haar mag geworden,*" Mother said.

I dialed the number. "Hello, Barbie? It's me. Hey, guess what . . . You'll never guess . . . No. I have a new baby brother . . . Yep! A baby brother. Born yesterday . . . Yep! His name's Ronald Lee . . . Uh-huh . . . Just a minute, I don't know . . ." I put my hand over the receiver. "When's he coming home?"

"Day after tomorrow," Gracia answered.

"Friday," I told my friend. "Yep . . . My Mom? She's fine . . . She's feeling fine. You want to talk to her? . . . Ah-huh. Sitting right here . . . No? . . . Well, I gotta hang up."

Gracia cleared the table. Mother warmed up the oven and turned on the television for Arie J so he could watch "The Buck Barry Show." She put the casserole in and I went upstairs to play with the baby doll in the corner of my room.

∾

The Sunday morning air felt fresh and pure, as if it had filtered through heaven just before sunrise. I took a deep breath, my head tipped toward the sky, while Father backed the station wagon out of the garage.

Three weeks ago, on Easter, I had worn my new dress for the first time. Made of soft baby blue cotton, the tiny tucks in the bodice were edged with white lace. So was the hem. I wore lots of petticoats underneath the gathered skirt and had to straighten them every time I got in and out of the car.

Father dropped us off in front of church before he drove around the block and parked, as usual, on the hill.

We met Mr. Kamps in the back foyer.

"Pearl! *Hoe ist?*"

Mother had on her new beige linen suit with matching pumps. She reached her hand out from under the baby blanket and shook Mr. Kamps' hand. He peeked in the bundle then shook mine and each of my brothers and sisters' hands before going upstairs to ring the church bell. Father walked in as the first bell sounded.

Reverend Piersma read the Form for the Baptism of Infants, the same form read for every baptism, the same form read on the first Sunday of every month. The form says we're all born in sin but baptism witnesses and seals that our sins are washed away through Jesus Christ. We're in a covenant with God by baptism and are "obliged unto new obedience, namely, that we cleave to this one God, Father, Son, and Holy Spirit; that we trust in Him . . ." Nor should we despair of God's mercy when we sin since ". . . we have an eternal covenant with God."

I knew the words by heart—despair, trust and love, God's mercy, Covenant. Covenant was one of our favorite subjects.

I took a peppermint from my purse and slipped it into my mouth. Father and Mother were in the very front pew, holding Ronald Lee. We sat three rows back—Arie J, Bobo, Babe, Deannie, Aunt Dienke, and me. Gracia and John were in the balcony where I wished I could sit sometime.

Reverend Piersma prayed about God saving Noah and his family from the flood. He prayed about the Israelites crossing the Red Sea on dry ground when Pharaoh and his Egyptian army drowned, which is where the sign of baptism comes from. I finished my peppermint while he thanked God that those who are baptized may always be comforted because they are God's children and in the Covenant.

My parents had to stand and answer sincerely if they believed their children ought to be baptized, if they believed in the Old and New Testament Scriptures, if they believed the articles of the faith taught in the Christian Church. They had to promise in front of God "to instruct . . . [this child] . . . in the aforesaid doctrine . . . to the utmost of your power?"

I had heard those words on the first Sunday of every month since I could remember. I straightened my petticoats and listened carefully.

"Mr. and Mrs. Griffioen, what is your answer?"

"We do," they said at the same time.

Father carried my baby brother to the wooden font with Mother following. Lifting the sleeve of his robe, Reverend Piersma dipped his hand into the bowl of water. "Ronald Lee Griffioen, I baptize you into the name of the Father . . ." He sprinkled Ronald Lee's forehead. ". . . and of the Son . . ." He dipped his hand into the bowl of water and sprinkled Ronald Lee's forehead again. ". . . and of the Holy Spirit." Once more, he dipped his hand in the water and sprinkled Ronald Lee's forehead. "Aah-men."

Reverend Piersma smiled at my parents. He turned to the congregation as the organist began the hymn and held the songbook for Mother and Father while they stayed in the front to sing.

> *Oh God, great Father, Lord and King!*
> *Our children unto Thee we bring;*
> *And strong in faith and hope and love,*
> *We dare Thy steadfast Word to prove.*
>
> *Thy covenant kindness did of old*
> *Our fathers and their seed enfold;*
> *That ancient promise standeth sure,*
> *And shall while heaven and earth endure.*
>
> *Look down upon us while we pray*
> *And visit us in grace today;*
> *These little ones thou didst receive,*
> *Thy precious promise we believe.*

I had permission to skip Sunday School. We returned home and used up an entire roll of film. Pictures were taken with a blanket around Ronald Lee, without the blanket, with his bonnet on, with it off. Pictures were taken with Ronald Lee in the buggy and some while he was held. Some with me and my sisters and Ronald Lee. Some with him and my mother, some with him and my father. Some were taken with him and my mother and father. A lot of pictures were taken with Deannie and Ronald Lee.

Which made sense to me because it was Deannie's camera.

Zeven

I learned to fold clean diapers and set them in straight stacks on the bassinet. I could sprinkle a baby's bottom with cornstarch and pin a fresh diaper as snugly as my mother. In the late afternoons just before dinner, I fed Ronald Lee his bottle and he gurgled with happiness. One month led into the other and another. My rewards were his smile.

I often walked Ronald Lee around the block in the buggy. Pushing the buggy one afternoon, I followed Arie J on his tricycle. He led the way as we rounded the corner and headed up Lynch Street. Most families on Lynch went to Grandville Avenue Church and sent their children to the Christian school. "Our kind of people," Mother would say. "On the right side of the antithesis," Father would say.

The Hoolsemas lived on Lynch Street. Sandy Hoolsema was in my fourth-grade class. Once after we went ice-skating together, Sandy invited me in. Glad to have a chance to thaw my toes, I stood on the rug inside the back entry the entire time, about five minutes. From there, I could see their kitchen, a huge mess that immediately made me uncomfortable. Newspapers, baby bottles, a hairbrush all among the clutter of dirty dishes. Two opened cans of Franco-American spaghetti stood on the counter. Orange sauce was spilled down the side of a pan on the stove. Cereal boxes sat on the table next to bowls still holding a quarter inch of milk. Fingerprints smeared the front of the Kelvinator refrigerator.

I wondered what the rest of the house looked like. I knew if I walked across the floor I would hear crunching.

The Hoolsemas had two teen-age girls, two teen-age boys, another boy, then Sandy, then Mary and Sally, then another boy, then a boy or a girl in a diaper, and then I lost track. I rarely saw Mrs. Hoolsema and I never saw Mr. Hoolsema. My parents said he wasn't home much.

Our ride this warm spring day had started with Ronald Lee sitting propped with pillows. By this time he had slid on his back, content to watch the sky and play with his toes. I sat him up straight again, eager for him to get the most from my tour and show him off to the neighborhood. Arie J pedaled in front of me, his legs working fast. He stopped and threw a stick, picked up a stone. He never got too far ahead, often slowing to admire a tree or a parked car.

Pushing the buggy, I thought about Mr. and Mrs. Hoolsema. Mrs. Hoolsema went to our church. Sandy was always in Sunday School. I followed Arie J's tricycle, thinking about my father's antithesis principle. I wondered if a man could be on one side of the antithesis and his family on the other. Then I asked myself if someone could be a Calvinist, on the right side of the antithesis, and still be so sloppy.

~

Every neighborhood had one and London Street was no exception.

We called her "*Klikkuiken.*" She had a gift—the ability to gather information about other people's affairs. With invisible antennae on top of her head, Klikkuiken picked up tidbits and sent them through the community as if she worked for WFUR radio. Sometimes she would even edit and moralize her reports first.

She was very short and small, with a large bosom. Her hair was cropped and curly, the result of wet hair pinned up in bobby pins from Saturday morning until Sunday morning just before church. Klikkuiken was Barbie's grandmother and lived next door to Barbie, the third house from the corner. She gave us root beer and cookies and let us roller skate in her driveway.

But when Klikkuiken asked me a question, as she often did, I instinctively answered, "I don't know."

On a warm morning near the end of August, we rolled down the car windows and waved to Klikkuiken, watching from her front screen door. Ronald Lee, now seventeen months old, sat in a canvas car seat, entertained by the plastic steering wheel with a red push-button horn.

We reached the church, took a left, and headed west along M-21 toward Uncle Frank's farm. My father was to butcher a pig today. We weren't allowed to watch the actual slaughter, but the ritual had other rewards, like the time last fall when I brought a pig's eye to school for show-and-tell.

I liked going to Uncle Frank and Aunt Jane's even more than going on picnics to Gun Lake with the Kamps. Mother called my uncle and aunt "Pa" and "Mama," though I knew they were not our grandparents. We were supposed to say Uncle Frank and Aunt Jane.

The farm covered sixty acres. Not a full-time farmer, Uncle Frank worked at General Motors and kept the farm with its few cows, pigs, and chickens for Freddie. Freddie was my cousin, 27 years old and "mentally retarded." But we didn't call him retarded, not even my mother. She didn't call him anything but Freddie.

"Why do you call Aunt Jane and Uncle Frank 'Ma and Pa' anyway?" I asked when we stopped for the light.

"When we came to America, I was only eight. Grootmoe was sick most of the trip. I was scared." Mother pronounced the last word with a "t" at the end. "Aunt Jane and Uncle Frank took care of me on the boat."

"But where was *Opa*?" I asked.

My father accelerated and the air rushing into the vehicle cut off the conversation.

"Eeeeuuw," Bobo said after we'd gone a good ten miles or so.

We were used to butcher shops and the smell of fresh meat, but not manure. Arie J and I wrinkled our noses. "Peee-uuuw."

The collie greeted us, barking as the station wagon rolled slowly over the stone driveway. Aunt Jane let the screen door slam behind her, wiping her hands on the ever-present hand-sewn apron tied over her housedress. The hem of the dress fell almost to her ankle.

"*Halte op, hond!*" Aunt Jane called to the dog. "*Halte op!*"

Her shoes were black-laced like Grootmoe always wore, the kind with heels one and a half inches square and the same measure tall. Aunt Jane wore her grey hair in a bun, but a bun fuller and looser than Grootmoe's. In fact, Aunt Jane looked a lot like Grootmoe, except bigger, fuller and looser.

"*Hoe ist? Hoe ist?*" She shook hands with my father using two hands.

"Haaallo," Aunt Jane said softly to my mother, and held her arm warmly as Mother returned the "haaallo" in a warm tone reserved only for sisters.

I think Aunt Jane was my mother's best friend. Mother didn't socialize with many other women besides my sister Gracia and Aunt Dienke—once in a while Mrs. VanderGoot from next door, sometimes Mrs. Kamps. Aunt Dienke had a driver's license. On Tuesday nights she and my mother would pick up Aunt Sena and Aunt Tina. They would ride out to Aunt Jane's farm for what they called "sewing club." I know Mother took her turn supplying the Cracker Jack, as Aunt Jane called it in her Yankee Groningen Dutch. Cracker Jack was actually Jack Daniel's.

We used our best manners and each said hello to Aunt Jane. Her accent would crescendo with her comment. "*Aach! Aach! Aach!*" She touched the top of our heads. "*Aach! Arme Kind!*" she said to Ronald Lee, stroking the top of his head.

"*Komest aan!*" With her arm coaxing, Aunt Jane waved us on to the back door.

A long, narrow rag rug softened the cement floor of the shed called a *hoekje*. The *hoekje* opened to a large square kitchen. We arranged ourselves around the silver chrome table beside a large picture window and the three adults started a conversation in Groningen Dutch.

"*Hier komt Freddie aan,*" Aunt Jane announced. Freddie came in and stood leaning in the doorway between the kitchen and the *hoekje*, smoking his pipe.

"Hello, Uncle Orie. Hello, Aunt Pearl."

"Well, hello Fred," my father greeted him from across the table.

"Hello, Freddie," Mother said and smiled. "Been working hard?"

"Yeah. Well, we couldn't get the other tractor started. But now it's set. Pa should be coming in a minute."

"*Aach ja jonge,*" Aunt Jane agreed.

Freddie walked into the dining room and placed himself in a stuffed chair to smoke his pipe.

After a second piece of raisin bread with almond paste, Babe asked if we could look around outdoors. Aunt Jane nodded.

"Keep your eye on Arie J," Mother commanded.

The dog got up as we passed through the *hoekje* and followed us. We let the screen door slam. Out in the driveway, Arie J stroked Lassie's long silky fur and cuddled his face close to her whiskers. "Good boy," he said, hugging her neck.

"Lassie means girl," I informed my little brother.

I began my traditional stroll around the two-story farmhouse. Spreading hostas hid most of the block foundation. Beginning in the freshly mowed backyard, I worked my way west, where I stopped for a moment to stare at the large old maples and their shade. Along the fence, enormous bright pink hollyhocks blossomed. Yellow daisies mixed with purple wildflowers where the screened porch met the living room.

In the front yard, closer to the house than to the road, a wooden windmill from Uncle Gerrit stood surrounded with marigolds and red geraniums. In the grass near the stone driveway, Aunt Jane kept two tulip chairs, the kind that bounced if you did, with arms and a high rounded back. Each chair was painted white and stood next to a short table made of wrought iron twisted into pretty designs, also painted white.

Just as we started a game of hide-and-seek, Aunt Jane called from the stoop. She held a tray loaded with cookies, biscuits, and cheese that she placed on the pine picnic table. She disappeared into the house and quickly returned with glasses and lemonade.

My brothers and sister settled to enjoy their treats, but I picked up my cookie, biscuit, cheese and drink and began to follow my aunt toward the *hoekje.*

"*Wil je binnenkomen?*" Aunt Jane turned around and smiled, maybe thinking I would follow her inside.

I walked past without reply until I reached the wrought iron table in the grass. I set my refreshments on the tabletop and looked up to see Aunt Jane's reaction.

She beamed and nodded her approval. "*Ja viegt. Hier als me'vrouw te zitten,*" which meant it is where the classy ladies sit.

I could hear my aunt chuckle as she returned to the house. I took a bite of my biscuit and cheese, sipped some lemonade, and nibbled my cookie. I tipped my head back against the high metal chair. My imagination floated like the light summer clouds above me.

"Janie! Janie!" Babe called me to join their game of tag. Then we played cowboys and Indians. Then we played follow-the-leader through the barn. After that, we ran through the alfalfa field, playing nothing in particular. We were not allowed near the lean-to or small shack where the pig slaughter took place. Instead, we took turns using the outhouse and decided to visit the three cows in the pasture.

I went inside to get Ronald Lee, took him by the hand, and walked him around the yard. In the driveway, I convinced him to pet one of the cats. He carefully placed two fingers near the fur and quickly jerked his hand behind his back when he felt it.

The boots and knives and aprons were already put away when Aunt Jane called us in. "*Eeten! Eeten!*" We washed our hands and gathered around the cherry-wood table, covered with a lacy cloth in the dining room.

Father said the blessing before the meal. When we finished dinner, Uncle Frank read a Psalm and prayed. In Dutch.

As the ladies began to clear the dishes, I stepped into the living room, not sneaking, but careful. I poked my head around the corner into the porch where Freddie sat to light his pipe. He saw me and nodded. I returned a hand wave but pulled back, left the living room and went down a short hallway.

Pushing one of the doors open a bit further, I tiptoed inside the room. A mahogany bureau against the wall held a spotted grey mirror. The two windows with lace curtains were open, the bed in between. A Martha Washington spread was pulled perfectly smooth over the mattress and pillows, its white nubs the same color as the patterns. At the foot of the bed, a small rag rug covered the wooden floor. The floor creaked when I moved. This was the room Grootmoe had occupied when she moved from across the street on London to Uncle Frank and Aunt Jane's. The room where Grootmoe lay sick for so long. The room where Grootmoe had died.

I tiptoed out, putting the door in the same position as I found it.

When I went back into the dining room, the last ritual of our visit was beginning.

Uncle Frank took the baby on his knee and bouncing him up and down asked, "Wat your *naam* is?"

"Ronald Lee," Arie J answered for his brother.

"Ja. Dat is zo." He placed a dime on the tablecloth and passed Ronald Lee to my father.

Arie J waited patiently at his side until Uncle Frank lifted him to a knee.

"You big boy already. Wat your *naam* is?"

Arie J nodded and answered "Arie."

"Ja. Dat is zo." He opened the small fingers and placed a dime in the palm. "Is for you."

Arie J climbed down while Bobo came closer, somewhat hesitant of this summertime Santa.

"Too big for da lap, ja?"

Bobo nodded.

"Wat your *naam* is?"

"Bobo."

"Ja. Dat is zo. Wat your other *naam* is?"

"Gerhard."

"Ja. Dat is zo." He pressed a quarter in his hand before offering a manly shake.

Babe's turn. She beamed and climbed onto his lap.

"You do school?" he asked her.

"Yes, but not in the summer," Babe told him.

"*Nee, in zummer niet,*" he laughed. "Wat your *naam* is?"

"Babe."

"Ja. Wat your other *naam* is?"

"Aleda."

"Ja. Dat is zo."

He showed her the quarter. "Is for you."

She kissed him on the cheek and climbed down with her coin.

My arm bumped his bulky middle as I sat on his leg. His eyes were bulgy. His ears and nose were hairy, his head mostly bald. The skin on his face full of tiny red veins matched his almost always-bloodshot eyes.

He was not afraid to show favorites. "*Mijn prinses. Oom* know wat your *naam* is. It is *goede naam*. It *beste naam*."

He put two quarters in my hand. I kissed his cheek, said thank you, and climbed down. There was still time to play on the hay bales if Uncle Frank would let us.

"Ja. You go. We have *koffie* and den surprise."

When my father called us down from the loft, we lined up in the driveway. Our eyes itched. Aunt Jane chuckled loudly while Mother picked and brushed hay off our clothes and hair.

Uncle Frank took Ronald Lee's hand and walked him down toward the lane to the chicken coop. "*Komest aan!*" my uncle hollered. Anyone could tell he was bow-legged even though he wore baggy, dark green work pants. He always wore baggy, dark green work pants. Except to church every Sunday. His short frame tipped to each side when he stepped, and Ronald Lee's arm swung to Uncle Frank's slow walking rhythm, up and down like the handle on the old water pump.

Uncle Frank waited until everyone reached the chicken house before he turned the wooden latch to open the door. We heard the peeping as soon as Uncle Frank hushed us. The lights in the glass box kept the chicks in an area warm and safe, Uncle Frank told us. Incubator, he said.

Register, I thought.

We all held one. Ronald Lee squealed then squirmed when the tiny feet scratched on his hand. I held the baby chick and gently stroked it with one finger, and though I could see the fuzz on the little yellow form, I could barely feel it.

We called same places when we loaded back into the station wagon. By the time we left the dirt road, I had stopped sneezing. When we crossed the railroad tracks, my eyes didn't itch as much. After we went four miles, it started getting dark. Before we reached the city limits, our swollen eyes were heavy. By the time we turned on London Street, Mother and Father were the only ones who waved to Klikkuiken.

Acht

The year I was ten, my sister Deannie moved to an apartment downtown with her friend Suzie.

Every time we visited, my mother made her disapproval known. "It's too rough around here," she said as we entered the third-floor apartment. "I suppose you never eat decent. Here. I brought you this toaster from Pylmans' rummage sale."

Deannie served coffee in free china cups she collected from boxes of powered laundry detergent. Arie J, Ronald Lee and I got to have Neapolitan ice cream from colored Melmac bowls. When we finished, Deannie took Ronald Lee on her lap and wiped the chocolate from his face.

"The neighbors are nice and so is the landlady," Deannie told us. "She lives on the first floor and lets us use the basement if we want to store stuff."

"It's a waste of money," Mother said. "You should know better."

Father spoke up, but he addressed Mother, not Deannie. "It's no business, that's all."

To me, the large old Victorian house looked exactly like the kind of place where I would want to live some day.

Mother repeated her criticism a while later when we were leaving. "Too many *sortje* around."

"You don't belong here, that's all," Father summed up.

Deannie ignored their comments, said good-bye to Arie J and me, and gave Ronald Lee a long hug.

Four months later, Deannie moved home again. She stayed most of the summer. Sometimes she would leave the dinner table crying.

A lot of door slamming and yelling went on.

Deannie alternated between London Street and apartment life, usually a few months at a time. I saw my sister's moves as brave adventures and hoped someday I could live in the kind of places she did.

One day, Deannie didn't stay in an apartment or in the bedroom across the hall from mine. She went to stay at the place where pine trees covered the grounds and shaded the buildings. The buildings with wire mesh windows in heavy doors that only opened with loud jangling keys.

We didn't talk about where she went. It was one of those secrets my family had, an anonymous shadow haunting the air. A fake smile, an artificial greeting, a stare from teachers or neighbors encouraged our silence. Many people in church avoided us altogether, as if we were our own little leper colony at 711 London.

It was Wednesday. I strolled over to catechism class along the sidewalk that separated the school and the church. I reached the concrete steps of the edifice and joined the other sixth-graders waiting. When the fifth grade was dismissed, we filed into the basement.

The room had two sections of brown wooden chairs with right arms that extended out for writing. Except I was left-handed and found the spread of the frame awkward.

"Let's have it quiet now, boys and girls," Reverend Piersma said. He wore a dark suit and looked only slightly less dignified without his black robe.

We hushed and folded our hands for prayer.

"Almighty God and Heavenly King, Thou art the Covenant God, the Father of Abraham, Isaac, and Jacob. And Thou art our God too . . ."

He took roll. Meanwhile, most of the children crammed for the upcoming questions.

"It is good we sing," Reverend Piersma said. Unless we were writing a test, we sang every week. Only one song and every week the same selection.

Tis not that I did choose Thee,
For Lord, that could not be;
This heart would still refuse Thee,
Hadst Thou not chosen me.

. . . .
My heart owns none before Thee,
For Thy rich grace I thirst;
This knowing, if I love Thee,
Thou must have loved me first.

"By the end of the year you should know it pretty well," Reverend Piersma said the first day. It might have helped if he could play the piano like he could preach.

My father's Sunday afternoon drills paid off now. I knew my catechism and I knew it well. I put my book face down on the armrest and listened as the minister began working around the room with questions.

"Jim. You are first today. Was the church very large at the time of the Flood?"

"No. There were only eight left that believed and obeyed God."

"Correct. Bruce. How did Noah show his faith before the unbelieving world?"

Bruce sat up straighter. "By building the ark as God had commanded."

"That is correct. Pamela. What did God do for His church in that day?"

"He saved his church from the wicked world by the Flood."

We were expected to answer exactly.

"Tina. What beautiful promise did God give to Noah?"

"God said to Noah, 'With thee will I establish my Covenant.'"

"Good. Linda. What does this promise mean?"

"That God would save his church and send the Savior," Linda answered.

"Robert. What becomes plain in the lives of Abraham, Isaac, and Jacob?"

"I don't know," Bobby Garrison said.

"Well . . . then, we'll go on," Reverend Piersma announced, marking his book. I was next.

"What becomes plain in the lives of Abraham, Isaac, and Jacob?" he repeated.

I answered exactly. "That God proves his faithfulness to his people in spite of their sins."

He smiled, nodding. If Reverend Piersma had an appreciation for my father's appreciation of the catechism, I didn't know. I only noticed his kindness to me. When he wasn't writing on the chalkboard, Reverend Piersma stood in one place, bouncing on his toes. As he spoke, his face flushed. What the minister taught about God's Covenant, His deliverance, His faithfulness, verified what my father had said Sunday afternoon. I liked the confirmation. Somehow, it made me feel included.

I walked home in a group with no one in particular. I turned at the corner, yelled good-bye and headed up London Street. Catechism day was the only afternoon I wasn't required to look after Ronald Lee. From time to time I resented that responsibility and occasionally complained. But most often I really didn't mind. In fact, on Wednesday afternoons I missed my little brother. But I didn't tell anyone that kind of thing.

∼

Days were warm with Indian Summer. Leaves from stately old trees on London Street had already changed color, fallen, and now waited in a pile as long as our lot to be burned in the curb. Mother would light the leaves with a torch of wadded newspaper and let us roast apples at the end of a stick from the same tree.

On Saturday morning, I watched as Aunt Dienke crossed London Street wearing her green flannel shirt. She opened our back door without knocking, walked through the kitchen, opened the door to the basement landing and poked her head in.

"*Koffie drinken!*" she summoned.

"Okay!" Mother called back.

Saturday morning routine was set. At precisely ten o'clock, Dienke would enter our house unannounced, march through the kitchen with determined importance, and call into the basement where my mother never failed to be working on the laundry. The ritual happened each Saturday, week after week, month after month, season after season, year after year.

Through the living room window, I saw Dienke cross the street once more and return to her house. I was waiting for Deannie to pick me up. She lived in an apartment again with Suzie and would come once a month and take me, just me, out for coffee.

Her bright red Chevrolet pulled in, the chrome and huge back fins shiny. I didn't mind that Deannie waited at the end of the drive-way and honked for me. I liked that Klikkuiken was watching. Klik-kuiken might think me pretty important to be driving to Chickie's with my big sister this warm November morning.

It was the following week that President Kennedy was assassi-nated. We were dismissed early from school that day. I listened and watched the reports with Mother and Father. School was canceled again three days later and we watched the processional—Caroline, John John, the horses, the casket on television. As the nation fell into mourning, we also mourned. My father had not voted for President Kennedy. Kennedy was Roman Catholic. We paid attention and wor-ried about our country, but from the other side of the antithesis.

I didn't know why my father's antithesis theory never applied to baseball. He always kept up with the standings. My father wouldn't listen to the Sunday games, but during supper on Monday evening, he'd fill us in on the final scores of the previous day and any important plays. Bobo knew the Detroit Tiger statistics as well as he knew his catechism. I knew all the names of the Tigers and their positions. Arie J even knew their numbers. My favorite was number 11—Bill Freehan.

We went to Tiger Stadium every summer because every spring my father received free tickets from the Herrud Meat salesman. Mother didn't care much about baseball, but she would fill the round, Scotch-plaid cooler with dried beef sandwiches and grapes, and load our canvas bag with suckers, cookies, washcloths and her thermos of coffee. Somewhere during the three-hour drive to Detroit in the sta-tion wagon, she would dig a harmonica out of her purse and entertain us with "She'll be Comin' 'Round the Mountain," "Oh Suzanna," or "When the Roll is Called Up Yonder," and we'd sing along.

Last summer, it looked to me like the whole city of Detroit was of the world, let alone the huge stadium at the corner of Michigan and Trumbull. Fat vendors sold food and trinkets and beer. I didn't know what side of the antithesis the third baseline was on, but my father didn't seem concerned. In fact, he bragged about our seats, bought us hot dogs and ice cream and seemed proud to give us such a good time.

~

Baseball being an acceptable worldly amusement, we played it often on London Street and on the school playground. One spring day when I was almost finished with sixth grade, I caught a fresh dose of baseball fever.

The bell rang, dismissing class. I ran down the steps to the exit, and passed my classmates Janet, Beatrice, and Doug, the most popular boy in the sixth grade. Which explained why he seemed to ignore me.

"Hey! Where ya goin'?"

I heard but paid no attention.

"Janie! Where ya goin? Don't be in such a hurry!"

So he was talking to me. I turned around to look.

"We're gonna hang around and play baseball. Ya wanna play?"

I thought for a minute before I answered. "I can't. I have to get home."

"How come?"

"Just do," I said.

"Why don't you go home and come back?" he asked.

"I don't know if I can."

"We got a whole bunch playing. You could play too." He practically pleaded with me, and my face flushed realizing it.

"I have to go home and baby-sit my brother. I do it every day," I explained.

"You can go get him and take him along. We'll start and when you come, you can be on my team."

"If I can," I answered.

As soon as I was off school grounds and out of sight, I raced the four blocks home in record time.

"Mom! Mom! Where are you?" I called, running into the house, disappointed not to meet her in the kitchen.

"I'm in the basement."

I called from the top of the steps. "Do I have to take care of Ronald Lee today?"

"Of course you do. You always do."

"I know I always do. So do I have to today for once?"

"Yes, you do." The answer was firm. She started up the clothes dryer.

"But they're going to play ball at school. They asked me to play. Other kids don't have to watch their brothers all the time. Please?" I begged.

"You have to watch your brother."

That was that.

I dared again. "Can I take him along?"

My mother thought a moment. "You better be careful. And change your clothes first."

On our way out, I stopped in the back porch and dug through an old milk crate for our baseball gloves. My mitt had a Jim Northrup autograph in the leather. Ronald Lee's was a hand-me-down from Bobo so the Norm Cash signature was nearly worn off.

Ronald Lee must have heard my argument with Mother. "I don't want to go to school," he complained as we rushed down the driveway.

"You have to. Let's hurry."

"I don't want to play ball."

"You can watch."

After going through the tunnel and up Roosevelt Park hill, we saw the game going on at the far end of the playground. I let go of Ronald Lee's hand as we walked across the sandy lot.

"Make sure you don't get in the way," I warned.

True to his word, Doug halted the game when we approached. He indicated a place for Ronald Lee to sit and told everybody I was joining his side. Dale, the captain of the opposite team, kicked the dirt on the mound, waiting impatiently as I found my place in the lineup.

As much as I liked baseball, I wasn't good at it. When my turn came to bat, I struck out. I played outfield, although I preferred third base because I had a pretty decent arm. At least in the outfield there would be fewer balls for me to miss.

We played three more innings before I noticed Ronald Lee becoming restless.

"Okay. Janie's little brother gets a chance to bat now," Doug said, and stopped the game once more.

"Oh, come on!" Dale yelled.

Reluctant, I helped Ronald Lee choose a bat. He wasn't a large five-year-old and looked silly facing the big brute Dale.

"I don't believe this," Dale moaned.

"Shut-up, Dale," Beatrice called.

"Okay. We have a rookie here! Let's make it nice and easy," Doug said.

I began to relax and enjoy the spectacle.

Dale threw a fairly slow pitch but high. Purposely high, I thought. Ronald Lee took a swing.

"Wait for him to send you a good one," Doug called.

The next ball came in the middle, but faster. Swing and a miss.

"It's okay, buddy," I said. "Wait for the right one."

The next ball was faster.

"He's out!" Dale hollered.

"Never mind. He can bat some more," Doug told him.

He swung and missed again, the ball faster than ever. Strike four.

Doug paced between home plate and first. "Come on, Dale, slow it down. Let him hit one."

Ronald Lee tapped the ball. It dropped fair. "Run! Run!" the team shouted.

He threw the bat down and ran toward first. The catcher retrieved the ball and in nearly slow motion, threw it to the first baseman, who fumbled the toss on purpose. Ronald Lee was safe. He joined the base runners.

Dale rolled his eyes and muttered. "This stinks."

My turn. I let two go by before I swung and hit a pop fly to second base. One out.

Beatrice flied to right field.

I watched the ball bounce off the fielder's glove and looked in time to see Ronald Lee rounding third base. Just before he reached the plate, Dale charged and socked Ronald Lee in the stomach.

Ronald Lee doubled over but didn't cry out. I ran to him. Others had seen it too and gathered around. I laid my hand on his back and he stood upright, tears streaming down his face. I wiped his wet face with my sweatshirt and tried to hug him, but he pushed me away. He let Doug put an arm over his shoulder, so I stepped away and looked at Dale.

I shouted so hard my voice broke and my throat hurt. "You stupid-ass bully!"

Walking back to Ronald Lee, I wiped my own wet face this time.

"Call this off." Beatrice picked up her mitt. "I'm going home."

"Me too," said Janet.

"You better take him home," Doug whispered to me. Out loud, he asked Ronald Lee, "Can you walk home, buddy?"

He nodded with a brave, stubborn expression.

"Hey, Doug." I wanted to kiss him. "Thanks."

Ronald Lee refused to take my hand on the way home.

Negen

Arie J was supposed to bring the church bulletin to Mr. Hoogeveen every week, but today he was home on the couch with an earache. Since I agreed to walk along, Mother said Ronald Lee could take the bulletin this time.

Mr. Hoogeveen lived on the corner of London Street with his wife, four teenage daughters, and Stephan, who was five years old. Even though they belonged to the Reformed Church and not the Christian Reformed Church, Mr. Hoogeveen liked to read over the births and deaths or sick and shut-ins from Grandville Avenue. His interest was different than Klikkuiken wanting to keep up on all the news. Klikkuiken was nosy and wanted to be first with information. Then she could enhance the stories, passing the gossip along to Bertha Feenstra, who'd pass it on to Albert Meyer or Rena Grasman. Mr. Hoogeveen just seemed to care about his neighbors.

Proud to be substituting for our brother, Ronald Lee rang the doorbell.

Mr. Hoogeveen opened the door, dressed in his familiar railroad overalls. "Well, well. What do we have going here?" he said. "Hello. So nice to see you."

Ronald Lee took a step forward and handed him the bulletin.

"Thank you so much. We are about the table, ready to have a little tea. Maybe you would like to come in for a cookie?" He opened the door further to let us pass through, but we hesitated. "It's okay. You like cookies? Come in."

The four girls and Mrs. Hoogeveen were sitting around the kitchen table. I recognized the oldest daughter, Marilyn because she was a friend of Deannie's. She was Stephan's mother and wasn't married.

Marilyn got up and offered her chair to me. "I'll get a couple more a minute."

There wasn't room for two more chairs. "Ronald Lee can sit on my lap," I said. "He doesn't mind, do you, buddy?" We settled in Marilyn's chair and she wedged one in for herself.

"Would you like tea?" Mrs. Hoogeveen asked and set two cups in front of us, like we were grownups but couldn't speak for ourselves. "Isn't it a pretty spring day?" Her housedress reminded me of Aunt Jane's. So did her gray hair, except Mrs. Hoogeveen wore her hair curly and loose instead of pinned in a bun. She poured the tea and set the sugar bowl within my reach.

Mr. Hoogeveen passed the cookies. Thick, round, homemade peanut-butter cookies.

"Would you like a gumdrop?" Mrs. Hoogeveen asked, handing Ronald Lee a small, pretty glass plate that held spearmint candies arranged on a doily. "Milk with your tea?" She asked politely. Ronald Lee and I answered with a nod or a shake of our head.

"You know Ron, don't you, Stephan?" Marilyn asked. "Remember Ron, Deannie's boy? You played with him last winter."

I heard it. For the first time. Clearly.

Having inherited the ethnic ability to conceal emotion, I set my cup in the saucer without choking on my tea. I picked up my cookie and bit off a piece. The chatting continued.

Maybe Marilyn is mistaken. Maybe she's confusing Ronald Lee with someone else. Maybe Marilyn's just plain wrong.

I knew she was right.

I picked up my tea once more, but wondering what Ronald Lee knew about all this, quickly set the cup down again. He continued to calmly eat his cookie on my lap. I gave him a slight squeeze, like I was the mother.

The Hoogeveens continued to visit. My unyielding arms wrapped around Ronald Lee in protection. Protection from what, I wasn't sure.

"Do you go to Sunday School, Ron?" they were asking.

He nodded.

"What age does it quit? Do you still go to Sunday School, Janie?"

I tried to focus, shrugging my shoulders.

"How old are you when you finish Sunday School in your church?" Mrs. Hoogeveen repeated.

"I'm not sure," I finally answered. "I think twelve."

I wanted to leave and go outside in the fresh air, in full daylight instead of the kitchen that now seemed crowded and smothering. I wanted to breathe deeply without anyone noticing, to exhale what I had heard.

I finished most of my tea. "So, we have to go. I told my Mom we'd be right back," I said. "Thank you for having us."

"Well, come again and you can play with Stephan," Marilyn said.

"Come again for cookies!" Mr. Hoogeveen called as we stepped outside.

"Thank you. Bye!" I answered for both of us.

Some kind of relief came over me—relief to walk along the sure, hard sidewalk of London Street, relief to see Ronald Lee kick a stone into the cemented curb, relief watching him point to crocuses in DeLeeuw's grass. The air smelled new and I could feel spring, warm on my face. I looked up to white clouds floating in the blue sky. The sun was bright and made my eyes water.

Or something made my eyes water.

We walked down London Street together, my clammy hand holding his. It was Thursday. There'd be pork chops for supper. Pork chops, potatoes with gravy, green beans, applesauce.

Ron. Deannie's boy.

I had never heard it before, but when I did, it seemed true, natural. Now that somebody said it out loud like that.

Pork chops ranked up there in my favorites, like Sunday dinner. But my eye stayed on Ronald Lee during supper. He seemed unaffected. I ate without appetite, without tasting, to avoid questions. I didn't ask. I wasn't sure I was supposed to know. And if Ronald Lee didn't know or understand, I certainly wasn't going to explain.

So I didn't ask him. And I didn't tell anyone.

That night, kneeling at my bed in pajamas and brush rollers, I prayed through "Now I lay me down to sleep." Then I added my own words. "Forgive me for not wanting to baby-sit Ronald Lee that day. Forgive me for taking him to school so Dale could hit him in the stomach. Dear God, help me not to give away today's secret. For Jesus' sake. Amen."

~

Teasing spring weather fooled us before changing back to winter. But after a few weeks, spring made an appearance once more and Deannie moved home again.

It was Sunday so we ate raisin bread with frosting for breakfast. Deannie prepared the roast with spices and put the pan in the oven. The potatoes, peeled the night before, were sitting in a pan of cold water on top of the stove. When we finished breakfast, I helped clear the table and went upstairs to beat my sisters to the bathroom.

I put on a slip and petticoat, white anklets, patent shoes, and my blue and white gingham dress. Tying a matching ribbon in my blond hair, I looked in the full-length mirror behind our bedroom door. "Plenty fine," I said to my reflection.

Dressed in trousers, sport coats and ties, Bobo and Arie headed downstairs. Their bedroom door was open, and after peeking first, I went in and sat on the bed with Ronald Lee. He was still in his pajamas.

"You know, Sunday School's almost done for the year," I told him, urging the *toefka* of his brush cut up and off his forehead with my fingers. "They don't have it in the summer."

"But I like Sunday School," Ronald Lee said.

"Well, we'll have lots of fun outside instead."

Usually someone helped Ronald Lee get dressed on Sunday, either my mother or my father, sometimes Deannie. I reached for the closet door and took down the hanger with a green and white pin-striped Eton suit. Ronald Lee put the white short-sleeved shirt on and slipped his little legs into the shorts. As I scrunched up a knee sock over his foot, Deannie came in the room.

"That's not what he's supposed to wear." Ignoring Ronald Lee, she walked to the back of the closet and came back with long pants and a seersucker jacket.

"But this is what Mom set out for him," I said.

She raised her voice. "He is going to wear this."

"That's ugly!"

"Ronald Lee, take off that shirt and shorts," Deannie told him.

"He just got it on and now you want him to take it off?"

Ronald Lee stood between us, caught and confused. Then he began to remove his shorts.

"Be a good boy and put these on instead," Deannie said, softening her voice.

I hated the way being good meant listening to Deannie. "He shouldn't have to," I said.

"Mind your own business!" Deannie told me.

"I don't have to."

"Just get out of here!"

"What's going on?" Father said from the hallway before entering the room. "We have to leave for church in a little while. Is this any way to prepare for church? You stop it, *hoor*?"

"I was helping Ronald Lee get dressed." I picked up the little green and white shorts and rammed my fists on my hips. "Until Deannie stuck her nose in!"

"I wanted him to wear this today," Deannie explained.

Father picked Ronald Lee up and hugged him close.

"You go downstairs," Father told me. "Deannie and I will handle the rest of this."

"This is stupid! I'm sick of it! What right does she have, anyway?"

I left the room. I knew what right she had.

≈

I took a long look outside the church, stretching my neck back until it hurt. The top of the steeple is hard to see unless standing across the street in Roosevelt Park or on the other side of Grandville Avenue. There's a large cross at the top, Father said a symbol of fear and fortress at the same time.

We filed into the third row from the front—Deannie, Babe, Aunt Dienke, me, my mother, Ronald Lee, my father, Arie J and finally, Bobo. The Pylmans took their place behind us in the fourth row. Mr. Bachuizen sat at the organ and began "*Alle Roem is Uitgesloten.*" After calling the song one of her favorites, Mother told me once it means, "All Celebrity is Excluded."

Last Sunday had been Preparatory Sunday. Over the next seven days, people were supposed to be especially mindful of their sins and their need of Christ's sacrifice. Today was a Communion Sunday. Communion Sundays are a big deal, observed only four times a year.

In front of the pulpit, the long elaborate walnut table engraved with the words "*This Do in Remembrance of Me*" was set with a beautiful shiny silver flagon, chalice and plate. Round silver receptacles the size of dinner plates had been carefully stacked on each end. Some contained bread, some contained individual miniature cups of wine. Mogen David wine.

"Grace, mercy, and peace be unto you from the Father and from the Son through the operation of the Holy Spirit. Amen."

We stood to sing. Mr. Pylman's rich tenor voice behind me, in my left ear.

> *My heart was glad to hear the welcome sound,*
> *The call to seek Jehovah's house of prayer;*
> *Our feet are standing here on holy ground,*
> *Within thy gates, thou city grand and fair.*
> . . . .
> *For all my brethren and companions' sake*
> *My prayer shall be, Let peace in thee abide;*
> *Since God the Lord in thee His dwelling makes,*
> *To thee my love shall never be denied.*

After Reverend Piersma read the Ten Commandments, the congregation sang Psalm 51 from the blue hymnal. We sang the Psalm slowly, sincerely, with penitence. The blue hymnal edition marked the denomination's one-hundredth birthday. At our house, the older red songbook still rested on our piano.

Scripture was read. The entire chapter of Ephesians 2. Then Lord's Day VII of the Heidelberg Catechism.

The Catechism says true faith is a confidence that our salvation is freely given by God, merely of grace and only for the sake of Christ's merits, which we heard over and over when Reverend Piersma preached. That's what Gospel implies. Assurance and comfort.

My father said reading the Catechism each Sunday guaranteed observance of the church year and kept Sunday morning sermons set accordingly. Reverend Piersma held the Heidelberg Catechism in as high and sacred regard as being Protestant allowed. In addition to structuring the church year, Reverend Piersma said the Catechism "sustained the congregation in a sense, it gave the congregation substance. . . ." I read that in the bulletin.

To avoid a pinch on the thigh or upper arm if I did not face forward, I watched Reverend Piersma during the sermon, appearing attentive. What I did for real was daydream about a new hopscotch pattern, imagining various arrangements of thick, chalky numbers.

If I had listened carefully, I might have noticed something the minister said to upset Deannie, but when she stood up and walked out of church during the third point, I didn't understand.

People didn't walk out of church.

People didn't talk to each other either, especially during the sermon. Even so, Mother and Father began to whisper back and forth. Then my mother left the sanctuary, distracting more than the entire front row she had to pass to reach the exit. I wiggled uncomfortably on the hard wooden bench.

When the sermon ended, the elders came forward to distribute the sacrament. There was so much to see. First, while we sang, the silver plates holding soft white cubes of bread were passed up and down the aisles like when the deacons collected an offering.

> Come, for the feast is spread, Hark to the call;
> Come to the Living Bread, Offered to all.
> . . . .
> Millions have been supplied, No one was e're denied,
> . . . .
> What-e'er thy want may be, Here is the grace for thee,
> Jesus thine only plea; Come, . . . come.

Reverend Piersma lifted his arms, the sleeves of his robe opening further. I could see the material of his black suit coat and the cuffs of his white shirt. He held up a strip of white bread. I watched closely, absorbed, forgetting Deannie and Mother for now. Reverend Piersma pulled the bread strip apart and announced, "The bread which we break is a communion of the body of Christ. Take, eat, remember, and believe that the body of our Lord Jesus Christ was broken unto a complete remission of all our sins."

At the same time as the other full members in good standing, my father placed his piece of bread in his mouth, chewing slowly and remembering atonement.

A slight, sharp clink could be heard as the remaining receptacles on the table were uncovered. The elders passed the wine and the aroma in the sanctuary captured me. This forgiveness of sins thing was important, powerful stuff.

> *Come, ye disconsolate, wher-e'er ye languish,*
> *Come to the mercy seat, fervently kneel;*
> *Here bring your wounded hearts, here tell your anguish;*
> *Earth has no sorrow that heaven cannot heal.*
>
> *Joy of the desolate . . . Hope of the penitent . . .*
> *Here speaks the Comforter, in mercy saying,*
> *"Earth has no sorrow that heaven cannot cure."*

After pouring wine from the silver vessel into the cup with an audible, ceremonial flow, Reverend Piersma lifted the cup and recited, "The cup of blessing which we bless is a communion of the blood of Christ. Take, drink ye all of it, remember, and believe that the precious blood of our Lord Jesus Christ was shed unto a complete remission of all our sins."

The members tipped their heads back and swallowed reassurance from the tiny glasses.

"Beloved in the Lord, since the Lord has now nourished our souls . . . let every one say in his heart: 'Bless Jehovah, O my soul; and all that is within me, bless his holy name.'"

The sacrament ended with prayer. Though I wasn't old enough to "partake," I knew enough to be sorry Mother and Deannie had missed it.

The service ended and we filed out from the aisles. I immediately left the building from the side exit. But Ginny Huizinga caught up to me. "I saw your sister walk out of church. My Mom says a lot of flu is going around."

"Yeah," I said. I knew her comment was innocent. "It's too bad."

"I hope she feels better soon. Your Mom, too!"

"Well . . . thanks."

It was going to rain. A good spring thunderstorm. I ran toward the station wagon, the white vehicle a contrast against the darkening sky. I climbed into the back seat and waited for the rest of the family. The clouds gave rise to rumbling thunder. A cruel sting rose in my throat.

Tien

From the tunnel underneath the traffic, I walked up the metal grid steps to daylight. I passed Treat's Drug Store, Jelsema's Hardware, Sid's and the parking lots. Spring was swaying toward summer and before long sixth grade would be finished.

With the afternoon mild, I thought we might take a bike ride when I got home. Ronald Lee and I would cruise around London, Lynch, and Hogan streets. We'd take a sweep down Roosevelt Hill where I'd take my feet off the pedals and lift my knees, letting the Rollfast race down at its own speed.

If riding bikes didn't sound good to Ronald Lee, we could play Wiffle ball in the street once the 3:30 Kelvinator traffic tapered off. Or it might be a good day to go over to the woods, a small grove of trees next to the railroad tracks by Griggs Street where we were in the process of building a secret camp with Arie J.

I cut through Kingmas' driveway, on to London Street, past the Hoogeveens and DeLeeuws. Mr. DeLeeuw was at the end of his driveway. I looked down, ignoring him as I passed. Klikkuiken was stationed on her front porch. I gave a routine wave to the old woman and then passed the DeBoers and VanderGoots.

I didn't recognize the car parked in front of our house, but it wasn't Wednesday and I didn't think much of it. Mr. and Mrs. Vander-Goot, Theresa and Henry were sitting on the front porch, so I didn't cut across their grass but waved to our next-door neighbors from the sidewalk.

I hiked up the driveway. Someone had forgotten to latch the white picket gate. As I entered the backyard, my oldest sister, Jackie, came from the back door and onto the stoop. Under one arm, she held an entire dresser drawer.

"What ya doin' here?" I asked. Not a silly question, considering how seldom she visited.

She stepped off the small cement porch. "Hello." Jackie nodded, one-half of her mouth curved in a delayed smile. Her buggy eyes resembled my father's. She was the shortest member of the family, slightly wide. Her hair was cut in a practical bob and she wore no makeup. Ever.

"Having coffee?"

My sister shifted the drawer to the other arm. "Nope. Can't visit. I'm here to help move." With a shrug, she headed through the gate.

I went inside. Gracia sat at the table but the table wasn't set for tea. I checked the den, popping just my head around the corner. There Mother sat in the chair with gold flecks. "Hello," I said. All she said back was hello. Mother's new dark-brown glasses made her face look stern.

I started upstairs and met Deannie coming down, a drawer with its contents under her arm. We nodded as we passed each other. From the landing, I looked into my sister's room and saw clothes strewn on top of the bed. Most of the drawers from the bureau were missing.

Deannie used to put her things neatly in boxes days before moving. She always talked about it in advance. Suzie always helped, not Jackie, and it always happened on a Saturday.

"Can I help?" I asked when Deannie came back and found me in her room.

"Well . . . here." Deannie opened a cabinet with socks inside. "Empty these into a bag and carry it out to Jackie's car."

We made more trips up and down the steps, packing the car.

After a thousand climbs up and down the stairway, I said, "I think that's everything."

"Not yet," Deannie said.

She walked into the boys' room and started pulling out drawers. She opened the closet and made a pile on the bed—little white and black saddle shoes, the Eton suit, corduroys, the white shirt with a bow tie, the Carter pajamas with horses printed on them. Blue jeans, a flannel shirt from the drawer. Deannie stacked them next to the clothes from the closet.

My stomach tightened. I just stood there watching socks and underwear pile up. The red tennis shoes, his Tiger baseball cap, a sweatshirt.

Jackie picked up a stack to take outside. I watched Deannie take the suit and the pile of shirts and carry them out. Jackie came back, picked up more. Deannie returned for another stack. Finally, there was only a pile with pajamas and underwear left. I picked up the pile, hesitated, and carried it outside.

On the front walk, Deannie took the pile from me and found a place for it in the back of the car.

"Thank you," she said.

"You're welcome . . . I guess . . ."

Father's station wagon pulled into the driveway. It was only 3:30—two and a half hours early. He drove up to the garage, but did not park inside it. He walked to the front yard, took one look inside the green and white sedan, then turned and faced Deannie.

"Where is he?" he demanded.

"He's not here. He left earlier with Suzie." Somehow Deannie sounded brazen and scared at the same time. "We met her at the corner."

He grimaced, breathing deeply through his nose, and stomped passed us into the house.

I stood on the sidewalk, staring at my sisters, then at the car packed haphazardly like their plan. A lump in my throat found its way down to my stomach. I looked back at Deannie but she offered no explanation. I looked at Jackie, who quickly turned away. I looked at the VanderGoots watching from their porch.

"We better go," Deannie said.

"Just a minute, young lady!" Father called as he came out of the house again.

Looking down at the pavement of the street, he walked right past Deannie and went up to Jackie first.

"That you would help in this . . ." He shook his head from side to side, slowly like he spoke. ". . . I don't know."

He turned to Deannie. In his usual reprimand stance, he lifted his index finger and pointed it in her face. But then he lowered his finger and said nothing.

I watched my father's anger change to frustration, disappointment, and despair, all while standing there in the middle of London Street.

Finally, he spoke. "After all this time . . ." his voice was nearly inaudible. "After all these years." I heard Father gulp. "Not even a good-bye."

It was the most dejected statement I ever heard my father make.

He turned, head down, shoulders slumped. He stepped over the curb onto the sidewalk, past the border of white bricks set along the drive, and through the picket gate. The latch clicked loudly while I watched and my sisters looked away.

Deannie and Jackie climbed into the car and I rasped out, "See ya later." They must not have heard me, because they didn't answer. Instead, they drove away.

I plunked down on the back stoop wiping my face with my sleeve. My stomach still hurt and so did my throat. I stood to open the screen door but let it slam as I sat down again to wipe my face some more.

Father left to go back to work in the same white, stained shirt. He paused in the backyard and quietly placed his hand on my head as he walked around me on the stoop.

I went inside. I didn't see Gracia and didn't care. In the kitchen, my mother stood in the corner on the register. It wasn't cold outside. The furnace wasn't even on. I doubted she saw me. Her gaze looked far, far away and her stance on the register uncomfortable. Without my after-school apple, I went upstairs to change out of my school clothes. I turned the clock radio on, hoping to hear the new Beatles song. I stretched out on the bed, opened my notebook and tried to do my homework.

From my window, I could see the VanderGoots still on their porch and I wondered what they were thinking. I wondered what Deannie and Jackie were thinking. I started to cry softly, wondering what Ronald Lee was thinking. I wondered about my mother. I wondered about God and his Sovereignty.

Then I wondered what Klikkuiken would say.

I wiped my face and went downstairs to practice my piano lesson. My hymn assignment for the week was "Take Time to Be Holy." I played my scales and songs through three times and heard my mother preparing supper. The smell of pork chops frying filled the kitchen, den, living room, and moved up the stairs, spreading over the house like Ronald Lee's absence. The void in the house reached from the basement to the roof's peak.

And Mother was frying pork chops.

It was Thursday. If the antichrist himself were manifest on Thursday, my mother would serve pork chops.

∾

I tried to keep to myself at home and in school. I didn't want anyone asking questions. We assumed Ronald Lee and Deannie stayed at Jackie's, although a week passed without any proof. Every night I prayed, "Dear God in heaven, I'm sorry I didn't want to babysit and then took Ronald Lee to school that day. I'm sorry for arguing about what he was going to wear to church." I swallowed to keep from crying. "Forgive me. Be with Ronald Lee. Keep him safe and from being scared. Please help Mom and Dad, too. And forgive me all my other sins. For Jesus' sake. Amen."

Stretched out under the covers, I faced the empty ceiling. Silent tears dripped into my ears and onto the curlers in my hair. The feeling was familiar. Not like a skinned knee or elbow, not like a bloody nose or earache or the flu. More like when my mother was gone and I didn't understand where or why or when I would see her again. Or if she knew I missed her.

On Saturday nights, my parents took their baths and peeled potatoes, like they always did. On Sunday mornings, they dressed and prepared for church as faithfully as the bell that rang in the tower after we greeted Mr. Kamps. Father ushered our family into the third pew of the sanctuary, as always. I listened to my parents sing Psalms. I watched my parents' audacity as they sang along with the congregation during a sacrament of baptism.

> *O God, Great Father, Lord and King!*
> *Our children unto Thee we bring;*
> *And strong in faith and hope and love,*

We dare thy stedfast Word to prove.

That's when I saw my mother relent. Right in the middle of Psalm 90. Tears spilling on her face. In church.

The place where Ronald Lee stayed remained uncertain. Mother stayed on the kitchen register a lot.

Reverend Piersma came to our house and I overheard him trying to comfort her. "But you loved him. He knows that. One does not forget such a thing. It will stay forever with him." I heard him remind my mother about baptism and of baptism's "indubitable" promise. I heard Mother's spoon on her saucer. I heard Reverend Piersma sip his tea.

My father went about suffering in his own silent way. I suspected his silence exaggerated my mother's difficulty. One night when I should have been asleep, I heard them.

"You don't care," my mother said.

"Yes I do," my father answered, his voice strained.

"You don't care," she repeated.

"Of course I do."

"But I know you don't."

"Yes I do."

I imagined my father kneeling next to his bed in his paisley print pajamas for nighttime prayer, like he always did. He must have prayed a long time. It was 11:30 and I began to drift to sleep when I heard my mother say it again.

"You don't care."

He raised his voice. "I do care."

"Shhhh! The kids will hear you."

"Of course I care. Don't be silly. Go to sleep."

"Sleep? I can't sleep. How can anyone sleep? How can you lie there sleeping and snoring every night? It goes to show you."

"That's crazy talk."

I drifted half asleep for a while until I heard noise coming from the bedroom below. Sobbing—a disconnected, haunting moan of three words repeated over and over and frighteningly over again. And it was coming from my father.

I lay under the covers shivering and listening but not wanting to hear.

"I do care. I do care. I do care."

"Dad. Dad," Mother whispered loudly. "Stop." She sounded scared.

"I do care."

"Dad. Dad. Stop."

"I do care. I do care. I do care."

"Please. Please stop, Dad," Mother pleaded.

He began to gasp loud and long, breathing in with a high tone, breathing out with lower sound, all in a rhythm that matched his words.

"I do care."

"Dad. Dad."

"I do care."

"Stop."

None of us got up. Not Babe, not Bobo, not Arie J, not me. We had been trained to mind our own business.

I could hear Mother crying. The clock radio said it was one o'clock. I thought about finding some music on the clock radio to cover the commotion downstairs, but I didn't want anyone to know I was awake.

"Please stop."

"I do care. I do care."

I heard Mother pick up the phone in the kitchen.

"Pete. It's about Orie. Can you come?"

He knocked almost immediately. When my mother let Mr. VanderGoot in, he must have gone directly to my father, whose words now ran together in a bizarre singsong.

"Orie."

"I do care. I do care. I do care."

"Orie. Orie. Orie."

I heard Mr. VanderGoot repeat the name, softly, gently, patiently over and over, rolling the "r" in a Dutch fashion I found somehow reassuring.

Again and again, he repeated the word in a comforting cadence. He spoke with the rhythm of my father, naturally inserting the name between Father's moans.

"I do care.

"Orie."

"I do care."

"Orie."

Mr. VanderGoot continued into the night. Mr. VanderGoot, the man who rapped on the window and frightened me with stern Dutch phrases he growled and I understood only by tone. I was afraid to touch his grass. And now I pictured the man holding my father, rocking him, soothing him, gently chanting again and again, "Orie. Orie. Orie."

Ever so gradually, at last the affliction seemed to diminish and the misery in Father's words lessened.

There was whispering, but I did not know what was said.

I heard Mr. VanderGoot leave and soon the house was silent altogether.

When I awoke and dressed, brushed my teeth and my hair, there was no indication of the night's events. I didn't feel tired after being awake most of the night. My father had left for work in the station wagon.

From the kitchen register, my mother watched me eat Cheerios and said nothing.

On the way to school, I cut across his grass, no longer afraid of Mr. VanderGoot. No longer a gruff old man guarding his green turf, but a shepherd tending pasture, heeding hurt.

Elf

I dawdled as I walked to school, thinking.

If Deannie is Ronald Lee's mother that gives her the right to say what he wears, what he eats, what he does. If Deannie is Ronald Lee's mother, it gives her the right to say, "This is Grandma. Janie's the aunt. I'm the Mother."

I stopped short and stared down at the sidewalk. It gives her the right to take him away. I didn't want anybody to notice my tears, so I brushed them away.

It doesn't mean she loves him more.

Maybe it was foreordained. Maybe my praying harder and harder finally helped, as if God operated on some sort of Richter scale. Or it could have been my sister's only option.

Deannie called and wanted to talk to me. She asked if I would baby-sit on Saturday. So I was chosen to see Ronald Lee first.

I kept counting the days until Saturday. They didn't talk about it but I could tell my parents were disappointed and hurt.

When Deannie came to pick me up, she waited in the car in the driveway. Father was at work. Mother stayed on the front porch, I supposed in case she could see Ronald Lee in the car. But he wasn't along.

We drove south about eight miles to a trailer park, turned down a side street and stopped in front of a brown and white rusting mobile home. I followed my sister inside.

"Hi, Janie," Suzie said.

"Hi. So where's Ronald Lee." My reply came out like a demand instead of a question.

"Playing in his room," Suzie said.

"Ron," Deannie called, "look who's here."

Ronald Lee flew down the long narrow hallway. "Janie!"

We hugged, hard and long, until Deannie interrupted.

"Let me give you some instructions before we go." She talked as if I never babysat anyone before. "You won't be able to reach me. If you have trouble, you can call Jackie. Or the nice neighbor there in the green trailer. You can make sandwiches for lunch if you walk to Shop Rite for some bread. Otherwise just heat up this can of soup. Pull Ronald Lee in the wagon if you want. I'll be back by suppertime. Suzie'll be here for supper too and you can stay and eat before I bring you home." She handed me three dollars for the store. "Ron. Say good-bye to your mother."

That sounded pretty awful. I wondered how it sounded to Ronald Lee. I doubted the word could transfer in a matter of weeks.

"Give your mother a hug and kiss. Mmmm. What a big boy. You be good. I'll be home by suppertime."

He hugged her back easily, naturally. Didn't cling or cry.

I took Ronald Lee to the window to wave. When the girls were out of sight, we sat at the table and shared some Kool-Aid.

"Janie, can we color now?" Ronald Lee asked.

"Sure. Whatever you want."

We went in his room. From under his bed, he pulled out a jumbo Disney coloring book, a new Roy Rogers one, and a box of forty-eight crayons. Most were still sharp.

"You can use Roy Rogers with me." He spread it open on the floor.

"Cool. Thanks. Let's find two together we like."

"It won't matter what side you take 'cause we both left-handed, remember?"

"You bet I remember." I lay down on the floor, reached over and gave him a short tickle. He giggled and my eyes started to tear up. "May I have the red?" I quickly asked.

Next we played Animal Rummy. Then we went outside and played cowboys. I hid behind the storage barn and heard him sneak up on me from the back.

"All right, stick 'em up!" He pushed the toy pistol into my spine. "Bang! You're dead."

I collapsed into the grass. Ronald Lee tapped his foot along my side to make sure I was a goner. I grabbed his leg and pulled him on top of me.

"Gotcha!" We wrestled on the ground. He climbed on my back and switched from sheriff to rodeo rider, grabbing my collar and wrapping his legs around my middle. I pranced around on all fours and stopped to rear up in a wild fit.

My mother had said she worried he wouldn't eat right and he would lose weight, but carrying around Ronald Lee didn't feel any different than when we played weeks ago. He had accumulated a few more freckles on his face, and his skinny little legs showed a tan mark where his shorts ended.

We played Wiffle ball, had a Popsicle and took a walk to Shop Rite. I pulled Ronald Lee in the wagon on the way to the store, and as we bumped along the sidewalk, I had a notion to just keep walking. It could take a long time to find us. Days or weeks. Maybe even never.

"That's where I'm going to first grade," Ronald Lee called out.

I stopped the wagon at the corner, along the chain-link fence. "What'd you say?"

He climbed out of the wagon and ran up to the fence. "That's my school!" He pointed to an "L" shaped, one-story building made of a light colored brick. Near the main entrance, a large sign said Gaines Elementary.

"Who said?"

"Deannie." He turned and said in a hushed voice, "I mean my mom."

I looked away and by squeezing my eyes shut, locked the tears and stopped the twitching around my mouth. I wanted so badly to pull him close to me, rest my chin on the top of his innocent little head and tell him "It's okay." But I wasn't sure it was okay.

Clearing my throat, I faced him and tried to smile. "Did you go inside? With . . . your mom?"

"Uh-uh." He looked through the fence. "Can we swing at the playground?"

I didn't want to think about Ronald Lee going to first grade here, making things so permanent. I picked up the wagon handle with one hand and with the other took Ronald Lee's. "Let's wait 'til on the way home."

On our way back, Ronald Lee pulled the wagon with a loaf of bread in it. We stopped at the playground to swing. While pushing him, I thought of my father. Last year, he had sent Ronald Lee to Christian kindergarten.

"Higher!" Ronald Lee called.

I pushed harder.

When we returned to the trailer, I made peanut butter and jelly sandwiches for lunch. We ate them outside on the step. We finished our milk and I asked, "Ready to take your nap now?"

Ronald Lee wrinkled up his nose. He smiled and his dimples showed. "I don't wanna take a nap."

"Okay." I winked.

Instead, he sat on my lap in a lawn chair with a book.

> *I am a bunny.*
> *My name is Nicholas.*
> *I live in a hollow tree.*
> *In the spring, I like to pick flowers . . .*

After I read it, Ronald Lee read it, remembering the story by heart from before.

Before, when he lived on London Street.

Drowsy, we cuddled and turned our faces toward the sun. Ronald Lee rested his head on my chest and soon fell asleep. I wondered if his dreams were restful or scary.

When they came back, Deannie and Suzie made hot dogs and instant pudding for supper.

"Say your prayer, Ron," Deannie told him when we sat down at the table. He folded his hands and covered his eyes with them. "Lord bless this food forJesussakeamen."

Deannie passed the food around. "No warm buns like Mom does it," she said to me, and before I could tell her it didn't matter, she went on. "This reminds me of the first week we were here. Ron wasn't eating his supper, so I sent him to his room with his hot dog until it was gone. After fussing a half hour or so, he came out. 'Is your hot dog gone?' I asked him. 'Yup!' he said. Well, the next week we ran across that hot dog at the bottom of the toy box, didn't we, Ron?"

I laughed with the others for a minute, until I remembered that first week after Deannie took Ronald Lee away. Suzie saw me scowl and stared at the ketchup bottle she tipped upside down to let the rest of the liquid drain to the cap. Deannie pretended not to notice my discomfort.

After dinner, we put the dishes in the sink. Deannie said Suzie would stay with Ronald Lee while she brought me home.

I gave him a kiss, and didn't want to let go when I hugged him. "Good-bye Ron. I'll see ya later." Deannie and I got in the car. He pressed his face against the kitchen window and didn't smile as he slowly waved his hand back and forth. It hurt me to watch him. "Good-bye, Ronald Lee. My forever brother," I whispered so Deannie wouldn't hear.

I fought tears all the way home. I didn't want my sister thinking I shouldn't baby-sit again or that I thought she had done the wrong thing by asking me. Mother must have been hoping for a glimpse of Ronald Lee through the side window. I saw her standing there when we pulled in the driveway. I walked in the door and didn't cry then either. I didn't want my parents more upset. I wanted them to let me go back if Deannie ever asked me again.

"He's back at the trailer with Suzie," I said.

"She lives there too?"

"No. She's just staying with him while Deannie brought me home."

I heard my father coming up from the basement. "Ronald Lee okay?" he asked before reaching the top step.

"He seemed pretty good."

"Poor kid," Mother said. She turned away, staring toward the window. "Was he clean, washed up?"

"Sure he was."

"How'd he eat? Did he eat decent?"

I sighed, shifting my feet before answering my mother. "He ate his lunch and his supper."

Father shook his head back and forth in slow motion and I saw his eyes well up.

"Poor kid." Mother dabbed her face with her apron.

I'd bust into tears myself if I didn't get out of there. "I'm tired. I think I'll go upstairs."

Father nodded.

I stayed in my room the rest of the night with the door shut, still thinking about Popsicles, *I am a Bunny*, the wagon ride. At bedtime I positioned my knees on the floor with my elbows on the bed and my hands folded. "Thank you that I could be with Ronald Lee today." I always said my prayers silently at night but still needed to stop to take a deep breath. "May that help him—not make things worse. Help Mom and Dad. Please keep Ronald Lee safe . . . and make Deannie take good care of him . . . don't let him be sad . . . he must be sad . . . he must miss us an awful lot he must be all mixed up . . ." I climbed on the bed and buried my face in the pillow, sobbing.

~

Drilling started again the next day.

"The trailer. What about the trailer?" Father asked.

"Well, it's fine. Clean. With furniture. Ronald Lee has his own room."

"Poor kid. I suppose it's all *sortje* around there," Mother said. "What did you do all that time?"

"The neighbors weren't *sortje*. It looked okay around there. We took a walk."

"What else did you do?"

"We played Animal Rummy, read a book, colored."

Father shook his head back and forth, slowly.

By Monday, I was sick of their questions.

"I wish you'd leave me out of this. Just leave me alone." I stomped upstairs and slammed the door. My conscience kinked with guilt. I made a secret vow to try to be kinder to my parents and more hopeful.

But I had inherited this capacity for a good deal of hope and a good deal of anxiety at the same time.

Twaalf

"Take your hat off at the table," Father greeted us on Sunday morning.

Arie J took off his Tiger baseball cap and set it on his lap.

Babe and I were allowed to wear our brush rollers. I had outgrown the pipecurls.

"Let us pray," Father said. "Gracious God and heavenly Father, we come to you this Sabbath morning hour . . ."

We ate our raisin bread with frosting. Babe prepared the beef roast. After cleaning up breakfast, I went upstairs and put on a flowered cotton dress with patch pockets in the front that I recently made in 4H class from a McCall's pattern, my first hand-sewn dress.

When I came back downstairs, my father took one stern look at me. "That is too casual, *hoor?* You must show respect when you go to church."

"Dad, this isn't disrespectful," I answered. "It's style."

"It is not respectful and neither are you, young lady. Besides, what will it lead to?"

I stomped upstairs and changed.

After Father dropped us off at the front of the church, he went to park the station wagon. Mr. Kamps met us inside. He held my mother's hand a long time when he greeted us today. "*Hoe ist?*" he asked. Mother returned his smile and answered something I could not hear. Mr. Kamps left to ring the bell, and as it pealed, Father walked into the church.

The Law was read. We sang a response. "Lord, like the publican I stand."

Reverend Piersma read from the book of Esther. After the reading, the sanctuary lights were dimmed. He stood in his black robe with his hands behind his back, bouncing up and down on his toes before he began the sermon.

"Brothers and sisters of the Lord Jesus Christ," he addressed us.

I put the first peppermint in my mouth.

Reverend Piersma bounced on his feet. "The book of Esther is actually about Mordecai."

The new family from Canada sat in the fifth pew, behind us to the right. Originally, three years ago, they came from the Netherlands. One of the five boys was in my grade, another in Bobo's. They lived on Griggs, the block south of London Street.

When Reverend Piersma started his second point, peppermint two went in my mouth.

I studied the stained glass window on my left with the three crosses on Golgotha and stared at the opposite window with the angel and the empty tomb until Mother nudged me with her elbow.

"Let us look at the third point."

Third and final peppermint.

I looked straight ahead.

"People of God." He bounced on his toes before continuing. "Mordecai is the mediator for Israel. This is the first Feast of Purim. Through Mordecai, God delivered Israel from the massacre of the Persian Empire. Mordecai is a picture of Christ and God's grace to His people."

On the stained glass window behind Reverend Piersma, The Good Shepherd looked over us. Forever etched into my memory from the third row.

"And, dear people, God's grace comes to us too." As he delivered the final sentences, his bounce relaxed and his speech slowed to a quiet, affirming Gospel.

During Sunday dinner, comments on the beef roast were complimentary. Comments on Reverend Piersma were too.

∾

When daylight ended earlier and earlier and autumn nights prophesied cold, we still weren't used to Ronald Lee's absence. We were beginning to understand we might never get used to it.

Seventh grade began junior high. This morning like every morning, my homeroom teacher, Miss Vredevoogd, made us sing. She waltzed up and down the rows, tapping a ruler on our desks in rhythm or slapping non-participating students on the hand. Ginny sat across the aisle from me. Ginny often got a rap from the ruler for whispering.

The bell rang for break. I took my time clearing my desk while my classmates rushed outside to play basketball. I couldn't shoot baskets for beans so I walked the circle of the schoolyard instead. Ginny caught up to me and walked along. We stopped near the basketball net in the parking lot to watch the boys play "Whoever gets the ball gets to shoot." Jim caught the ball and handed it to Ginny to shoot, which meant he liked her.

"Oh rats," she said when the ball hit the backboard first and landed on the blacktop.

Jim grabbed it, dribbled a few paces and took aim.

Corky got the rebound and gave it to me.

For lunch hour, I was expected to go home because we lived only four blocks away.

"Why are you in such a hurry today?" Mother asked.

I gulped the rest of my milk and set my dishes in the sink. "Ginny and I are going to hang out before the bell."

I walked quickly along London Street and Clyde Park and soon entered the tunnel. Sometimes at school I felt more like an alien than the new boy from Canada must have. And there was this fear of divulging our family secrets. But Ginny said she would meet me at the parking lot. And maybe Corky would give me the ball.

∾

On Friday afternoon while I worked on our geography assignment in homeroom, my mind drifted to the weekend, home, and soon to Ronald Lee. There was never a day I didn't think about him, but today his absence felt more pervasive. So did my sadness.

Assigned seats in homeroom were in alphabetical order, so Corky sat behind me. He tapped me on the shoulder, and I had to blink a few times to keep tears from running out of my eyes before I turned around. I shrugged my shoulders, indicating I wasn't up to number six yet and faced forward again.

Soon there was another tap on my shoulder. When I ignored him, I heard a whisper. "Janie. You okay?"

Without turning around, I nodded.

I waited for my eyes to dry and my geography concentration to return. Miss Vredevoogd was busy with her wall maps, rolling them up for the weekend. I turned around. Corky stopped his work. Boldly, he lifted his pencil and twisted a piece of my hair with it.

Corky, if I could tell you, I would. Of all people, I would tell you. I would tell you how I lost a brother. Well, I didn't lose him. I mean, he isn't dead. You see, he's gone. He's just gone. My brother is gone. Well, he's not my brother, I mean, not really. He's my nephew. But to me, he's my brother, at least he always was. He still is. Anyway, he belongs to my sister, but he actually doesn't because really he belongs to us. Never mind.

I could never say it aloud to him. I could never say it aloud to anyone.

∾

Autumn advanced and we continued our attempt to adjust. Sometimes Ronald Lee's absence was less noticeable, but at other times the void would poke its head around the corner like a mean, corrupted game of peek-a-boo. Late afternoons I stayed in my room pretending to do my homework, hiding my hurt from a mother unable to help, a mother trying for her own relief on the kitchen register.

November came and wore on. Mother made pork chops, casserole, pea soup, and sought consolation at her post on the register.

∾

On Thanksgiving Day we went downtown to watch *The Sound of Music* at the Midtown Theater. Mother, Babe, Aunt Dienke and I. Father refused to come along and was disgusted that we went without him. Hollywood was still of the world. "A place of Sodom and Gomorrah," he said. The opposite side of the antithesis.

"But what about the music, Dad? There's beautiful music in the movie," I said. "And the mountains. You would love the mountains."

"Do they open with prayer?" he asked me loudly, to be sure my mother overheard.

"Nooo," I answered as if I had to think first.

"That's a good indication you don't belong there," he said.

"They don't open with prayer at Tiger Stadium."

"Never mind. Hollywood is trash. It's all trash. Everyone wants to be part of the world. It's horrible, that's all. Just horrible."

But Father loved a good story. So I kept arguing.

"It's only a movie, Dad. About a widowed man with children who gets married again. With nice mountains and lots of Catholic nuns and pretty music."

"Yes. And full of idolatry. Catholics and idolatry," he said. "And what will it lead to?"

My father took Bobo and Arie J bowling that Thanksgiving, just the three of them. I'm not certain if Aunt Dienke ever went to the theater again in later years, but I know it was the first and last time for my mother.

~

On a Sunday morning in February, Reverend Piersma announced he was taking a call to the First Christian Reformed Church in Sioux Center, Iowa. When he preached his final sermon, he used the text from Genesis where God establishes an everlasting covenant with Abraham and his seed through all generations. ". . . baptism is a seal and indubitable testimony that we have an eternal covenant with God."

I had heard it many times. "I will be your God, you will be my people." One more time Reverend Piersma spoke this comfort. But every covenant has two parts and I couldn't help but think of the vow my parents took when Reverend Piersma baptized Ronald Lee. I couldn't help but wonder how they could do justice to their part of the bargain.

When the farewell service finished, cake and coffee were served in the church basement. We took our place in line to say good-bye after refreshments.

Father held up the line for some time, talking while Reverend Piersma nodded agreement. When Ronald Lee was born five years ago, my father had disputed and overstepped Reverend Piersma's advice. Through the floor register in my bedroom one Sunday night, I overheard Father talking with the Kamps. Reverend Piersma had told my father that both clergy and social authorities recommended putting Ronald Lee up for adoption. Father refused.

Now they shook hands firmly, conveying what looked to me like mutual respect.

My mother accepted the Reverend's hand and grasped his forearm with her left hand, resisting an urge to embrace. But she couldn't stop her tears.

"Good-bye, Dominie," I heard her say.

Then it was my turn.

"Good-bye, Reverend Piersma," I said, but "bye" was the only sound my throat did not choke away.

He grimaced as he always did when he preached and made a face in pain or disgust for emphasis. "Is that all you can say? Bye?" He leaned back and tipped his head sideways.

I knew he was teasing, but I was embarrassed as he took my hand. This man is what Sunday means to me. This man drinks bourbon *slokjes* with my parents in our living room. He gives pardon from the pulpit and mercy from our kitchen table.

And all I could say was "Bye."

∼

Before winter was over, Reverend Piersma was gone.

Before winter still wasn't over, my mother was gone.

Father said Mother was in the hospital. The same one as before. Like the other times, he went to visit her several times a week. Like the other times, we didn't talk about it much at home.

No one at school talked about it. No one at church talked about it—to me anyway.

This time Reverend Piersma didn't visit my mother. Neither did I. I chose not to.

Although this time the silence about it all left me more frustrated and desolate than ever, a part of me was relieved no one spoke about the hospitalization. It would be too humiliating. I didn't know my mother's clinical diagnosis, only the customary conclusion—people in that place either had had a nervous breakdown due to lack of faith and strength, or they were plain crazy.

Or both.

We somehow managed a routine similar to my mother's, although the casseroles on Wednesday gave new meaning to Dutch blandness. Bobo called Thursday's pork chops ping-pong paddles. With a little help from my father, Sunday dinners remained intact for the most part. Babe had learned to prepare beef roasts since Deannie had been gone anyway.

One Saturday, Father took the time to show me how he made his pancakes. His ritual of mixing batter in a certain bowl with a certain amount of milk, with a certain fork, for a certain amount of time, was as important as the way he greased the griddle with butter and poured out the batter in small disks.

A few times while Mother was gone John and Gracia invited us for supper. Sometimes Dienke brought us a meal. After Father arrived home from work, Dienke walked across the street wearing potholder mittens and marched into the kitchen without a word. She set a potholder on the table and placed a fresh hot casserole down on top of it.

"*Eten*," she announced and left.

Not that we didn't ask her. Dienke always refused the offer to eat with us. But my father would thank her later and she would nod and answer "*Ja.*"

∾

Our teachers liked their seating charts in alphabetical order, which meant Corky usually sat behind me. He would make up questions to ask me about homework, make jokes about our teachers, or just smile and not say anything when he sensed my sadness. He seemed to like me even though my mother was in the mental hospital.

One Friday while Mother was still gone, Corky asked me after New Math, "Want to go to the movies tomorrow afternoon?"

"I don't know. The movies?"

My father had continued to remind us how the movie theater was a place of the world. Just plain wicked.

"Uh-huh," Corky said. "I'll come by and we can walk over together."

"Um. Sure. I'd like to go . . . maybe I should meet you there."

"How about at the door by the 28th Street parking lot side? 1:30?"

My cheeks were burning and I'm sure he noticed. "Okay."

This theater wasn't one of those large old downtown places like the Midtown but a new one next to the new mall, the first mall ever in our area. Mother was still in the hospital. I lied and told my father that Ginny and I were walking to the mall to look at the snow boots on sale. A forty-five minute walk from London Street.

How easily one can cross over the line of the antithesis.

In spite of my guilty conscience, the large screen and the sound track of *Stagecoach* mesmerized me. Corky actually laughed out loud and so I did too. And Corky held my hand in the dark through the whole second half of the film.

We met again the following week. Corky waited for me by the fence at the ball diamond near the far end of the school playground. A few inches of snow had started to pile up.

Junior high girls seldom wore hats. It just wasn't cool unless we were sliding or skating. The collar of my corduroy coat was lined with a heavy soft fleece and I pulled it up around my ears. I slipped my hands into my large square pockets. We didn't wear mittens or gloves either.

"Hello," Corky said. He didn't wear a hat either. His nose was red from the cold.

I liked that he didn't talk much. We walked across the baseball diamond, the lines now lost under the snow. He offered his arm to me, but I refused it with a shake of my head. When we turned the corner behind the community house, the building blocked the wind. We stopped.

Corky looked at me, but I quickly looked down. We each had our hands in our pockets. It was cold and I stood trembling. Then he leaned forward and kissed me. On the lips. I didn't resist, but didn't kiss back, either. He could feel me shaking. He put his hand behind my head and gently forced it down on the shoulder of his coat. He put an arm around one side of me. Then he went and put his other arm around my other side.

He didn't hug me—he held me—now and then rubbing the back of my coat, sometimes moving his hand to the back of my head, mostly just holding me still. He held me a long time. My trembling stopped. He put his hand under my chin, lifted it and kissed me again. This time I kissed back. My winter-chapped lips warmed.

A few minutes later I noticed the afternoon sky getting dim.

"I need to be home."

"I'll walk with you," Corky said.

He lived in the opposite direction and I said, "You don't need to."

In spite of the cold and the snow falling around us, Corky thought it best. As we walked through the darkening tunnel under the street, I was glad he had insisted.

He lit a cigarette and offered me one.

"No thanks."

At the corner of London Street I stopped. "It's best if I go on myself now."

"Well, good-bye then." He pulled a stocking cap out of his coat pocket and stretched it over his head and ears. He lived over a mile away, one of those boys who rode the bus home from school.

"Hope you're not too cold walking home," I said.

"I'll be okay."

London Street lay hushed with new snow. No hat, no mittens, no boots or scarf, only that very first kiss keeping me warm as I stepped through the small drifts forming in the twilight.

Dertien

O n the way home from school the following Monday, Arie J and
I decided to climb a giant snow bank the plow had left in the
Kelvinator parking lot. The pile stood as high as the roof of our garage
on London Street and, although almost fourteen years old, I couldn't
resist. We reached the top just as Ginny crossed the street. She stopped
to watch. I stuck my arms out, performance style, and slid down on
my feet to the very bottom where I landed on my butt.

Arie J was close behind me, sitting down to slide, he steered
himself with his hands, stuck tight in puffy nylon mittens that made
scraping sounds like the back of his snow pants.

"Nice play," Ginny said as I brushed myself off. She looked down
at her skirt and knee socks and then eyed the pile. "I should've worn
my slacks today." She stood in one place, kicking at the snow with the
heel of her shoe boot. "So, um . . . um . . ."

I looked at Arie J. "Go on ahead," I told him. "Wait for me at the
corner."

"Um . . ." Ginny continued to hesitate.

"What is it, Ginny?"

She kept kicking at the snow. "Well, I just wanted to tell you . . .
I'm sorry your mom's in the hospital."

"Oh yeah . . . That."

"Yeah . . . Well, you know, my mom was there a couple years ago."

"Really? . . . Well."

Ginny nodded a couple times, turned and started down the sidewalk. Struggling to say something, anything, to show my appreciation, I called after her. "Hey, Gin. See you at school tomorrow."

~

I tried to get used to the idea that Ronald Lee's absence wasn't talked about. But more and more, my anger festered as people I saw everyday kept quiet about my mother.

On Sunday, we sat as usual on the west side of church in the third row from the front, without my mother. We sang a song asking God to look on us favorably and, in his kindness, guarantee his grace. I couldn't exactly define the grace, but somehow knew it and was glad I was there in God's house.

I couldn't exactly define the sense of being left out either, but that's how it felt. Although there we sat in the middle of everyone, right in the third row from the front.

And as the separation between our family and the people from church increased, I could tell the gossip they reveled in did too.

Albert Meyer was a friend of Klikkuiken and one of the elders of the Church. He stood under the exit light when the service ended, acknowledging each of the churchgoers as they were leaving. He extended a hand for me to shake, his face stuck in a smile.

"Good morning. How are you?" he asked, his voice thin, his eyes darting to the person next in line.

I answered as a proper young lady would answer a righteous church representative. "Fine. Thank you, Mr. Meyer."

I wondered what he would say if I told him how I really was. Or worse, how I thought he really was.

~

Tulips bloomed. I felt a mild spring breath soften the harshness of the winter. Maybe because my mother came home again, making my family seem more like a normal family to me. The spring seemed to rub off on her, like humus for lilacs, making her a bit brighter and stronger.

~

Babe had a boyfriend.

Quiet and polite, Tom sat on his hands a lot during Sunday dinner. If he wanted something, he would lean over and whisper to Babe,

"Please pass the beans." His hair curled over his ears and on his neck in the back. While reading the Bible at the table that Sunday, my father inserted the eleventh chapter of I Corinthians right in the middle of the book of Ezekiel. "Doth not even nature itself teach you, that, if a man hath long hair, it is a dishonor to him?"

It didn't scare him away.

Tom took Bobo and me to swimming holes, county fairs, car shows. He played Rook with our family on Sunday nights, joined us for a card game of Pit when Gracia and John came over, and attempted to beat my father at canasta.

One Sunday afternoon while we were sitting on the front porch waiting for Tom, Mother asked Babe, "Where will you go to church tonight?"

"We'll go to Tom's church."

"With his mother and father?" Mother dunked a windmill cookie in her tea.

"Probably." Babe had told me once that his parents hardly went to church twice on Sundays.

The noisy red Plymouth pulled up in front of the house. Tom turned off his car, the silent air a contrast. He slammed the car door and climbed the front stoop.

"Don't tell me," Mother said. She got up from her webbed chair and latched the screen door. "Oh no you don't."

As Tom reached to pull the door open, Father stood up.

"What?" Babe asked, stepping between my father, mother and the door.

Mother put her hands on her hips and explained through the screen. "You don't come to pick up any daughter of mine on Sunday dressed like that." The tone of her voice sounded like "of course."

"What are you saying?" Babe asked.

"'Tis *Zondag* still."

Tom looked down at his blue jeans. "You mean these?"

"Go back home and put something decent on, young man," Father added.

"But Dad!" Babe said.

"Never mind. We are not of the world. I won't have it."

"After all," Mother said by way of further explanation.

Tom ran down the steps. "I'll be right back!"

The Plymouth roared away. My sister ran in the house, flew up the stairs and slammed the bedroom door.

The discussion about the noisy car, the long hair, and the blue jeans continued on the porch. I feared Tom would be discouraged for keeps.

But he didn't give up. That autumn, Tom signed on with the Marines. A few days after, he and Babe were engaged.

∽

My paternal grandfather died in March, the same week as Babe's wedding, the first weekend after Tom's boot camp.

Tom's orders were to report to Camp Pendleton, California, five days after the wedding. Initially, my father questioned the appropriateness of the celebration, but on Wednesday he decided, "The wedding should take place as planned."

Thursday was the funeral. Friday was the wedding.

It was a small wedding. About thirty people. We held it in the church's fireside room.

My father escorted Babe through a short aisle made between a few rows of straight-back wooden chairs. Babe wore a white gown, snug at the waist and full to the floor. Her face was hidden behind a shoulder length veil of lace. Father's face was beaming. I heard him repeat more than once during the day, "This is as it should be."

The new minister at our church, Dr. Palmer, came from Westminster Theological Seminary near Philadelphia. "A strict disciplinarian from the East Coast," Father said. Dr. Palmer had been a first lieutenant in the Marines in World War II. At Babe's wedding he gave a sermon entitled *Semper Fidelis*. He talked about the faithfulness required of a Marine, the faithfulness required in marriage, and God's faithfulness.

Vows were spoken. For a recessional, Bobo played the Marine Hymn on his trumpet while I accompanied him on the piano. Tom took Babe's arm and marched to the back of the room in his dress blues, black spit-shined oxfords, and a shaved head.

After the festivities, Babe and Tom packed their red Volkswagen Bug parked in the driveway on London Street.

"Well, I finally get a bedroom to myself," I teased my sister.

"And I finally won't have to share my clothes," Babe answered. "Now give me a hug."

We waved and watched them drive away. I let myself cry. It frightened me to think of my sister so far away in California.

A few days later, they called long distance to say they arrived safely at Camp Pendleton. "In that little red car of theirs," Mother said.

That very same day Deannie phoned and announced her engagement.

We met Bill late one Thursday afternoon. He drank coffee with Deannie and my parents around the kitchen table and spoke of the wedding they planned for July. I ate a chocolate chip cookie at the counter and could tell my parents thought Bill was a decent person. Except he was not from our Christian Reformed denomination but "merely Reformed."

"And what about poor Ron?" my mother finally blurted.

"What about *poor* Ron?" Deannie asked.

"You know. What will happen to him?" My mother tried to clarify herself.

"I intend to adopt Ronald Lee," Bill explained. He didn't expect approval or admiration for his statement, and he didn't receive it. Deannie must have warned him my parents weren't the type to praise anybody for performing an obligation in the first place.

Mother rose from the table to check the pork chops in the electric frying pan.

"What about school?" The interrogation continued now through my father.

Sure enough, Bill must have been rehearsed because I could detect eagerness in his answer. "We plan to send Ronald Lee to the Christian School."

As they finished their coffee, Mother put the pork chops on simmer and came back to the table. "You and Ronald Lee could move back home again until the wedding," she told Deannie. "You'd save money and you could finish building up your hope chest."

Deannie's eyes opened wider. She looked at my mother, then at Bill, then at my mother again. "Maybe," she said. "Maybe. We'll see."

I was happy for Deannie and Ronald Lee. I was happy for my mother and father.

And yet the idea frightened me. If Bill is Ronald Lee's father, it gave him the right to say what Ronald Lee does, where he lives. Who he sees and doesn't see. It gave him the right to take Ronald Lee—anywhere. To say, "I'm the Father."

But it didn't mean he'd love him more. Not more than we do.

Veertien

M y father said the unsettling summer of 1967 brought the antithesis closer to home.

We knew about hippies and long hair, flower children and free
love. We knew about Rock 'n' Roll. I had a Beatles album stashed in
my underwear drawer, hidden so my father wouldn't break it in half
and throw it in the trash barrel like he did to Deannie's Elvis Presley
album a few years before.

We knew the name Martin Luther King. Father listened to all Dr.
King's speeches on television. Once a year, always in the hot summer,
Father took us to Wealthy Street Baptist Church on a Sunday night.
Not to participate in their spontaneous "Amens," or hands clapping
and lifted to hallelujahs. We didn't follow the musical processions into
the aisles. But the hymns and voices were so beautiful, we did join the
singing from where we stood in our pew.

"I like that preacher, " Father said by way of explanation. "Fuller
is a Biblical, good conservative man. Reminds me of King."

Of course, we knew about Vietnam. We knew the unrest on college campuses. We knew the name Bobby Kennedy.

What we didn't know was how the tension, protests, and violence
would affect our little Dutch neighborhood.

Before I started high school, that summer I worked a part-time
job at George's ice cream stand. Besides the lunch hour regulars from
the Pepsi, Kelvinator, and Keeler Brass factories in the neighborhood,
exceptional summer heat brought a continuous string of patrons or-
dering ice cream and soda pop.

Across the country, the summer sun also heated inner-city hostilities. In July, rioting broke out in New Jersey and Des Moines. Illinois called on the National Guard to help quash outbreaks there.

We heard about it on the news and read it in the paper. But we were occupied with another wedding.

∽

When Deannie was in the hospital, she had found the guidance of a kindly chaplain there helpful. She stayed in touch with him these four years and was delighted when he agreed to officiate her marriage vows.

And so the wedding took place in a cool, shaded chapel in a large clearing of pine trees on the hospital grounds. Though no one asked me, I thought the setting an awful choice at first. But when we arrived, I recognized what a lovely little church it was.

My mother had spent the money to get her hair done at the beauty parlor. She looked unusually contemporary in her pink linen sheath dress—Jackie Kennedy style with cap sleeves—heels and pearl button earrings. The beaded pocketbook, held over her arm by a small golden chain, glittered in the sun.

"Wow! Don't you look nice!" my father said as we left for the wedding. Mother blushed.

There were maybe thirty-five guests total and they were already seated. An usher brought my parents to the front pew of the chapel. Arie J, Bobo, and I were escorted to the row behind them. The organ began to play "Praise to the Lord, the Almighty, the King of Creation." I gave Arie J a gentle nudge with my elbow, his signal to pay attention.

Bill, pale as the white jacket of his tux, walked to the front of the church with the chaplain. Next, Ronald Lee came down the aisle. Hair slicked back, wearing a bow tie, black patent shoes, pants and jacket identical to Bill's. Ronald Lee held a small pillow-like cushion, covered in white lace, two gold rings tied to the top. He grinned as he passed us.

Everyone stood up and turned to watch Deannie. A short veil covered her face. The color of the veil matched her dress, a simple yellow taffeta gown. Even her shoes were dyed light yellow. It looked to me like she squished her face into a pinch to avoid smiling too hard.

She carried a bouquet of pink tea roses and came down the aisle alone. Her choice.

A celebration for sure, but during the ceremony I found myself thinking beyond today and whether or not Ronald Lee would be all right a year from now when he was seven, or the year after that or a year after that.

Deannie and Bill repeated their vows. When he took the ring from the pillow and slipped it on my sister's hand, I saw Bill wink to Ronald Lee. That wink said a lot to me.

Outside on the lawn afterward, cake and ice cream were served under a canopy. In the arch of the chapel doors, I saw my father speaking with the chaplain, nodding with what I took to be approval. My brothers and I stood on the grass with my mother. Bill pointed us out and Ronald Lee headed our way. He appeared to cross the lawn deliberately slowly, trying to act as nonchalant as a six-year-old could.

"Good goin', man," Bobo said. He shook Ronald Lee's hand in four or five exaggerated pumps.

"Yeah. Way to be," Arie J said.

I waited patiently to congratulate him, finally getting to wrap him in a hug.

"Come here, boy," my mother said softly and put her arms out toward him. He ran to her and she held him long and hard—in front of everyone there. And the whole time, he hugged her back.

The photographer asked to take a picture, both of them facing forward with my mother's arms around Ronald Lee's shoulders and their hands holding each other's.

All afternoon and evening my mother conducted her role as Grandmother quietly and with such poise, I knew right then and there what kind of woman she was. And it wasn't crazy.

~

Two days after Deannie's wedding, riots exploded in Detroit and forty-three people died. Governor George Romney had to ask for federal troops and President Johnson ordered in 5,000 U. S. Army paratroopers. Buildings burned and tanks rumbled through Detroit streets. Like the rest of the folks on London Street and our neighborhood, the violence frightened me. As close as Detroit. That close and that real.

And then the following day the governor issued a curfew in Grand Rapids.

My boss at the ice cream stand came early to cash out that day. He paid me directly from the till. I made $3.75 that evening, and as I walked home, the three quarters jingled in my pocket. Within five minutes, I reached the corner where Grandville Avenue, Chicago Drive, and Clyde Park came together. I took the crosswalk instead of the tunnel.

I headed south down the sidewalk, running the quarters noisily through my fingers. A few cars went by. I was the only pedestrian in sight. I passed Crofton and glanced across the street to the four-storied Kelvinator factory. The sun was going down behind the building, but as I looked up at the roof, the sun wasn't what caught my attention.

Just to make certain, I looked again.

My heart beat faster and I sucked in my breath. I counted eight men. Some were standing, some walking back and forth. They were all in uniforms like policemen and they all held rifles. Three of the men knelt, one knee down on the roof, and held their rifles in ready position, aiming down at the very street where I was walking.

I knew about the curfew, the restriction on gasoline sales and the alcohol ban. But circumstances couldn't be this bad. This wasn't Chicago. This wasn't Detroit. This was Grand Rapids. And yet, as I walked toward London Street, watching the men on the rooftop with their rifles, I knew this was serious.

Ronald Lee was spending two weeks with us. One week while Deannie and Bill went on their honeymoon and another week while we took our annual summer trek to the cottage. Deannie asked ahead if I would sleep in the room she and Ronald Lee shared on London Street the last few months. Just in case he needed any extra attention or reassurance while she was gone.

Tuesday night, after we roughhoused and read a chapter from *A Wheel on the School,* I tucked Ronald Lee into his bed like I had done the last couple of nights. I left the room. When I returned an hour later and climbed into Deannie's bed, Ronald Lee was sleeping.

The night was still quiet when I first began to doze off. I slept a couple of hours before waking up to sirens. I lay in my sister's bed, listening.

Sirens continued on and off and when the blaring rested, I heard shouting. Then shooting.

Father climbed upstairs to use the bathroom. When he came out, I poked my head out of the bedroom door.

"Dad?"

"It's all right," he said in a hushed voice. "It won't come this far."

Bobo stood in the hallway. "How do you know, Dad?"

"I saw the police blocking Hall Street after work today."

"Hall Street's so close," I said.

Father reached and patted the top of my head. "Go back to bed, kids. I'll let you know if things get worse."

We did as we were told. As the night dragged on, I heard more shouting and more gunfire. Sirens sounded over and over. I thought the sun should be coming up by now. It was as if this never-ending night had some power over morning. Ronald Lee slept soundly until morning—an innocent, peaceful sleep on a far from peaceful night.

At breakfast Wednesday morning, my mother kept the radio tuned to the news. The reports said police armed with rifles and bayonets struggled all night to control yelling, fighting, smashing glass, the torching of buildings.

Father's boss, Bill Pastoor, phoned and told him not to come to the plant. Bob and Jim's Market had burned, Bill said, and smoke could still be seen coming from a house at the corner of Pleasant and Jefferson.

The *Grand Rapids Press* reported, "roving mobs." Fire trucks, hoses and police cars filled the streets. Black and white photos showed city police, firemen, and Michigan State Troopers. In the *Press*, all the enforcers looked white. All those arrested looked black.

Three hot miserable days and nights passed before the destruction wound down and the governor called off the curfew. The restrictions on gasoline and the ban on alcohol sales were lifted. The rioting in our city was moderate compared to Detroit. No deaths were reported in Grand Rapids, but dozens of injuries and over 300 arrests had been made.

On our Sunday afternoon drive, Father took us up Division Avenue, down and over on Wealthy. We could see Wealthy Street Baptist wasn't damaged, but other buildings were charred black, a lot of broken windows half disappeared or totally gone, some already boarded up. I saw a storefront that appeared unharmed. It had boards over the windows with words spray-painted in red. "Negro Owned."

"That's part of the problem," Father said. "White people own the shops and the houses but they don't live here. They don't hire the Negroes. Banks won't lend Negroes money because they don't have jobs."

We drove to Eastern Avenue and turned south, passing Pastoor Meats at the corner of Franklin. From there we took side streets and ended up on Hall Street. The two-story second—hand shop at 200 Hall had burned. Arson, the police suspected according to the *Press* report. Or firebomb.

Father took some more side streets between Jefferson and Lafayette as we headed back home. Buckley, Cass Avenue, Pleasant. This area was mostly residential. We had the car windows down. I counted at least ten houses that had been burned.

Like it was any other warm summer Sunday afternoon, people in white shirts and white dresses sat outside on their front porches. All of them were black people.

"*Aach . . . Aach . . . Aach . . .*" was all Mother said.

~

As Deannie and Bill headed back from their honeymoon, we drove north to the cottage my father had rented on Silver Lake.

He considered this year a splurge. "Everyone's growing up. Won't be long and we can't do this," he said to Mother.

There were seven people in the station wagon, including Ronald Lee and my brother Bobo's best friend, Case. Father's experience in packing the car made it bearable for us to make the two-hour trip. We found places to sit between boxes of clothes, towels, sheets, groceries, beach toys, and lawn chairs, too excited to mind the inconvenience. Heading down London Street that warm, end-of-July day with a car carrier stuffed and the station wagon's open tailgate loaded and sagging, we gave Klikkuiken an eyeful. Enough to satisfy her for the entire week we'd be gone.

Silver Lake is an inland lake separated from Lake Michigan by mounds and mounds of sand dunes. Scientists call the dunes "moving sand" that settles depending on wind and water and erosion. You can't hold Michigan sand. It runs through your fingers. It's sugar sand, fine granules of quartz left long ago by ice glaciers, according to my science text. My parents said God created the dunes and the Great Flood made the dunes what they are today.

Father rarely took us to the beach along Lake Michigan, where once over the top of the dune, the sandy shore looked long, flat, and forever. Mother hated the beach and "all that hot sand." She preferred Gun Lake, where grass grew up to the edge of the water and there were plenty of shade trees.

In that way, I wasn't like my mother. There was something about the sand and beach I loved. The way the sun parched the sand. The double warmth—one from direct sunrays browning my flesh and one from lying in the bleached granules already roasted. My body soaked it up and took it in like I was standing on the kitchen register.

On the first day of our vacation, Arie J, Ronald Lee, and I took a paddleboat along the side of the lake to the dunes. We climbed the tallest dune and ran down again until we landed, splashing in the water. Then we climbed it again. And again.

"Let's roll down this time," Arie J said.

Ronald Lee spread out in the sand. "I'll beat you," he said and took off.

"That's gross! The sand will stick!" I yelled, following them anyway. I ran zigzag down the dune, my arms flailing. "Watch out, here I come!"

One early evening before dark, Arie J and I took Ronald Lee out fishing in the rowboat. We grabbed our coffee can of worms, two bamboo poles for me and Ronald Lee, and Arie J's reel rod. After I rowed out a ways, we dropped an anchor and rocked gently on the water's surface.

"Pass the coffee can," I said. Arie J found it under the seat and handed it to me. "If I catch anything, you have to take it off the hook."

"Long as you put the worm on yourself," he said.

"I can do my own," Ronald Lee told us. "Worm and fish."

"We'll see," Arie J said. He reeled in his line and cast further out.

I put a good inch more space between my sinker and the bobber, and tossed the line over the side of the boat. Ronald Lee copied me. Each time we adjusted our lines, he grinned at me. Whenever he moved, the back of his neck scraped the top of the orange life jacket tied over his sweatshirt.

We sat quietly watching our bobbers until I asked, "So, Ron. How ya doin'?"

Without hesitation, he answered, "Good."

"I mean, how's it goin' with all this wedding business and stuff?"

"Good." He fidgeted in the tackle box, then closed it and scraped it across the aluminum bottom, back under his seat.

Arie J's reel clicked slowly. He made another cast and we heard the end plop through the top of the water.

I shifted my weight and looked over the lake. "Miss your Mom?"

"A little." He scratched the top of his head and didn't look at me. "Mostly, I want to move to my new place."

"Sure." I smiled at him and nodded.

My throat tightened and I swallowed. He doesn't get much choice, just does what people tell him. Move out with Deannie—move back in with Deannie—wear a tux—carry a wedding ring—go to the cottage with us—

"Better check your worm," I said.

We had a few nibbles but didn't catch anything. It began to get chilly as the sun went down. I twirled my line around my pole, pulled up anchor, and rowed back to shore while Arie J and Ronald Lee trolled.

Wednesday afternoon Bobo and Case took the rowboat to the dunes across the lake and invited me along. The three of us climbed mound after mound, up and down and up again until Lake Michigan came into view. When we reached the water, the guys shed their t-shirts and jumped in. I waded up to my knees, content to watch their horseplay. Our trek back to the boat took up the rest of the afternoon. Bobo said I was a weakling and didn't let me row. I kind of liked the idea that maybe Case was being a gentleman by not letting me row. Maybe it was dawning on my big brother that his friends didn't consider me just a stupid little sister.

I rowed over to the dunes alone the next day. Pulling the boat on shore, I climbed one of the hills and, this time, rolled over and over in the sand, all the way down. I climbed to the top of the highest dune and looked down on the lake below. Other vacationers unpacked picnic lunches at the bottom of the mammoth slope where the sand met the water. The soft wind mingled with the sun, while small waves and sailboats filled the lake's silvery landscape.

I sat down and watched with feet buried in the sand. My head rested on my crossed arms that were resting on my knees. My long legs were tanned. The breeze played with my blond hair that was slowly turning whiter with the summer sunlight. Independent, alone on the high dune. The peacefulness, the ease in the air, the luxury of warm velvety sand and the intimacy of the sun awoke in me a sensation fanciful, dreamy and pleasant.

Vijftien

Tom received his orders for Vietnam that September, a few weeks after I started high school. Babe moved back home with us. She was five months pregnant.

We asked father to hang a new, better full-length mirror on the back of our bedroom door. To dress by, to do our hair without tying up the bathroom, to follow the expansion of Babe's tummy.

After we watched the evening news with Walter Cronkite that night, I went upstairs to do homework. Babe stayed and watched "Daniel Boone" with Arie J and "My Three Sons" with Bobo. Later she came up, entered our bedroom and shut the door. The new mirror swayed, its wire hanger on a single nail. I closed my biology text and grabbed a shopping bag from the top of the dresser.

"Check out these new curlers. Big as tin cans."

"Cool." Babe threw her sweater on the bed and opened the closet. "Don't you like the way we iron our hair?"

"Yeah, but Mom will kill us if she finds out."

We heard my father cough as he came upstairs. He never knocked but always coughed again before opening the door.

"You girls get to bed now."

"I just finished my homework and have to do my hair yet," I said.

"Well, hurry it up, *hoor?* Goodnight."

Although he left the door ajar, I closed it all the way as soon as I heard him reach the bottom of the stairs. In front of the mirror, I separated a section of hair, combed it, and sprayed it with my water bottle. "*So Mama—tell your children—not to do as I have done—Spend your life in sin and misery . . .*"

"Let's play the radio." Babe said, dressing for bed. Her belly looked bigger in her nightie and she'd been leaving her bra on all night. She adjusted the radio dial, picked up her socks off the floor and balled them together. I recognized the lone harmonica ending to "Eve of Destruction" on the radio just before the station began Peter, Paul and Mary. Slipping one of my curlers over her wrist, Babe began dancing. "I Dig Rock and Roll Music."

"Gimme that!" I stomped my foot and she whipped the curler across the room.

"Turn that trash off!" we heard Father yell from downstairs.

Babe lowered the volume and took her stationery out of the headboard. With a pillow behind her back, she settled on the bed to write a letter to Tom like she did every night.

I had to use two bobby pins to hold one curler in place and it took me awhile to get the hang of it.

"How you gonna sleep in those?" Babe asked. "I'm writing Tom how silly you look."

"Least I don't sleep with a bra on."

A pillow hit me from behind.

I turned around with the spray bottle and aimed it at her face.

"Don't get my stuff wet!"

My father coughed at the bedroom door again and poked in his head. "Shut off the light and go to bed. I don't want to say it again." He left, closing the door all the way. We looked at each other and giggled.

Babe wrote five pages. I finished my hair and went in the closet to change.

"Shit!"

"What?" Babe asked

"I can't get my nightie over my stinking head!" I stood in the doorway with my arms stuck in the nightshirt. Babe shrieked and had to hold her stomach as she laughed.

"It's not funny." I leaned against the doorframe, laughing with her.

"Shhhh!" Babe tried to talk. "Dad's gonna have a fit."

Bobo yelled "shut-up" from across the hall.

I struggled out of the nightie. When I looked at Babe, we started to laugh all over again. We put our hands over our mouths, trying to settle down.

Still snickering, Babe addressed her envelope. I put on a pair of pajamas with buttons down the front. Putting the sealed letter on her dresser, Babe took a deck of cards from the drawer and started shuffling. "Okay. What's it gonna be tonight? Rummy or Spit?"

"Whatcha got to play for?"

"Nothing."

"Let's play Rummy. You can owe me."

We sat cross-legged on the bed. Five minutes into the game, I laid down three aces.

"Oh man!" Babe said. "Are you cheating?"

I shook my head. "Never." I bounced on the top of the bed and belted out the first line of Janice Joplin's "Piece of My Heart."

"All right, that's it!" my father called. "If I hear any more, I'm coming up and taking your light bulb!"

We looked at each other and howled.

"Never mind you two! I mean it! *Horen?*"

I rolled sideways on the bed and pounded my fist on the mattress.

"Maybe we should quit." Babe's voice was hoarse as she laughed.

"We need a playoff," I whispered. I shuffled the cards and handed them to my sister. "Deal 'em."

The radio played "Ode to Billie Joe." I put a consecutive row of diamonds down on the bedspread with just one card left. I threw it on the discard pile. "I win."

"Dog-gone it! That's the one I was waiting for." She flashed two kings.

"You owe me a bag of M&Ms. Plus the ones you ate last night."

"No way! I won those fair and square." She picked up the cards and put the rubber band around them.

Father came into the room without even coughing first, a wet washcloth in his hand. Without a word, he unscrewed the light bulb and took it with him downstairs. We fell backward across the bed, our hands over our mouths to cover the shrieking laughter.

Finally we got up to use the bathroom and brush our teeth. Afterward, I crawled under the covers and quietly waited for Babe. She always took longer than me to say her prayers.

"Good-night," she said as she climbed into the bed.

I let out a long sigh and turned on my side. "Good-night."

Babe cleared her throat and rolled over with a heavy oomph.

I sighed again and turned on my back. "Oh crap!"

"Now what?" Babe whispered.

"One of my curlers fell out."

Babe buried her face in her pillow. After ten minutes or so, I could still feel her shoulders shake the bed as she stifled more giggles.

Unless she was crying.

~

Over the holidays, we watched the "Bob Hope Christmas Special" on television. We didn't see Tom, but we saw a lot of other servicemen. During the song "Silent Night" at the end of the program, the camera scanned the audience slowly, showing the men still, hushed, and weeping. Bobo and Arie J didn't move, didn't make a sound. My father cried. Openly. Babe and I cried too, quietly, wiping the tears off our faces quickly because this kind of display was new for us. My mother was at Ladies Aid Society and missed it.

The baby was born on New Year's Day, 1968, the first baby of the year in the city of Grand Rapids. The local newspaper and radio stations gave the event special publicity because the baby's father was "currently serving our country in Vietnam." The Red Cross passed the information along to Tom's battalion. Bobo and I called the local rock n' roll station. They broadcasted a message of congratulations and encouragement, thanking Tom for "the patriotic sacrifice he was making." We recorded it on a cassette tape and mailed it off to him the next day.

And my mother and father welcomed a new grandson into our home. Again.

~

Mother and Father respected Dr. Palmer, the minister who took Reverend Piersma's place, but never fully agreed with his method. Dr.

Palmer emphasized Bible memory work instead of doctrine in our catechism classes. The very fact he had "a method" at all meant he was a teacher and not a preacher, according to my parents.

Every week, we were required to write out assigned verses on a 3x5 card and memorize them. We were tested at the end of each year. We had to write out over fifty verses by hand, word for word, and where they were found in the Bible. I had already mastered several lengthy passages required at school—the Creation story, the Christmas story, the Easter story, dozens of Psalms, and more. Now the verses were also committed to my memory.

Dr. Palmer stressed a "spiritual growth," a term and its implications not used in Grandville Avenue Church at the time. He encouraged Bible study groups, individual Bible study, and he preached with an open Bible in his hand, turning the pages, quoting from various books, chapters, and verses.

In other words, he was an Evangelical. Or so my father said.

Dr. Palmer left our congregation eventually to head the group of scholars that published the New International Version of the Bible. My parents considered a new Bible version unnecessary and even harmful. They didn't mind Dr. Palmer leaving. But I missed him when the Detroit Tigers played in the World Series. When Detroit lost the American League Pennant by one game the year before, Dr. Palmer had posted the scores in the window of the parsonage after each inning so we could see it from our schoolrooms.

Father preferred Reverend Hellinga, our next minister. At high school level, Reverend Hellinga instructed us in the entire Heidelberg Catechism, full and undiluted. Man's misery and deliverance. Guilt, Grace, Gratitude. Sin, Salvation, Service. It was as simple as that.

It was very complex.

Of course, my father continued to teach me the Catechism. Not only did he find it fitting to explain each week's lesson in detail, he also gave me ongoing thorough reviews.

"'What is your only comfort in life and death?'"

"'That I, with body and soul, both in life and death, am not my own, but belong unto my faithful Savior Jesus Christ;'"

"'How many things are necessary for you to know, that you in this comfort may live and die happily?'"

I always answered correctly. "'Three; the first, how great my sins and misery are; the second, how I am delivered from all my sins and misery; the third, how I am to be thankful to God for such deliverance.'" I got it exactly right.

I began to learn how meaning and understanding rises with repetition. Father drilled me every Sunday afternoon after dinner. I would have rather skipped it, but at least his lectures got me out of doing the dishes.

Other doctrines of the Reformed tradition were included in my father's lectures as well. The Belgic Confession. The Canons of Dordrecht. Originally the "Five Articles Against the Remonstrants," the Canons later became known as the five points of Calvinism and summarized as T.U.L.I.P. Not to be confused with the Dutch tulip bulbs buried next to the windmill along the side of our driveway.

"Total Depravity, Unconditional Election, Limited Atonement, Irresistible Grace, and Perseverance of the Saints," Father said. He leaned forward in his grey, upholstered chair while I sat on the footstool. "Now. These are very, very important, see. But not most important."

I nodded my head and asked the question I knew he wanted me to ask. "So, what's most important?" I pushed the footstool further away from his chair and crossed my legs, figuring this was going to take a while.

He pointed and shook his finger as he spoke. "The Sovereignty of God. The Sovereignty of God is the most important."

"Oh, yeah." I answered. "I remember."

"Even before the beginning of the world, God decreed whether or not a person is elected to be saved or if he is condemned. Everything that happens in the world is fore-ordained by God, because God is sovereign."

"Yeah." I straightened my legs, rested my chin in my hands with elbows on my knees. "And what about the bad stuff?"

My father reached for the green and silver foil bag of Half & Half tobacco and packed his pipe. I already knew what he was going to say next.

"Well, remember. In the Old Testament, when his brothers sold him to the Egyptians, Joseph said, 'You meant it for evil, but God meant it for good.'" He put the end of the pipe in his mouth and sucked. I waited while he held a kitchen match over the bowl. *Puut . . . Puut . . . Puut . . .*

After a couple of good draws, he leaned back in the chair. "The Apostle Paul says all things work together for good for them that love God and are called according to His purpose." He sat up straight and, with his pointed finger, poked himself on the top of the leg four times while he talked. "The Sovereignty of God means God is all-powerful, all-knowing, immutable and impassable."

I wanted the lesson to be over.

"Of course, you can't forget Common Grace and the problems there."

Odd that the idea wasn't "A Doctrine of Special Grace," but instead the rejection of "The Doctrine of Common Grace." I didn't bring this up. I wanted to be finished for the day.

"There cannot be two loves of God. There cannot be two graces," Father said. "It makes no sense, see. 'Jacob have I loved, Esau have I hated.' One love. One hate. One grace. And it's saving. It's as simple as that, that's all."

I had heard all this Common Grace stuff before. It was regular dinner conversation.

~

Tom returned home from Vietnam that summer. After a two-week leave, he and Babe packed the little red Volkswagen for California where he would be stationed once again. This time the little car was loaded down significantly more than the first time they traveled to California. This time it was even harder to say good-bye to my sister. This time Tommy Jr. rode along.

Late one night three months later, my father got a long distance phone call.

"Yes, this is Orie Griffioen. What's that? Yes. Yes." Father was talking very loudly. "Yes, operator. I'll accept the charges . . . Is that you, Tom? Yes . . . What's going on?"

I heard Mother's footsteps. Our phone hung on the wall just inside the kitchen, across from the stairway. Bobo and I got out of bed, met on the landing and came down. We sat hiding on the third step to hear what we could.

Father listened for a long time. ". . . Oh yeah . . . Oh yeah . . . Where is she? . . . I see . . . Ah-huh . . . think you're probably right . . . Yes . . . Yes, we can do that . . . Well, tell her we talked . . . Yes . . . We'll figure something out . . . Call back in an hour or two . . . Okay, Tom."

The phone clicked on the receiver so Bobo and I entered the kitchen. My father rubbed his chin, gathering his thoughts, then looked at my mother.

"Babe's not doing so well," he said.

"I knew it," Mother replied. She stood at the kitchen counter with her arms crossed. Bobo and I lined up next to her.

"Tom says it might help if someone comes out there. From the sound of it, I think he's right."

"Where is she?"

"Tonight she's in bed sleeping for the first time in days. She hardly eats anything."

"And the baby? Who's watching the baby?"

"The lady from the downstairs apartment is there most of the time."

"I remember one of Babe's letters mentioning her."

"She's from the church out there. Tom says she's real helpful, but it's not enough." Father pulled out a kitchen chair and sat down, staring at the tabletop.

"I knew something like this would happen," Mother said.

When my father turned from the table and crossed one leg over the other, we knew he had already made a decision.

"I can't leave the store with Connie out of town. The best thing is to see if Bill and Deannie can go. Bill can get away the easiest." He got up and reached for the phone again. "I'll call Gracia and John first to let them know."

After Father talked with Gracia, he called Bill. Bill said he could make arrangements in his schedule. He and Deannie would drive out to California. Ronald Lee would go along.

"Can I go?" I interrupted my father while he was still on the telephone. Holding the receiver with his shoulder, he waved his hand and shook his head.

"I could help with Ronald Lee and Tommy." How cool would it be to go to California, no matter what the circumstances were.

Father looked at me and shook his head again.

"Please! Pleeese!"

This time, my father dropped his arm to his side, still holding the receiver. "No, Janie. No. You be quiet now, *hoor*?"

I stomped through the dining room and into the living room, as far away from the kitchen as one could get in the house. There was no point in arguing. I looked out the window but could only see wet, geometrical shapes in the streetlight. I shifted my weight from one foot to the other, crying, angry and worried.

The next morning, Sunday at six-fifteen, Bill and Deannie pulled into our driveway. Everyone was already up and we all went outside when we heard the car.

"I can give you forty dollars," Father said. "It would help some."

Bill took the money and Mother nodded.

I could see Ronald Lee in the back seat. Books, puzzles, a quilt and two pillows were stacked next to him. He held a small Mickey Mouse duffle bag on his lap. I tapped on the window and he rolled it down, showing me a plastic baggie of Fruit Loops.

"Yummy!" I said, and poked my head into the open window. I gave him a smooch on the forehead. "Hope you have some fun, Ronald Lee. Get yourself a sun tan and a surfboard." My eyes started to burn, so I turned away.

We went inside. My father never added anything to his usual prayer. "Gracious God and Heavenly Father, we come unto you this Sabbath morning . . ." We ate our raisin bread with frosting and then went to church.

On Monday, I went to school with swollen eyes I tried to camouflage with mascara. I hated when people asked questions that were none of their business. In class, my mind kept wandering to Babe, like it did last night when I was trying to sleep. I attempted to study. I didn't want anyone asking about the tears I wiped back as quickly as they surfaced.

A week and a half later when Deannie, Bill and Ronald Lee came back, Babe and Tommy Jr. came with them. Babe and Tommy

Jr. stayed with my parents for three days. On the fourth day, Babe entered the hospital.

Zestien

Father gave me permission to use the car on Sunday afternoon. I said good-bye to Mother, noting the significant time she spent on the kitchen register lately. It seemed a long time ago since I found my slippers and nudged my way onto the register with my mother where we nestled together against a nameless despair.

Maybe her endless evaluations on the register did her more harm than good. Or maybe she bolstered her perseverance there. I don't know. For a brief moment, I considered what would happen if I joined her.

The curtains swayed as I closed the kitchen door. I passed through the white picket gate, locking it from habit, and waved to Mrs. VanderGoot. I backed the Chevy Impala out of the narrow driveway between the borders of white bricks. Shifting into first gear, I moved down London Street with a jerk. Second gear wasn't any smoother.

Eight miles south, past the first grove of pine trees, I turned. The rectangular building was six houses wide and four windows tall. It stood on one side of the drive that opened into a parking lot with another border of evergreens. I parked the car, locked the doors, and walked across the lot.

Climbing the six concrete steps, I passed through the first set of doors and up the three steps with the silver finish on the edges. The second set of doors closed heavily behind me as I entered the lobby.

I remembered the high ceiling and the cement floor with the marble-looking finish. A cold shiver ran through me. There stood the long backless bench in the center of the room. The green vinyl chair placed next to the desk. The double wooden doors with their big brass

116

doorknobs and large keyholes underneath. The windows with wire mesh in between the glass.

I wished I could stop shaking.

A lady in a white hat and uniform sat at the small desk with the green vinyl chair next to it.

"I came to see Babe," I said, approaching her.

"Pardon me?" the lady asked.

"I came to see Babe. Aleda Griffioen."

The nurse ran a finger down a list she had clipped to a notebook.

"I don't see anyone by that name. Could you spell it for me?"

"G-r-i-f-f-i-o-e-n. Babe. Aleda Griffioen. My sister. A-l-e-d-a. No, wait. Vandenbosch. She's married now. V-a-n-d-e-n-b-o-s-c-h."

"Yes. Yes. Here we are. We have an Aleda Vandenbosch. Hold on please."

She dialed two numbers on the desk phone. "Hello. Marge. Aleda Vandenbosch. Her sister is here to see her." She placed the receiver back and commanded, "Follow me."

The nurse walked over to the double doors on the left, her white thick-soled shoes silent as she moved.

But her jangling keys rattled loudly.

The woman opened the doors and directed me to the right.

I climbed more steps until coming to another double wooden door. The interior doorbell had a loud buzzer that startled me when I pushed it.

Jangling keys rattled on the other side of the doors.

A nurse held the doors open as I passed through. Then the heavy doors shut behind me.

"Fifth door on the left, down the next hall."

I turned the corner, entered the dim hallway, and walked slowly while my right hand felt the way along the wall.

I heard Arie J blabbering. I stopped and turned around.

Only the lobby and the nurses.

I listened hard before I continued.

The fifth door on the right. I wished the lighting was better.

I heard rubber boots scraping along the floor. I felt my father take my hand. He said "shhhhh" and we all walked a little slower, a little more quietly.

I wished the hallway wasn't so long.

I stopped in front of the opening and peeked inside the faintly lit room.

From the doorway, I saw a figure in the chair.

"Mama?"

~

"Hey, Hi!" my sister greeted me.

"Hey, Hi." I'd lost my courage and stood at the door, awkward.

Babe didn't get up. "Well, come in. Sit down."

I took an orange vinyl chair directly across from her. A round coffee table separated us. No beds in the room. It had been changed to a sitting area. A television that wasn't turned on took up one corner. Near the TV, a woman with gray hair who looked to be about sixty smoked a cigarette.

Babe had pulled back her hair and tied it with an elastic band at the neck. She looked thin, her skin colorless, yet her green eyes searching mine appeared less terrified than they did two weeks ago.

I stared at the thin green tiles of the floor. They reminded me of school just after the janitor ran over them with his damp mop.

I cleared my throat and came up only with, "So, how's the food here?"

"It's not bad. They want to make me gain weight."

"That'll be the day." My laugh took an effort, but Babe didn't seem to notice.

"One of the nurses is really fat. She works the night shift and she's always eating something. But she's pretty nice."

The orange vinyl chair squeaked beneath me as I shifted. "So, Mom says they make you play volleyball, even if you don't want to."

"Yeah. Mostly after supper. But it's okay."

My sister yawned and I asked her, "Is this supposed to be nap time?"

"No. No. They don't schedule much on Sundays. Except church."

"You go?"

Babe shook her head. "They don't make you because I guess a lot of people freak. It's pretty dorky, anyway."

"Huh." I crossed my legs and bounced my foot up and down, trying to give Babe plenty chance to talk if she wanted to.

After a minute or two, I said, "Mom told me you're doing some embroidery."

"They make you do stuff like that. It's a dresser scarf."

"Sounds nice."

The woman in front of the television left the room.

"I brought your mail," I said, rummaging through my purse.

"Thank you."

Babe shuffled the envelopes, two of them edged in red, white and blue, from Tom. She laid them on the table, unopened.

Every time I shifted positions, the orange vinyl chair sounded like it was breathing. My eyes wandered around the room for a while before they fixed on some pink carnations and yellow snapdragons in a vase on a bookshelf.

"Nice flowers," I said.

"Yes. They are. How's Tommy?"

"He's good. He's real good."

"Good."

If she wanted to talk about him, it must be okay to talk about him. "I fed him his lunch today. He ate it all."

My sister smiled and looked eager for more news.

"I make a bigger mess when feeding him than you or Mom."

We both laughed.

"He sleeps real good at night."

"Yes." Babe nodded slowly. "Yes. That's good."

"I took him for a ride in the stroller," I said. "He loves to be outside."

"I know," my sister said quietly, her eyes downcast.

"I know you do." I whispered, so sorry for my mistake.

We sat quietly. Craning her neck, Babe studied the ceiling. "Jeez," she finally said.

"What?"

She glanced my way and shrugged. She turned her face to the side for a while and seemed to stare at nothing at all. When she finally spoke, her voice was dull. "The equipment was scary."

"Not sure what you're saying, Babe."

She continued to stare off to the side. "They zapped my head."

I chewed the end of my thumb and with the other hand, fingered the strap of my purse. I shifted in my chair, cleared my throat.

As if just waking up, my sister looked at me, blinking. "I'm so spacey. Sorry." She leaned back in her orange vinyl chair. "Want a brownie? I stashed one from dinner."

"No. Thanks. You might wish you could nibble it in the middle of the night or something."

The same woman with the gray hair came back into the room. Without turning on the television, she plunked down in her chair with a lengthy sigh and lit another cigarette.

I checked my wristwatch. "I should get going. Dad will want the car for church."

"Sure. Yeah. Okay."

"See you soon, though." I stood and fumbled in my purse, wishing to say something reassuring. "We'll take good care of him."

"I know you will." She stared at the letters on the coffee table. I figured she would have gotten up if she wanted to hug or anything.

The lady from the desk opened the double doors for me. At the bottom of the steps, I knocked at the mesh wire windows of the heavy double doors with the large brass keyholes underneath. Keys jangled on the other side and the doors opened.

I crossed the terrazzo tile floor, opened the heavy wooden doors, went down the three steps, through one more set of doors and reached the outside.

The sunlight made me squint. Squinting holds tears back. I took a deep breath, attempting to clear my lungs and the heaviness in my chest. Crossing the parking lot, I dug in my purse for the car keys. When I unlocked the car, I turned toward the building, estimating where the sitting room was.

I wished the windows didn't look like jail.

And I wished my sister hadn't mentioned the electric shock treatments.

Zeventien

The sun disappeared behind the Kelvinator factory as I walked to church. I had left the house by myself before the rest of the family, but waited for them in the vestibule like I promised my father I would.

Mother would have walked with me but she didn't like to wait in the back of church. She said she didn't want to run into any tongue-waggers. There were exceptions to Mother's sense of alienation. The VanderGoots, Mr. and Mrs. Kamps, Mr. and Mrs. Berends, maybe the Pylmans. They had *verstond*, mother would say—a certain kind of understanding and manner with which my mother felt comfortable. But they never lingered in the back of church either.

We sat in the third row of the church in the evenings, exactly like we did in the mornings, which gave me a kind of solace that helped offset the gossip. At least we were in our own place here on the west side, third row from the front, right where we always were, right where we belonged. Something like squatters' rights.

George Vander Woude led singing before the evening service. We sang, "Far and Near the Fields are Teeming," followed by "We Have Heard the Joyful Sound—Jesus Saves." Still an Arminian, my father would say.

The congregation spoke the Apostles' Creed in unison. From the row behind us, I could hear Mr. Pylman's clear tenor voice reciting. Next to the Pylmans, the Berends were sitting and in front of them, the Bruinwoods. Across the aisle sat "Issac Two-Loves-of-God DeMay," or so my mother would say because Mr. DeMay was so Arminian.

Reverend Hellinga read the Scripture. As he preached in his full, black robe, the minister's cheeks contrasted red. Behind him the evening sun lit the stained glass. The Good Shepherd window.

Somewhere—not within the song service or the offering or the congregation or the long prayer omitting my sister's name, but somewhere in spite of these—there was grace. I knew it, recognized it. I was glad to be in the House of the Lord.

~

Officially sixteen years old, I started dating Case, Bobo's friend from the family from Canada who was originally from The Netherlands. I was now included in my brother's group, "The Do-It-Nothing Gang." We hung out on Sundays. Donald, Case, Bobo, Chuck, Liz, Ginny and me. Our parents didn't know we went to Big Boy's after church in the mornings. Occasionally, our parents let us sit as a group in the balcony. Sometimes we skipped evening church and visited Anazeh Sands pool hall instead. Church or not, the gang would gather in someone's living room for a night of "Bonanza," "The Smothers Brothers," and ice cream without parental interference.

One Sunday when the Do-It Nothing Gang settled into the living room for a night of television, I followed Ginny into the kitchen to get snacks before the episode of "Mission Impossible" started.

"How are the plans for your folks' 25th anniversary coming?" Ginny asked.

"We have a room at the Stagecoach Restaurant reserved." I poured a bag of pretzels into a bowl. "Deannie and Gracia's idea."

Ginny covered vanilla scoops of ice cream with frozen strawberries. "That will be in November?"

"Yeah. November 25. They were married on Thanksgiving Day that year."

"Cool."

We counted out eight glasses. As I filled them with cola, my brain clicked like the ice we just added. I stared at the fizzling soda. "You know, I never thought of this . . ."

"What?" Ginny asked.

"Well . . . it's my Mom and Dad's twenty-fifth anniversary."

"Yeah."

"Funny . . . Gracia is going to be twenty-nine in the spring."

Ginny looked at me long and hard. She emptied a bag of potato chips into a Tupperware bowl.

"It's weird, you know? I hadn't thought of it, " I said. "I don't get it."

Ginny's hand went over her mouth. She set the potato chip bag on the table. "It only dawned on you now?" She stared at me. "Janie. You don't know?"

I said nothing.

"Okay." Ginny squinted. "Okay. Gracia is your mother's daughter," she said very slowly like a teacher in first grade. "Your mother had her before she married your dad. Gracia is your mother's daughter, Jackie is your father's daughter. You knew Jackie was your father's daughter, right?"

I nodded. I didn't want Ginny to know I didn't know.

Of course Jackie is my father's daughter. But my mother isn't her mother?

"When your dad's first wife died, he married your mother. Your mother already had Gracia," Ginny said.

Forget what Ginny thinks. "My dad was married before?"

"Yeah."

I released a long, fatigued sigh. The sound of my mother sobbing in the night years ago came back to me. Of course. I'm so stupid.

"My mother's first husband died too?" And how the hell was it that Ginny knew so much about it when I didn't.

"No, Janie. She wasn't married."

I dropped my gaze to the floor and stared at the muted pattern on the indoor-outdoor carpet. My face grew hot from anger, or confusion, or embarrassment, not sure.

Then I shrugged, picked up the bowl of chips, walked to the living room and pretended to watch television.

Ginny had the *verstond* not to say anything.

So Jackie wasn't my full sister. It wasn't that. So Gracia wasn't my full sister, it wasn't that. It wasn't that my father wasn't Gracia's father. Or even that my mother wasn't married when Gracia was born. I probably would've figured it out eventually.

Like with Ronald Lee.

But I wished someone would have told me.

~

Babe was home again and my mother had been scheming for the last three days.

"After all, he's already been in Vietnam," Mother kept repeating. "What more do they think they need from him?" She set the coffee pot back on the stove, turned the burner on low and looked at my father.

He pulled far enough away from the table to set the chair sideways. He crossed his legs and took a sip from his steaming cup. "I think you're right. You should try it, *hoor*?"

While Babe went upstairs to give Tommy Jr. his morning bath, Mother took out a pen and a lined notepad. She sat down at the kitchen table and began her letter. By ten-thirty, she sealed it and addressed the envelope to our congressman, Gerald R. Ford. Clipping the leash on our Chihuahua, Tiny Joseph, she said to me, "Let's go for a walk."

Mother loved walking. As far back as I can remember, most Wednesday afternoons she walked five blocks to the bus stop and then rode downtown. After shopping and she caught the bus again, she walked back to London Street. Mother let me go with her sometimes. When I was little, it was hard to keep up because she walked so fast. Almost as fast as Aunt Dienke walked.

That morning we clipped along the sidewalk at an equal pace. When we reached the mailbox, a block north of London Street, my mother handed me Tiny's leash. The drawer squeaked when she pulled the handle. My mother paused with her eyes closed as if she prayed. Then she dropped the letter into box.

Tom obtained an honorable discharge from the United States Marine Corp because of Mother's correspondence with Gerald R. Ford.

~

When I was a junior in high school, my cousin Warren was drafted into the army. Bobo was next. They were both stationed in Fort Knox and that summer, we went to visit. We left on a Friday in the station wagon—my mother and father, Arie J and me, Case Berends, and Linda, Warren's recent new bride.

We stayed in army housing and picnicked near the barracks in the hot sun. We teased Bobo about his shaved head and his eyebrows, bleached invisible, though in my opinion, my brother looked handsome and official in his khaki uniform.

We traveled home on Sunday, typically a sin Father and Mother would say. Except this time. I asked myself what it would lead to and I asked myself about the antithesis. There we were, traveling *op Zondag*. We even stopped to buy gas and food on Sunday.

~

The summer between my junior and senior years of high school, I drank my first beer. I went on dates with boys who owned motorcycles and I smoked cigarettes if they were offered. Many of my friends smoked marijuana, although I didn't. Not yet, anyway.

During my senior year, one of the boys that sat next to me in study hall the previous year was wounded in Vietnam. He was never able to walk again. That same school year, two young men who had been in school with me were killed in Vietnam. My cousin Warren was assigned to duty in Vietnam. When I was a senior, Case's oldest brother became a chaplain in the Army and went to Vietnam. He returned an atheist.

Then it was Bobo's turn to go.

Reverend Hellinga came to our house for tea with my mother one afternoon before Bobo left. I interrupted them unintentionally when I came into the kitchen after school that day.

"Come. Sit. Join us," the minister invited, smiling with his red cheeks and speaking his Dutch brogue.

"No, thank you," I answered. "I have a lot of homework to do. I need to start right away." I lied. To the minister. I grabbed an apple and climbed the knotty pine stairway to my bedroom, leaving the door slightly open.

"I must go soon, Mrs. Griffioen," he said to my mother. "But first, we will read a Psalm."

> *I will lift up mine eyes unto the hills,*
> *from whence cometh my help.*

My help cometh from the Lord, which made heaven and earth.
He will not suffer thy foot to be moved:
he that keepeth thee will not slumber.
Behold, he that keepeth Israel
shall neither slumber nor sleep.
The Lord is thy keeper:
the Lord is thy shade upon thy right hand.
The sun shall not smite thee by day,
nor the moon by night.
The Lord shall preserve thee from all evil:
he shall preserve thy soul.
The Lord shall preserve thy going out and thy coming in
from this time forth, and even for evermore.

Bobo's leave home to London Street was short. Already on Monday, he had to report to Fort Sill, Oklahoma. From there, Vietnam.

He wore his dress uniform to church that Sunday, not because he wanted to but because my mother and father insisted. Instead of reading Psalm 121, Reverend Hellinga asked the congregation to sing it. I stood in the pew between my mother and brother, his mellow voice singing in conviction and Mother holding her lacy white handkerchief to her face. My throat would not allow any sound to escape.

I often thought of my brother's tanned forehead worried in wrinkles, his eyebrows white and high, his pupils wide the morning he left on the airplane. I wrote him at least once a week, affectionately and cheerfully, about news at school, Tiger Baseball, the Do-it-Nothing Gang, trying to include what might be interesting or fun to him, and avoiding what might be hurtful for him to miss, or cause him more homesickness.

I hated that damn war. Some of my classmates went to marches and protests. It seemed I would betray my brother if I joined them.

Ever since Bobo had been in the service, my mother wrote him many times each week. Now that he was in Vietnam, she wrote him every day, whether the post office liked it or not. She wrote at least two or three pages each day at the kitchen table with Tiny Joseph at her feet. When she completed the letter, she folded it, placed it in the envelope, and let Tiny lick it to moisten the seal. Then the two walked down the block to the mailbox, the dog on the leash and Mother with her letter.

This was the routine for months.

Often, we petitioned in church—we had this in common with some of the others at least. We prayed at the dinner table. We knelt at our beds. I wondered and worried if God would do as we pleaded, and I'm sure my mother wondered and worried, too. After all, there were other mothers and fathers who prayed and their sons were killed anyway.

Despite having the dog lick the envelopes, despite teasing Tom that even a Marine could not surpass her son, despite her insistence on the flag in front of the house, despite Psalm 121, the paint on the grate of the register in the kitchen wore thinner.

During those months Bobo was there, so many young men died, so many young soldiers disappeared. Reverend Hellinga frequently had us sing Psalm 121 in church. Mother always held her white handkerchief as we sang. I had trouble blocking my tears. Sometimes I just went ahead and cried.

When Bobo was "short," he wrote my parents he would soon be home and that he had a surprise. For days Mother worried the surprise was a Vietnamese wife who would come home with him. As it turned out, he had mail-ordered a 1969 silver Corvette Stingray.

We welcomed Bobo at the county airport—the Griffioens, the in-laws, the Do-it-Nothing Gang. We cheered, shouted, cried. We grabbed him, hugged him, congratulated him, grabbed and held him some more. We thanked gracious God.

But my cousin Warren came back from Vietnam in a flag-draped casket.

Achtien

When students completed a three-year study of the Heidelberg Catechism, they were expected to make a public profession of their faith and become full members of the Church. With that intention, I waited outside the consistory room with nine classmates for my turn of examination.

A few of the girls sat on the floor, whispering. The rest of us stood and leaned against the wall of the church basement, shifting back and forth on opposite feet, silent. I chewed the end of my thumb and Ginny twirled her hair around her finger.

When they called my name, I entered the carpeted room. Twelve men, the church elders, sat in chairs upholstered in green leather around a long rectangular mahogany table. The head of the table belonged to Reverend Hellinga. I recognized the other men, including Mr. Prins, Mr. Kladder, Mr. De Boer, Mr. Meyer, my father.

Reverend Hellinga introduced me and then began the procedure.

"We understand it is your desire to make the Public Profession of Faith."

I nodded.

"Young lady," Reverend Hellinga said. "Why is it you want to make this Public Profession of your faith?"

I took a deep breath and my face flushed before I spoke. "Because God in His mercy has graciously included me in His Covenant." I pulled some of my answer from the catechism and some of it from the baptism form and some of it from I wasn't sure where.

Reverend Hellinga addressed me again. "What do you mean by 'Covenant'?"

"The situation between God and man where God comes to man and says 'I will be your God and you will be my people.'" Once more, the question and answer were not verbatim from any text, yet I answered without hesitating. I began to relax a little. This was my best subject.

"Which of you gentlemen would like to ask a question?" Reverend Hellinga scanned the faces in the room. He wore a suit and tie with a white shirt, not his robe. All the men wore suits and ties and white shirts.

Mr. De Boer lived on London Street, between the VanderGoots and the Vander Kloks. He looked at me from across the polished table. "How do you know your sin?"

I answered, "From the Law of God."

"Who is Jesus?" Mr. Prins asked, while making a note on the white paper in front of him.

"Jesus Christ is the God/man who died on the cross to save his people from all their sins."

Mr. Prins looked up and asked another question. "Is He your Savior?"

"Oh, yes." I thought that was a given. I thought his question was silly. "My only comfort in life and death is that I am not my own but belong to my faithful Savior, Jesus Christ," I added, this time quoting exactly from the Catechism, just to show him.

I wondered if my time was up. There were still six more classmates waiting in the hall. Reverend Hellinga looked around the consistory again.

"Gentlemen?" he asked, giving everyone a last chance.

"What do you think about dating unbelievers?"

Damn, I thought, flashing a dirty look at my father.

I saw Reverend Hellinga watch me, waiting for an answer, frowning over my father or frowning over me. It was hard to tell.

"What do you mean?" I asked Father.

"Do you date unbelievers? Will you continue to date unbelievers?"

We had engaged in this tangle at home, ever since my father had been aware I was dating Greg. Greg didn't have any Reformed affiliations. In fact, Greg didn't belong to any church at all. But I couldn't believe Father would bring it up here.

He had caught me off guard, but not for long. I faced my father straight on. "Yes, I do. And yes, I probably will."

"How is it you can do that? Do you intend to convert them?"

Looking down at the table, I took a deep breath. He hadn't asked that part before. "I suppose that's possible." I bit my bottom lip, stiffened my back. "But it's not my intention to date unbelievers so I can convert them. It's not my place to convert anyone."

He wouldn't argue with that. That would make him Arminian.

"How can you embrace the world and still be a child of the Covenant? What about the antithesis? Do you know the verse in Corinthians, 'Be ye not equally yoked together with unbelievers'?"

How can I not know it, I thought. You've been quoting it to me since forever.

"Dating an unbeliever does not make me equally yoked with that person." My cheeks burned brighter than Reverend Hellinga's.

Mr. Kladder shifted in his chair and coughed.

"You would walk so close to the edge of the cliff, you would risk falling off?" Father asked.

I answered on impulse. "I thought we believed in Perseverance of the Saints."

"That's pushing the doctrine, young lady. And you know it."

Reverend Hellinga cleared his throat. I thought he was going to interrupt on my behalf.

Still, Father persisted. "What does it mean, then, to be equally yoked?"

I lifted my hand and rubbed the tip of my thumb across my front teeth. It took great effort to keep a steady, hushed tone. "It must mean to have the same beliefs."

I looked at the table. If I weren't so angry, I'd be crying.

"We must move along, gentlemen." Reverend Hellinga turned to me and said, "You are dismissed."

I left the chamber, shaken.

Jesus.

Late Tuesday afternoon the church appeared deserted. I knocked on the door of the study, relieved there was no one around to see me arrive.

"Good afternoon." Reverend Hellinga said when he opened the door. He pointed to a library chair across the desk from his and I sat down. "I am pleased that you accepted my invitation to speak together for a few minutes."

I could smell the leather of his burgundy, high-back chair. I noticed it swiveled when he sat down. The office seemed small for a man of his importance. Behind him and on both sides, the walls were covered with books, neatly arranged in expensive looking cabinets. I recognized titles like in my father's bookcase—John Calvin's *Institutes,* Louis Berkhof's *Manual of Christian Doctrine,* Herman Bavinck's *The Certainty of Faith.*

"So now," Reverend Hellinga said. "You are a lady who knows her Catechism well." He paused.

I hadn't said anything so far.

"You know other theology too, do you not?"

"Yes, Dominie. I mean, Yes, sir." I put the tip of my thumb against my mouth.

"Your father." Smiling slightly, he raised his eyebrows. "He can be a difficult man."

I looked down, embarrassed. "Yeah." I stared at the geometric patterns of white squares and purple rectangles in the material of my skirt.

"Your father is a good man . . . with good intentions."

Reluctant, I looked up after a moment and slowly nodded.

He leaned back, folded his hands. I thought maybe he was going to pray. A new smile crossed his face, one of kindness that reminded me of Reverend Piersma.

I didn't say anything.

"I will ask you. You date more than one person?"

"Yes, sir."

"You also date some who do not belong to the Church?" His face turned serious now and matched his voice.

"Yes . . . sir."

"And why?"

I sat up straighter and tugged my skirt, making sure my knees stayed covered. "I don't understand why not."

"Do you understand the dangerous potential in these things?"

"Like the edge of a cliff my father talks about?"

The minister nodded.

"Maybe." I shrugged but didn't mean disrespect. All week I'd been considering this scenario. Still, I spoke carefully. "I don't understand the connection. I believe in Jesus Christ. I believe in my baptism." The rest of the words more or less gushed out. "I still want to join the Church, take communion. After all, I'm still in the Covenant."

I pushed my lips tightly together to stop.

What seemed like a long awkward silence might have been only a moment, the time it took for Reverend Hellinga to form his reply. I heard benevolence when he spoke. "You are right, of course."

My eyes stung, my face already flushed. "Thank you," I whispered.

The walnut table with the elaborate lettering "*This Do in Remembrance of Me*" was on constant display in the front of sanctuary just below the pulpit. On communion Sunday, the elders draped the table with white linen cloth on which they stacked covered platters of silver.

> *What-e'er thy want may be*
> *Here is the grace for thee, . . .*

The elders lifted the covers and passed the platters up and down the pews.

Reverend Hellinga lifted the strip of bread into the air and broke off an end. "The bread which we break is a communion of the body of Christ. Take, eat, remember, and believe that the body of our Lord Jesus Christ was broken unto a complete remission of all our sins."

Everyone put their cube of bread in their mouth at the same time. Unexpected softness lingered on my tongue when I first tasted the bread and swallowed.

The elders passed the polished silver containing individual glasses of wine. Each tiny glass held one swallow. I held mine between my index finger and thumb, like my parents always do. Because we were the third row from the front, I had to hold it quite a while until everyone in the church was served.

> *Here bring your wounded hearts,*
> *. . . . .*
> *Hope of the penitent, fadeless and pure.*
> *Here speaks the Comforter, in mercy saying,*
> *"Earth has no sorrow that heaven cannot cure."*

The minister lifted his arms high and we watched the wine pour from the ornate silver carafe to the chalice. "The cup of blessing which we bless is a communion of the blood of Christ. Take, drink ye all of it, remember, and believe that the precious blood of our Lord Jesus Christ was shed unto a complete remission of all our sins."

We each took our tiny glass and swallowed our share.

Mogen David looks as dark and bloody as it tastes thick and sweet.

Negentien

M y parents believed college was a waste of time and money for a girl. Even if they could afford to help me with tuition, they maintained a girl ought to settle down with one of our kind. Raise children. If anyone were going to college, it would be Arie J.

"He's going to be the minister in the family," Mother said.

In high school, I had concentrated on typing, bookkeeping, shorthand, and business math. After graduation, instead of riding the school bus, I caught the city bus downtown each day and worked full-time in the credit office of a small jewelry store. The Protestant work ethic I had inherited paid off. I learned eagerly, worked dependably, won the confidence of my superiors.

By the summer of 1971, I had saved enough to purchase a used 1964 black Volkswagen Bug. I spent free weekends at the beach with Ginny. Usually we registered the VW at the campground and made do, me in the front with my sleeping bag, Ginny with hers in the back. From time to time, we slept in our sleeping bags in the dunes with the open sky above us. One Friday night, along with three other guys we'd gone to school with, we snuck through an unlocked window of an abandoned cottage and spent the night there.

I still preferred boys with motorcycles. When my date zoomed up the driveway, I could see Mr. VanderGoot or Henry or Theresa watching from their window. I pulled on a helmet and off we drove. The curtain on VanderGoots' window would move aside again when we rumbled back just before my midnight curfew. I imagined they scowled the day six of my friends roared up the driveway on their bikes all at the same time.

The vibration must have interfered with Klikkuiken's reception.

My parents made a habit of questioning my dates when they came to pick me up. They wanted to see if he was our kind of people. "Where do you go to church? Who are your parents? What school did you attend?" After everything short of "What is your only comfort in life and in death?" they'd inform him of my midnight curfew. "Don't be late, *hoor*?" Father would say as we left. "Don't forget who you are," Mother would add.

In spite of my parent's opposition, I registered for classes that fall at the Community Junior College. My boss in the jewelry store offered part-time work to keep me on, but I took a position as a grocery cashier instead, making more dollars for fewer hours.

Leaving the grocery one afternoon, I found a note on the windshield of my Volkswagen from one of the baggers at the store, written with magic marker on a paper plate. "Will buy you coffee if you meet me at Big Boy's. Jerry."

We had bantered back and forth during our shifts the last couple of weeks and earlier that day, Jerry told me he switched places with someone so he could pack in my lane. I tossed the paper plate on the floor mat and drove across the street to the restaurant.

Jerry waved to get my attention. "I didn't know if you would come," he said when I slid into the booth.

His grin and dimples eased my jitters. "I liked the paper plate."

Jerry's silky hair parted naturally down the middle, coming to his shoulders and flipping in the back. He had a habit of letting his silver wire-rimmed glasses slide a bit on his nose. While at work, when I counted out change or pushed apples or a box of cereal his way, his eyes distracted me, the kind of soft brown eyes that slant down slightly and wrinkle in the corners when he smiled.

"You like the store all right?" he asked.

"I miss my friends from the office sometimes, but I sure make better money here."

The waitress brought me coffee and refilled Jerry's. He stirred in two sugars.

"I heard you mention school in the lunch room a while back."

"I go to JC." I blew on the surface of my coffee and took a sip. "You graduate?"

He nodded. "High school. Sixty-nine."

"Where'd you go?"

"Rogers. What about you?"

"Calvin Christian High."

Bringing his cup up to his mouth, he laughed. "I knew you were one of those cute little Dutch girls."

I gave him a disgusted look and turned my attention to the hostess escorting a couple of senior citizens to the booth across from us. Jerry began to flip through the selections of the jukebox behind the condiments on our table.

He fished for some change in his jean pocket. "You like Dylan?"

"I like him a lot."

He dropped some coins into the player and selected "Like a Rolling Stone" and "Just Like a Woman" before he punched A29 for Kris Kristofferson.

We listened for a time without speaking. I sipped my coffee.

"Wanna go out sometime?"

I set my cup back in the saucer. "If you don't call me a cute little Dutch girl."

Picking up his napkin, he wiped the sides of his mouth slowly, trying to hide a smirk. "Deal." Arms crossed on the table, he leaned forward. "How about I pick you up Wednesday afternoon—we'll take the bike if the weather's nice."

"Hmmm. I have class on Wednesday afternoon."

"How about Thursday then? I only have to work until noon. About 1:30?"

"Sounds good."

We left when someone else's music came on and walked through the parking lot together. I pulled out my car keys to avoid any kind of awkward lingering. He held the driver's side door open while I pushed in the clutch and started up the VW. "Thanks for the coffee. Catch ya later."

~

The weather on Thursday was perfect for riding. We zipped through town, up the expressway north, then turned east and stopped for a stretch along the side of the blacktop road next to the river. Jerry removed his helmet and leather jacket and put them on the seat of the bike. I took my helmet off and let my hair fall past my shoulders onto my blue jean jacket. He took my hand and I followed him through a narrow row of trees and into a clearing along the water's edge. We stood quietly at the riverbank, still shy, and watched the sun warm the violets in the new spring grass.

When we walked back to the bike, Jerry picked up his leather jacket and noticed I was struggling with the clasp of the helmet. I dropped my hands down as he took the strap and fastened it under my chin. He brushed a hand along my face and with three or four attempts, gently pushed the stray piece of my hair back inside the helmet. I imagined kissing him.

He brought me home and switched off the bike in the driveway.

"Hey, thanks. I enjoyed that." I handed him the helmet.

"You're welcome. I dug it, too."

I wanted him to kiss me, but then again, thought he should go before Father came out and started his sermon about Jerry and the wrong side of the antithesis and holes in people's blue jeans.

"Wanna do something next week?"

Next week seemed like a long time away. "Sure. Okay," I said. "Cool."

He climbed on the bike and as he kick-started it, I stepped back. He turned the cycle around, rolled down the driveway, and zoomed off down London Street, past Klikkuiken, and around the corner. I waved to Mr. VanderGoot as I danced across the driveway, unhitched the gate of the white picket fence, and went in for a pork chop supper.

Sunday nights were for the Do-it-Nothing Gang. Ginny and I made plans when and how we would rent an apartment together. I kept my job at the grocery. Every few weeks, Case and I went for a cup of coffee. Otherwise, I spent my time with Jerry.

We were stretched out on the floor in Jerry's living room one night, drinking Old Milwaukee and listening to Jefferson Airplane. His friends, Roger and Suzie, were snuggled up together on the couch. Suzie tucked her stocking feet up under her legs and laid her head against Roger's flannel shirt.

"I've got some really good stuff," Roger said, reaching for an ashtray.

Jerry leaned back on his elbows and crossed his ankles. He looked at me, then at Roger. "Yeah?"

"Yup. Real good stuff. You smoke, Janie?"

"Depends."

The living room filled with the sweet, greenish smoke while we sipped in puffs from the pinched joint and held our breath as long as possible.

My mother and father had been interrogating Bobo about marijuana lately, after they'd heard that most guys who spent time in Vietnam had tried it. They threatened to search Bobo's room if he ever "acted funny." Bobo never had and never would touch the stuff. He knew that Ginny and I had been smoking marijuana on the weekends, but didn't narc on me.

Suzie decided on a glass of milk about eleven thirty and I reminded Jerry I needed to be home by twelve. The motorcycle climbed the driveway precisely at midnight. Jerry walked me to the gate. Father flashed the yard light on and off and so we said goodnight.

The next afternoon, I slipped on my jean jacket and a helmet again as Jerry revved up the cycle. Climbing behind him, I placed my feet on the rear pegs and, rather than holding the passenger rods along the sides of the seat, casually wrapped my arms around his midriff. We rode about an hour before stopping at a service station. Jerry bought cigarettes while I used the restroom.

"Townsend Park is about six miles from here. Wanna check it out?"

"Yeah, but I'll need to be home by five-thirty for supper. And I have a biology test tomorrow."

We weren't the only ones at the park taking advantage of the mild weather that day in late April. Picnic tables were still lined up winter style, in the grass, but people didn't seem to mind. They used them where they were.

Four or five tables were empty toward the end of the row. We sat on the top of one and each lit up a Marlboro Green. We noticed a footpath going into the oak trees and decided to walk it. In less than a quarter mile, the path opened to a clearing of grassland and a field flowering in narcissus and wild yellow daffodils.

Jerry stretched out on his back in the grass and I went and picked a few of the flowers. I came back and sat on the ground, knees bent and arms around my legs. Jerry sat up and shifted his legs Indian style. The breeze tickled the flowers in front of me. Sighing lightly, I smiled back at the sun. Jerry rested his arm on my shoulder and ran sections of my hair slowly through his fingers. A kiss would be safe now. I knew it would be sweet.

"I like your dimples," he told me.

"That's funny because I like yours."

He kept his hand in my hair, drew me closer and kissed me on the forehead as softly as his fingers had touched my face the week before, as softly as he said my name.

We kissed until the grasses and the earth under my hands were impressed on my palm.

~

I picked Jerry up in the Volkswagen five days later. The air had turned cooler again, below average for the first of May. We drove to the state park and decided to walk along the beach, nearly deserted, before the sun and the day disappeared.

We plodded through the loose sand until we reached shore. It smelled fishy. We stood quietly and watched the waves of Lake Michigan clamor up, hesitate, then roll back again. Behind us, a man and a woman played catch with two golden retrievers. We walked side by side past the concession stand, still boarded up until Memorial Day. When we were a few hundred feet beyond the boathouse, Jerry stopped.

He turned to face me. "Janie," he said in a serious voice, "I need to tell you something."

"Okay," I shrugged.

He dropped his eyes and stared at the sand for a moment. He looked up at me again then further out over to the pier. "I'm married."

"What?"

"I'm married."

"I heard you," I said quietly and looked away. I threw my head back, staring at the sky, determined not to let him see he had just crushed me. I stepped closer to the water, away from him, with my hand shoved into my blue jean pockets. I faced the lake. Waves licked my shoes.

I took my shoes off.

"Damn," I whispered loudly, up at the sky.

Stubborn, deliberate, I tramped forward along the water's edge. Jerry followed me. I thought of my father's admonitions. We walked without speaking, while I stared at the evening sky or down at my bare toes.

I kicked at the sand. He reached for my arm and I shoved his hand away.

"I'm sorry," he said.

I stopped and stared at him.

"I was going to tell you sooner."

"Like hell you were," I said. "Then you decided to charm me first, right?"

"Not really."

He squatted a couple feet from the water line, hands grasped around his knees. I parked myself a good arm's length away, scraping my index finger deeper and deeper into the sand.

"What the hell were you thinking?" I asked, squinting.

He watched the waves. "It's not like you think. She and I have been separated a long time now. We're getting a divorce."

I gathered my hair in a bunch with one hand, and rubbed the back of my neck with the other. "I don't think that helps at all." Letting my hair fall back in place, I reached in my pocket for a cigarette.

We each lit up. I exhaled loudly.

"Kids?"

"Nicky. My son. He's two."

The sun slipped below the water line. I watched him doodle with his finger in the sand, from time to time looking at me with those eyes of his, dejected and pleading.

Soon, it would be dark and the park would close. I stood abruptly and brushed the sand off. "Let's leave."

We walked to the car at a dirge-like pace.

There's always a vacuum inside the little Volkswagen Bug but it seemed more noticeable as we drove home that night.

"Can I buy you a beer?" Jerry asked. "Coffee?"

"No. No thank you."

When I pulled up to the curb, I shut off the engine, took a deep breath and a long look at him. He looked back blinking his eyes. I stared out the window on my side of the car, putting my hands tightly on the steering wheel until the blood drained from my knuckles.

"What's her name?"

"Lisa," Jerry said in a whisper.

"Hmm." Pretty name. Way prettier than Jane. I looked up at the leathery, cream-colored ceiling, ventilated with hundreds of tiny holes. "Well, good night."

"Can I see you again?"

I waited, looking out of the windshield as if an answer was out in the street someplace in the night.

"Maybe."

He surprised me with his quick kiss on my cheek then slammed the door behind himself.

There was that vacuum sensation again.

Twintig

S unday afternoon, the phone rang.
"You okay?" Jerry asked.

"Yes."

"Will you talk with me?"

"No."

"Are you angry?"

"Yes."

"Can I call you tomorrow?"

"No."

"When can I call you again?"

"Maybe never." I waited.

"I'll try Tuesday," he said.

I hung up, feeling a measure of revenge. He had hurt me. And lied. Never forgiving him would be justified.

Over the next two weeks, my self-righteous reasoning started to fade. I missed our evenings together, our lazy time on weekends. Sometimes I spent a day alone with Ginny, or a few hours with Case. I studied. Jerry had never excluded me from anything he did or planned and I missed his attention. I missed his shiny hair, his eyes, the hole in the knee of his jeans.

I tried to convince myself that seeing him would be okay. Maybe God wouldn't even mind because God knew all about love and stuff of that sort. Maybe we could work it out.

My parents had disliked Jerry all along—never liked his hair, his clothes, his bike. Even though he often went to church with me on Sunday nights, they had objected that he wasn't Christian Reformed.

If he was at least Reformed, they might have gotten used to the idea. He wasn't even Baptist. Jerry was brought up Roman Catholic. He'd have been better off if he were nothing. Or so Father would say. If my father knew.

~

Jerry made a decision to move in with Roger and Suzie and I drove there three or four times a week for dinner. Dessert was usually pot.

One Thursday night, Roger, Suzie, and Jerry convinced me to try mescaline before we went to a Fleetwood Mac concert out at Grand Valley College on M-45. On the way to the concert, we passed around a bottle of Monk Berry Moon Delight.

"What's in this stuff?" I asked before taking a swallow.

The car radio was blasting and Suzie shouted from the front seat. "Stop being so paranoid and take a swig. It's only wine." She laughed and added, "Wine with a little punch."

I took a gulp and passed it to Jerry who took a gulp and passed it to Roger, our driver, who took a swallow and passed it to Suzie. We finished off the bottle at the same time we pulled onto the campus.

The fluorescent lights in the crowded gymnasium looked like a glowing spectrum of bright primary colors. Bleachers were full and hundreds of people sat on the floor. An immediate claustrophobic feeling gripped me.

"Over to the left here," Roger said.

We joined the people on the floor where, even before the concert began, I saw the heads of people right in front of us let go of their bodies and start to float up toward the ceiling. "Holy shit." I looked at Jerry, then at Roger and Suzie, then back at the ceiling. There were more heads, all different glowing colors. These were not floating. They were smiling and bouncing around like the little ball on top of the words for a song. "It's impossible. The heads." I stood up. "Their heads—up there. Holy shit."

"Far out," Roger said.

Jerry grabbed my hand. "Sit down. It's okay."

"I gotta get out of here." I looked around for an exit, but every time I moved my eyes, everything followed along. I sat down again.

The necks on the headless bodies started to grow longer and longer, like Jack-in-the-box springs. "I'm gettin' the hell out of here." I jumped up. "Out . . . of . . . here . . ." I couldn't move any further.

"She's freaking," Roger said.

Jerry took me by the arm and told Roger, "You guys stay."

I shut my eyes while he led me through the people. Things looked pretty much the same whether my eyes were open or closed.

Once out in the fresh air, we started along the gravel shoulder of the road. The view looked more normal, except the trail of red streaks behind the few cars that passed.

Jerry stretched out his arm, stuck a thumb into the air, and started walking backwards.

I froze. "What are you doing?"

"Catching a ride." He kept going.

"Stop," I yelled and ran after him. He waited for me to catch up. "What the hell? I can't hitchhike!"

"You're gonna have to."

"No way. I can't. Why don't we just walk? It can't be more than fifteen miles or so."

"No." He started walking backwards again. "We'd be walking forever. Literally forever."

"But . . . I'm afraid."

He stopped and reached for my hand. We stepped further away from the pavement.

"Janie." His stern voice made me cry. He put both his hands on my shoulders as if he was going to shake me. "Janie, look at me." Staring straight in my eyes, he spoke a tad more soothingly. "We can't walk. We'd never get home. Trust me."

Jerry said later that the way my wavy, long blonde hair fell on my jean jacket was why one of the first cars coming by pulled over and picked us up.

We climbed into the back seat of an old Chevy Impala. "Going as far as Grand Rapids?" Jerry asked the man at the wheel. Although he wore a cowboy hat, I could see his face well enough. He wasn't much older than us.

"Where 'bouts?"

"Downtown's good, if it's not out of the way."

"Not a bit."

"Cool. Thanks, man."

I sat as close to Jerry as I could, my hands folded on my lap, my eyes wide open, looking straight ahead.

"What's with the chick?"

Jerry put his hands on mine. "She'll be all right, once we get home."

"Street?"

"Union," Jerry said as if the guy was a taxi driver.

"Goin' right by . . ."

Jerry was right. The ride took forever. Walking would have been an eternity.

"Here 'tis. Corner okay?"

"Very cool. Thanks again, man."

"Take care of the girl."

Inside, I kept my jacket on and stood by the door. "It's late," I said. "I gotta get home."

"It's only quarter to ten," Jerry said, flopping down on the couch.

I didn't move. "I'm still scared. Really scared."

He got up, put his arms around my waist and held me. "You're so beautiful." He ran his hand through my hair a couple of times.

I pushed away. "I sure as hell don't feel beautiful."

"Come here and sit by me," he said and led me to the couch where I sat in my jacket.

"Seems like two in the morning at least."

I drank some milk and smoked cigarettes, drank more milk, smoked more cigarettes, tried to calm my insides down.

A long, long time later, Roger and Suzie returned.

"This is hell," I said. "What time is it?"

"Eleven-thirty," Jerry answered.

"I want to go home."

"You're parents will put you in the loony hospital if they see you like this."

That was the last place on earth I'd want to be. Even hell must be better.

"Well, when?" I asked.

"It'll go away. I don't know how long."

We sat on the couch together. I smoked Marlboro Green after Marlboro Green to convince myself I was normal. When I wasn't smoking, I sat up straight, still in my jacket, my hands holding the top of my arms crossed on my chest.

"What's it feel like, Janie?" Roger asked.

"Scary. Damn scary." I looked around the room at the three of them. "Don't you know?"

"We don't get off like you did," Jerry said, squeezing my hand.

Shit, I thought, lighting another cigarette. I'm really not normal.

Roger put on a Kris Kristofferson album. "Comin' down music," he said.

At twelve-forty five, I asked, "Now?"

Jerry looked at me straight in the eyes like he was an optometrist, and shook his head. "Not yet."

When it was two in the morning, I insisted. My parents had probably filed a missing-person report by now.

"Can you handle it?"

"I'm very good at acting normal," I said.

He drove until we came to the corner of London Street. "I'll get out here," he said. "You make it okay?"

"Sure."

He held my face, stared into my eyes a few seconds, then quickly kissed my forehead. As he walked away, I wondered if it was his ass he was saving all along.

I parked the Volkswagen in front of the house and found I could walk just fine. Father met me at the door. I did not argue over releasing my car keys to him.

"You're alone at this hour?"

"Yes."

"Where is he?" Father demanded.

I stood trembling, genuinely afraid of my father. "He's not here."

Perhaps it was my cooperation with the keys or maybe my quivering voice that caused Mother to say, "Let her go, Dad."

Father stepped aside. I raced upstairs, undressed and stayed in bed awake until my alarm went off at eight. Then I got up, called in sick for work, and went back to bed.

My father was at the meat plant. My mother left me alone.

~

If I'd left the house a few minutes earlier, I could have avoided my father. But when I grabbed my jean jacket early Wednesday evening and headed downstairs, I met him in the kitchen. It had been three days since he confiscated my car keys.

"Where are you off to?"

My father's clothes smelled of smoked and cured hams and bacon.

"I'm going to Jerry's," I said.

"I still have your keys."

"You could give them back."

"No. And you are not going to Jerry's."

I said the words in a mocking tone. "Yes, I am."

"How will you get there?"

"I'll take the bus."

"The buses don't run after six."

"Then I better get going. It's a long walk."

He stepped in front of me. "You have no business being with that man, and you know it. He is a son of the antichrist, that's all."

And you don't know the half of it, I thought. "It isn't fair to blame him. I have a mind of my own, you know. I can think for myself."

I reached around him for the door handle but he blocked me again. This time, my arms across on my chest, I shoved my father.

He grabbed my arm.

"Let her go, Dad!" Mother shouted.

"I'll be home late." I ran out the door.

A four-mile walk lay ahead. The bus going north displayed "To Garage" in the window.

I hiked quickly—past Hall Street School, up Grandville Avenue, past Franklin and on to Wealthy. I crossed the expressway over the viaduct and came to the corner of Division. Impoverished. Worse than *sortje*. A few blocks south were where ladies stood in front of boarded-up stores and ramshackle bars. Who knew who or what else.

I reached the vicinity of St. Mary's Hospital and felt somewhat safer. Only a few more blocks.

I climbed the steps to the front porch and knocked on the door.

"You walked?" Jerry asked. "That's so cool." We went through the swinging wooden door into the kitchen for privacy. "Don't do it again."

"You saying you'd worry about me?"

He kissed me instead of answering. After a time, I laid my head on his chest and we just stood that way quietly.

Jerry borrowed Roger's car to bring me home. "Will your parents lock you out?" he asked.

"Naw. They wouldn't do that," I said. "They may think about it, but they never would."

"Really? But they're so damned straight."

"My mother says no matter what, we can always come home."

"Rad. Why?"

"Well . . . I guess . . . it's something like when the minister talks about Covenant . . ."

Jerry slowed the car, nodding as if the comparison made some sense.

It took a second to get the full realization myself. "It's . . . it's because I'm their kid . . . who I am . . . where I belong . . ." I breathed in and exhaled loudly. "They'll make me wash windows, mop the basement floor, write out five pages of Calvin's *Institutes*, give me sermon after sermon, even take my keys . . . But they won't turn me away . . ." I faced away from him, embarrassed. "Damn it," I whispered.

~

Father returned my car keys two days later. He seemed reluctant, but I supposed he finally figured keeping them wouldn't stop the relationship.

I watched Jerry struggle to please my parents and not succeed. Father held his tongue if Jerry showed up for evening church services or when I invited him in, yet still referred to him as a "son of the antichrist" when Jerry wasn't there.

"I don't know what to do about your parents," Jerry said one Saturday after I asked him to Sunday dinner.

I laughed. "It's the million dollar question. I never know what to do about my parents."

"It's not funny." He got up and headed for the kitchen. Roger and Suzie were out and we had the house to ourselves. After a few minutes, I went and found Jerry sitting at the table with his milk and a Marlboro Green. I stood behind him and slid my hands through the sleeves of his T-shirt.

"They don't even know about your divorce," I said, running my fingers along his biceps.

"They don't?" His arm tensed. "How come?"

"They would murder me. They would murder you."

He put out his smoke. I followed him to the sink. Rinsing his glass, he set it on the counter and turned around. "Janie. Please. Come here."

Our mouths touched and lingered together.

"I want you," he said with a temporary hoarseness.

My arms encircled his neck, my fingers caressed his hair. "You have me. I'm yours."

The outline of his mouth brushed my forehead and my cheek, until resting beneath the curve of my chin.

"You know what I mean," he whispered. "I want you all the way."

"We can't." I pulled away, stepping backward toward the living room.

He took me by the arm, placed his opened hand along the side of my face and kissed me.

"I can't do this," I said.

"I love you," he whispered.

"I still can't."

"You think God won't like it. He won't be angry, Janie. He knows all about love."

"Maybe . . . but it's wrong."

He lifted my hair, brushed my neck with his lips. "It's so right, baby. It's so right."

I pulled away only slightly. He put his hands on the back of my jeans, kissing me again. And for the first time in my life and the last time in our relationship, I gave myself fully to a man.

Een en Twintig

Jerry came to church with me more often after that. Eyebrows rose when he'd join us on Sunday mornings in the third row from the front. Klikkuiken would notice the pea coat instead of suit and tie, the long hair over his ears, past the navy blue collar. Mr. Meyer elbowed Mrs. Meyer and whispered. Mrs. Meyer would mention it to Mrs. Feenstra who would later discuss it again with Klikkuiken who would pass the observations on some more.

Some kindness was evident—a handshake from the Do-it-Nothing Gang, a nod from the Berends, Ginny's greeting, a smile from Mrs. VanderGoot or the Kamps.

We heard the same Gospel from Reverend Hellinga as I had heard from Reverend Piersma. Once during an evening service, Father allowed me to sit with Jerry in the balcony, separate from our family. The balcony's wooden seats folded with a soft knock when we stood to sing.

> O Lord of hosts, how lovely Thy tabernacles are;
> For them my heart is yearning In banishment afar.
> My soul is longing, fainting, Thy sacred courts to see;
> My heart and flesh are crying, O living God, for Thee.
> Beneath Thy care the sparrow Finds place for peace and rest;
> To keep her young in safety, The swallow finds a nest.
> Then, Lord, my King Almighty, Thy love will shelter me;
> Beside Thy holy altar My dwelling place shall be.

Jerry didn't know Psalm 84. Even his respectful non-participation drew attention from those around us.

Reverend Hellinga read the Scripture and gave the sermon. Jerry and I sat hand in hand.

We were on the third peppermint.

"Brothers and sisters, we must consider the Church on earth, here and now. We are in a battle. Not like our young men overseas, although they share the battle and we continue to pray for their safety, for God's mercy to return them safely, and to bring an end to the horrid circumstances in Vietnam . . ."

From the balcony, I could see the back of my father's head. My mother, purse on her lap. Bobo, Arie J, Aunt Dienke.

When the sermon was over, Reverend Hellinga lifted his black-robed arms and pronounced the Benediction. "The Lord bless you and keep you. The Lord make his face to shine upon you. The Lord lift up His countenance upon you, and give you peace. Aah-men."

We stopped in the church basement to chat with the Do-it-Nothing Gang and verify the date for a gathering.

We were in the Volkswagen. I drove and parked in front of Roger's house. We walked around to the side door and into the kitchen. Jerry poured a tall glass of milk before taking off his coat. In the living room we found Roger and Suzie cuddled on the couch.

"Hey, babe," Roger said. "Ditch your coat and stay awhile."

"Might as well. Can't dance." I tossed my coat over a chair and broke into a move of rhythm and blues. "Oh yes I can!"

Roger lifted his chin, pointing a red, short beard at Jerry. "Where ya been?"

"Bet I know," Suzie teased. "Church."

"Yep," Jerry answered.

I blushed again.

Roger sat up and lit a cigarette. "Tell me, Jerry. How do you do it? I mean, it's not like you, man—putting up with this churchy business."

"It's easy man," Jerry said, reaching for a smoke. "I just get high."

I must have misheard. "What did you say?" I asked.

"I said I get high. It's far out."

He wasn't teasing.

"You do? You get high?" My voice squeaked. "You get high? Always?"

"Always what?"

I closed my eyes and sighed loudly through my nose. Then I enunciated the words to be certain he understood. "Do—you—always—get—high—for—church?"

"Yeah. It's a gas. And the stained glass windows—they're so rad. You should try it."

"Oh, right." Disgust broke my voice and I didn't try to hide it. "Sure thing." I marched to the kitchen, letting the wooden door swing behind me.

I poured milk in a tall glass, took a long gulp before closing the refrigerator, sat at the table and lit a smoke. When finished, I lit another. As much milk as I drank, the calories never fattened me up. Or so my mother would say.

Jerry came in and slipped into the chair across from mine. "You angry?"

I didn't answer.

"You're upset, I can tell."

"I'll be all right."

I stayed reticent. We joined Roger and Suzie in the living room and listened to Jefferson Airplane, Santana, Canned Heat. I went to fetch my coat earlier than usual. Part of me wanted to put my arms around Jerry, kiss away the stupidness, the ache inside me. Jerry looked puzzled. I held my tongue and without so much as a touch, stepped outside to leave.

He followed me and quickly pecked my cheek. "Drive carefully, Janie. It's starting to rain." I fled down the steps and into the Volkswagen. He waved from the porch. Ignoring him, I switched on the wipers and drove away.

~

I hated how confused the reasonable and the ridiculous could be. I wanted to bridge the span between us and hated that I couldn't. Three days later, I told Jerry. "It'll never work."

Eventually he stopped asking me to explain. Eventually, the days between seeing each other widened. Eventually, he called less. Eventually, a long time, actually, I missed him less.

Twee en Twintig

"You be sure you're in on time, young lady."

"But Dad, it's Friday night."

"I don't care. I don't want you in late any more, *hoor*?"

Father was at the kitchen table finishing the potatoes Mother had fried up. We didn't wait with supper on Friday nights when he worked his second job at Lou's Market Basket. Mother would never serve Father the rice with raisins we ate earlier anyway. Good food for poor people, or so Mother would say. Not good for a meat and potato man.

I dug in my shoulder bag for my keys. "How come Bobo doesn't get yelled at when he's home later than twelve?"

"That's different." My father pointed his fork at me as he spoke. "A girl has no business out after midnight and you know it."

"Yeah, right." I rolled my eyes. "Well, crap. I left my keys upstairs."

He raised his voice while his fork shook at me like a pointed finger. "Ladies don't say that." Taking another bite and smacking his lips, he added, "And you look like an Indian with that coat on."

Father was referring to my brown suede coat trimmed with fringe on the front yoke, the back and the sleeves. Mother had warned me. "I don't know why you spend your hard-earned money on something like that. Better not let your father see it."

Father took more applesauce. "Nothing but an Indian or a Hippie."

"What's that supposed to mean?"

"You dress like the world. Can't tell you apart from the rest of them. I don't know anymore." He scraped his plate clean. "And that

153

Jerry. He should be ashamed the way his hair looks. And his ripped jeans. It's terrible, that's all. Just terrible."

"For Christsakes! He hasn't even been around!" I screamed, and headed for the stairs.

Father slid his chair away from the table. "Don't you talk that way! I'll have no blasphemy in this house!"

I stomped up each step of the stairs. "I am so sick and tired of all your fucking rules."

He took the steps two at a time. When we both reached the landing, I crouched and covered my face with one arm, my head with the other. He smacked me three times. Then, with his hand still in the air, he stopped. He pointed and shook his finger at me. He lowered his voice, not yelling but stern. "Don't you ever let me hear that coming from your mouth again."

He turned away, walked down the steps, and took his rage with him.

~

Ginny tried to fix me up with her boyfriend's buddy, Scott. We assessed him over a couple of rum and cokes one night. "On the pudgy side but adorable," I said. The four of us ran around together a few weekends, but as soon as we went out alone, all Scott wanted to do was park and make out and take my T-shirt off.

I ran into Denny, a high school classmate, at a pizza take-out. We made a date for the movies. "You okay with James Bond?" he asked when he picked me up later. I sat bored, kicking myself for agreeing to come. At Big Boy's afterward, Denny gobbled a hamburger, onion rings and a chocolate shake while I drank the coffee I ordered and watched.

Eddie was an old classmate, too. He dressed in kakis and polo shirts, lived in the suburbs and worked for his father, who owned his own business. "I want a Corvette, but I'm saving for a motorcycle. I smoked pot three times." Eddie listened to a lot of Neil Diamond.

I went out with Richard a few times. My parents hadn't noticed but I smelled alcohol on his breath when we got in the car. He could have at least waited for me.

Ginny and I rarely smoked dope any more. She broke up with her boyfriend and started going to grassers—outside beer parties held in a small, hilly field south of town. Ginny kept inviting me to come along, so one Saturday night we drove out together.

A person had to have been there before to find the two-track through the woods leading to the clearing. Ginny carefully steered her Plymouth to the right until the trail widened and a couple dozen vehicles came into view.

The night air smelled like a campground. A guy named Al played the stereo system from his pickup at the edge of the makeshift parking area. Railroad ties were placed in a circle near the huge bonfire. My guess said forty, maybe fifty people were there, more guys than girls. For two bucks, girls could have as much beer from the kegs as they wanted. Guys paid three.

I followed Ginny around for a while, feeling conspicuous. She kept introducing me to everybody. I excused myself and went to refill my plastic cup.

"Great hair," said the guy pumping the keg. He eyed the natural wave my hair took on in the August humidity. "I'm Jim," he said. "I don't think I've seen you here before."

"I came with Ginny. My name's Janie." I nodded and took the refill.

"Ginny's a cool chick."

"She's my best friend." There were people waiting in line. "Catch ya later."

I wished for more than my jean jacket over my T-shirt. I went and sat on an empty railroad tie near the warm fire. Across from me, a couple snuggled close, their hands intertwined. They nodded a how-do-you-do and returned their eyes to the flame. Before long, Ginny took a spot next to me.

"Janie, see that guy over there?" she whispered. "The tall one in the corduroy shirt talking with Al. He asked me your name and if you were going with anybody."

"You know him?"

"Yup. Used to be engaged to Luanne from work. Name's Walt. You can't tell from here, but he's boss."

"Engaged?" I took a swallow of my beer.

"Yeah. He called it off a couple of months ago."

"Hmmm. I don't think so."

~

Case and I shot pool together regularly. We listened to George Harrison, drank coffee at Big Boy's and drove up to the Silver Lake sand dunes, where we discussed Abraham Kuyper, Richard Nixon, and argued whether a Honda, a Harley, or a Royal Enfield were better models. We watched Barbara Streisand movies. No romance between us. Case was a good friend and I was in love with Elliot Gould.

Ginny and I kept busy secretly checking apartments for rent. We had saved enough to make a deposit. With newspaper ads on our lap, we rode around town jotting down addresses.

Walt and I went out after all. He came inside to meet my parents on the first date.

"And where do you go to church?" Father asked him.

"Well, sometimes I go with my mother to First Christian Reformed in Cutlerville, but usually I go to my dad's chapel."

Mother's face lit up. "Your dad's chapel?"

"He's the lay minister at the Ridge Grove."

Not the son of the anti-Christ. The son of a preacher.

The following weekend I went out with Robert, who I knew from Junior College. Case and I went for coffee Saturday and, on Sunday, the Do-It-Nothing Gang got together at Ginny's. The next Friday, I was out with Richard until my midnight curfew. On Saturday morning, my mother stood waiting at the kitchen sink when I came down for a bowl of cereal. Dumping the dishwater, she handed me a towel and said, "That nice boy Walter called last night."

Drie en Twintig

We said good-bye in the kitchen.

"I don't know, Janie. It's no good."

"Mom, don't worry. I'm nineteen. I'll be fine." I planted a smooch on my mother's cheek. "I'll be back on Sundays for dinner."

During the three weeks since telling my parents Ginny and I had made a deposit on an apartment, a type of unexpressed moratorium developed between us. My parents seemed to realize there wasn't much they could do to stop me. I tried not to rub my excitement in their face.

My VW was parked at the apartment. Ginny waited in our driveway on London Street with her Plymouth running. Mr. VanderGoot was at the window, my father was at the gate of our white picket fence.

"See ya soon, Dad." I wanted to get this goodbye over with, but while I gave Father a kiss, he slid his arm around my back and hugged me. I quickly hugged him back then pulled away. "I'll be okay. You'll see."

There were tears in his eyes, and just like when he watched television, he didn't try to hide them. "Good-bye, little girl."

I gave him another peck on the cheek, waved to Mr. VanderGoot, jumped in Ginny's car and slammed the door. "Let's get out of here," I said. "Hurry the heck up, let's go." My hands trembled as I lit up a Marlboro.

We drove down London Street—past the Richters, DeBoers, Kingmas, Hoogeveens. Nearly a whole twenty years in this neighborhood. No denying I would miss it in a way, Klikkuiken and all.

∽

Our apartment took up the entire bottom floor of a two-story house in an old neighborhood on the opposite side of the city from London Street. Spacious rooms with high ceilings, the doors and trim stained deep walnut. Long rectangular windows let in extra light and the sills were wide enough to hold pots of the ivy and spider plants. An enormous kitchen held endless cupboards, skinny and so tall we couldn't reach the upper shelves unless we stood on a chair. Ginny and I each had our own bedroom with walk-in closets we could tell had been added at some point, given the windows enclosed inside them.

No bad smells but the place was filthy. We didn't let any one see it, especially our mothers, until we trashed newspapers and magazines, cleaned crumbs from cupboards, tossed socks from the closets, fished paper, hair clips, dirt, and rubber bands from the registers. We sanitized porcelain, washed windows, scrubbed and painted walls.

When I missed the old neighborhood at all, second thoughts were nullified by the adventure of being on my own. Ginny and I lived on milk, bread, eggs, nineteen-cents-a-box macaroni and cheese, and monthly Burger King coupons. Independence was worth the deprivation.

My parents came only on invitation, about twice a month. On each visit, Mother brought something with her as if an on-going housewarming gift was needed as an offering. A frying pan, an end table from a garage sale, "a lost rug" that mysteriously re-appeared in the basement on London Street, a jar of homemade pea soup.

Ginny and I were compatible and complementary. I'd pick up, Ginny would clean. She liked to cook, I'd rather do the dishes. We went together like *brood en brie,* meat and potatoes. We shared the same friends and on the weekends, partied at the same places.

My Volkswagen became a convenient vehicle for roading-it. I'd learned to change a flat tire, change the oil and replace the filter. I could not, however, stop the rust from eroding a hole in the Bug's floorboard. So Ginny and I took advantage of the vented flooring, disposing our empty beer cans through the hole under the mat.

We reaped what we sowed one rainy Sunday morning. Ginny's Plymouth started with difficulty on wet mornings, so we jumped in the Volkswagen, dressed in our best. Both of us had faithfully continued attending Grandville Avenue Church. Soon we were on our way to Sunday services.

I accelerated to fifty miles an hour, preparing to merge onto the highway when the Volkswagen hit a mammoth puddle. Mud and water splashed through the cavity in the floorboard with a force that stopped the car, immersing us like a couple of Anabaptists.

With the exception of a Sunday during flu season and once when afflicted with serious hangovers, that was the only time we missed church.

~

After the first few weeks Ginny and I lived together, Walt started dropping in. I asked Ginny how she felt about it, if she was okay with me dating him and with him hanging around.

"Okay? I was the one who introduced you, remember?" Ginny said. "I think the two of you together's boss."

We dated during that winter and steadily the following spring and summer. Claiming John Wayne as his hero, Walt came off sure of himself, a bit cocky. Broad shouldered, he stood just over six feet tall. His coarse, dark hair waved naturally and he had a habit of rubbing his hand over the top of his head to smooth it. I found this habit sweet, a hint that there might be a little self-consciousness underneath all that confidence.

Walt's grandparents came from Germany, which is about as close to Groningen Dutch as you can get. He was born and raised in our denomination, his father a minister. "Our kind of people," my mother often reminded me.

Walt met Ginny and me with a group of mutual friends at a pizza bar where we regularly hung-out. One Thursday night as we passed around pitchers of beer and sang with the piano man on stage, Walt lifted his mug and put an arm around Ginny. Up to my ears in jealousy, I knew then and there I wanted to marry him.

~

"Janie, are you ready?" Ginny called, knocking on the bedroom door. "Walt's here."

"Be right out." I took a last look in the mirror and grabbed my jean jacket off the bed.

"You ready for dinner?" he greeted me.

I smooched him on the mouth. "Where we going?"

"How about Melvin's? I'm in the mood for a steak." Walt dug in his pocket. "Oh, here ya go. I saved this for you." He tossed me a small square wrapper from a Cracker Jack box.

"Last of the big spenders, I see," Ginny said.

He laughed. "Open it, Janie."

I ripped the paper apart. "What is this?" I took the small gold object between my fingers. "My gosh." I turned it over then held it up in the air. "A ring! Ginny! It's a frickin' diamond ring!" My arm fell to my side, the ring still between my fingertips. "Walt, what does this mean?"

"It means I want to marry you, dummy."

We hadn't discussed it. The presumptuousness made me stall.

"I don't know what the heck to say."

"Say yes," Ginny said.

"You knew about this?"

"Maybe," she answered.

Walt bent down on one knee. He didn't take my hand but lifted his together like he was praying. "Janie, will you marry me?"

My eyes were watering up so I looked at Ginny. She wiped tears from her face and started giggling. I turned to Walt and said, "Yeah, yeah, I will." I handed him the ring. "But first you'll have to ask my dad."

He got up and kissed me on the forehead. "No problem. How many Indian blankets are you worth?" Then he grabbed my hand and slipped the engagement ring on my finger.

Vier en Twintig

Case folded the newspaper and stretched his long legs under the booth. "I went to the basketball game with Bruce the other night."

"How's he doing?" I smeared my cinnamon roll with butter. "I haven't seen Bruce in a coon's age."

"He's working for a lawn maintenance place. Says this winter he can plow snow." Case poked the yolk of his egg with a piece of toast. "He was surprised to hear you're getting married."

"I don't think he's met Walt."

"He said too bad."

"Too bad?" I set my cup of coffee on its saucer.

"He's been thinking about asking you out."

Leaning back against the booth, I smiled. "Well, that's sweet." I nodded to the waitress passing with the coffee pot. "He sure took his time."

We finished our breakfast. When the table was cleared of everything but coffee, we set a clean ashtray in the middle. The restaurant was emptying, and the hostess was switching cardboard breakfast menus to laminated lunch ones.

"We're not going to be able to get together like this after the wedding," Case said.

"It won't be the same, will it? You and Walt will talk sports and stuff."

I didn't have expectations that Walt would fill in for Case or for Ginny or for anybody. Although Ginny and I swore we wouldn't let it, marriage always changed other relationships.

"So, Case. What do you think?"

He cleared his throat but didn't say anything.

"No, really. What?"

"All right. Let me ask you. Why the heck get married now?"

"Come on, Case," I laughed. "Why not?"

"I like Walt and all, don't get me wrong. But for one thing, we're young." He shifted his legs so they stuck out into the aisle. "Tell me. Specifically."

"We're not young. I'm twenty. Lots of people our age are already married and happy about it." Case waited while I blew on my coffee and took a sip. "I want to settle, have a house, have a family. Walt's a good guy. He's ambitious, good-looking, fun, belongs to church." We each had a cigarette going in the ashtray. I picked mine up and took a long drag. "I want sex," I added before exhaling the smoke.

He grimaced. "That's no reason to get married. You know that."

"For crying out loud, Case. Of course I do."

"Besides." Case smashed out his cigarette. "I'll have sex with you whenever you want."

"Not funny." I reached in my purse. "You know, I don't care much for his mother, but I like his dad. And Walt gets along with my family. My parents are nuts about him."

"And you?"

"And me what?"

"Janie, he's everything they've always wanted for you. Of course your parents are nuts about him—but are you? You love him?"

"Sure."

I snapped my purse closed and set a ten spot on top of the check.

~

My two-and-a-half week vacation started the first day of spring. In three days I was getting married. My father had asked me to have lunch with him. After a stop at the florist to confirm delivery of the wedding flowers, I drove to the wholesale meat plant where Father worked for the last nine years. He was waiting at the door.

"My car's in the other lot," he explained. I followed him across the street.

I thought my father would drive over to Maggie's up the block or maybe to the McDonald's on Eastern. But when I climbed in, I saw his tin lunch bucket on the front seat.

"Mom packed an extra fried egg sandwich," he said, opening the container.

I wondered if he was going to pray or read from the Bible, but he just handed me a sandwich and a baggie with potato chips.

"I haven't had a fried egg sandwich since I moved out." I turned sideways with my back against the passenger door and looked at my father. His head was bowed and I realized he was saying a silent prayer before eating. So I did the same.

"You'll have to share my coffee. I forgot an extra mug." Father poured the steaming liquid into his thermos cup and set it on the dashboard. "Help yourself."

"I'd forgotten how good these are," I said and meant it.

Between bites, my father dug around in his lunch bucket. He handed me something wrapped in a paper napkin. "I saved you a cookie from morning coffee break. And here's an apple."

"Oh, that's okay. You eat them. I had a good breakfast."

He started the car and turned on the heater. "That's better."

When I finished my sandwich and a hand full of chips, I took a sip of the coffee and passed it back to my father. "Thanks."

With the car still idling, he packed up our trash. He cracked the window, pulled his pipe from his pocket, lit it and winked at me. "So. My little girl's getting married."

"Yup." I smiled back at him, nodding. "Got any cigarettes?"

"You shouldn't smoke. It doesn't look good on a woman."

I just shrugged.

"They're in the glove box."

I took a Camel out of the package and my father pushed in the lighter. Usually I don't smoke cigarettes without a filter, but this was a special occasion.

"You wanna make sure you get up, have breakfast or coffee together in the mornings."

"Yeah?" I squirmed, thinking this is where the sermon comes in.

"Don't start the day without praying."

He was looking right at me, but he didn't point his finger or any-thing. Even so, I had to look away. I flicked my ashes out the window.

"Have Walt pray out loud."

"Oh."

"It makes a difference," he said.

We smoked quietly for a minute.

"And read the Bible at suppertime."

"Okay."

After a few more drags off the cigarette, I tossed it through the crack in the window.

Father turned the car off. "Walt's a good man."

We got out and he walked me to my car. My father hugged me then and said, "Bye little girl." His eyes got red and watery.

In the rearview mirror, I watched through my own tears as my father re-entered the plant.

～

Of course Ginny was my maid of honor. We were up by eight o'clock Friday morning, making coffee and giggling like a couple of little girls.

If I still lived at home, I imagined my mother and I would be in the kitchen together this morning, my wedding day. I'd be eating Cheerios at the table and she would be standing on the kitchen register, arms folded over her chest, worrying if I'd be happy the rest of my life. She'd probably say something like "I don't know, Janie." I'd reassure her things would be fine, and in an attempt at some sort of blessing, she'd say, "Well, he's our kind of people."

I called Mother before Ginny and I went out for breakfast.

"Umm . . . just thought I'd call a minute."

"Well, that was nice."

"You and Dad all set?"

"The question is, are you?"

"Oh, yeah. I'm set."

I wondered if there was something special I should say, and my mother was likely wondering if there was something special she should say.

I heard her sigh before she spoke again. "I don't know, Janie."

With the phone still to my ear, I shook my head, smiling. "It'll be okay, Mom."

We were both quiet and could hear each other breathing through the receiver.

"Are you sure we don't want to warm up the ham on buns?" Mother asked. "The Ladies Aid said they'd come a little early and put them in the oven if we want."

"No. I think they'll go better with the potato salad if they're just room temperature."

"Dad still wants everybody to sing before cake and ice cream. Aunt Grace said she'd play the piano. He wants 'Beautiful Savior' and Psalm 103."

"You think he's jealous that Walt's dad is marrying us?"

"No, I don't think so. It's not like Reverend Hellinga can be there."

"True . . . Well, about the songs, I guess it's all right."

I checked my watch. In less than a half of a day, I'd be married. "Think Walt will show?" I teased.

"I sure hope so." Her tone said she didn't think it was funny.

"Well, me too."

"You be careful today. Thanks for calling, honey."

Vijf en Twintig

Walt and I lived in a new mobile home on a small lot meticulously kept to blend with the yards of our neighbors. Our back yard bordered Plaster Creek, the same creek that ran eight miles north along my old church, school, and playground. Only here in the suburbs, the color of the creek didn't change depending on the waste Kelvinator dumped that week. Here, the stream ran clear and attracted mallard ducks that woke us in the early morning.

We didn't entertain fairy-tale dreams about love and happiness and marriage. We were in love, but not blinded. We expected the usual trivia newly-weds face—how to squeeze the tube of toothpaste, who took out the trash, where to set the furnace thermostat at night.

We attended Walt's church, the same denomination as Grand-ville Avenue. The one-story architecture stretched out in fresh, unattractive suburban brick. Any high and mightiness was limited to the apparent affluence most people there enjoyed. I soon preferred to leave when the services were finished and wait in the car while Walt conversed with his friends.

On our way to service one Sunday morning, Walt asked. "Why don't you mingle some, Janie? Get to know some of the people better?"

I flipped down the visor to check my lipstick. "Easy for you to say. You've been here a long time."

"We've been here together nearly six months now. I thought you'd make some friends."

"I'd like to have a cigarette when church is over. You guys can do that out on the sidewalk. Imagine the reaction if I went out there with the men and lit up."

"Please don't."

"Discussions of wallpaper and curtains are a drag. As are golf outings, fashion and cruise ships. It's either that or babies, which is worse yet."

"Can't be that bad," Walt said.

We pulled into the stadium-size parking lot with its glossy black-top. "Feels like a country club," I said.

No need to lock the car. We walked into the expansive vestibule while the recorded church bells played and brought me an aching for Mr. Kamps.

Every week I told myself I'd get used to Providence Christian Reformed Church.

The congregation sang psalms and hymns faster than I could catch my breath, as if that made their church contemporary. A song like "When I Survey the Wondrous Cross" is supposed to be contemplative. When done tempo allegro it becomes *spoterie*, and *spoten* was somewhere between a spoof on God and blasphemy.

Same with Communion services. After whizzing through "Just As I Am," the minister didn't read the traditional liturgy but a short pamphlet for the "special occasion." Far from dignified and hardly sacramental. I wondered if such a holding of the Means of Grace actually stopped the channel for it.

When I asked Walt what he thought, he didn't get the question.

Walt's brother and sister-in-law worked as houseparents in a group home for twelve mentally handicapped adults. When they took evenings off, we subbed for them. We were married just over a year, when Walt's brother and wife decided to move to the state of Washington where her family lived. We sold our mobile home and took their place.

Our small apartment annexed the group home. As housemother, I carried most of the everyday responsibilities for the residents and was paid a salary. Walt received a small stipend as housefather and took a more traditional role, continuing his job employed outside of the home. He was a cement cutter these days.

Each resident had a mandatory classroom or job they reported to every day, Monday through Friday, giving me some free time until three in the afternoon. An aide came five times a week to help with cooking and cleaning, and an activity therapist was assigned to the group home two evenings each week. Our residents had free access to all facilities on the grounds—the chapel, the workshop, the coffee shop, the volleyball courts, the embroidery classes, the trails in the pine trees.

Walt and I lived on the same grounds where my sisters had been hospitalized, the same grounds where my mother had been confined in that building with windows that looked like jail and interior doors only loud jangling keys could open.

Not that I ever mentioned it to him or to anyone.

~

"Wind's blowing, Jane," Donnie announced in his deep bass voice. He arrived home from the workshop precisely at three-fifteen every weekday.

Donnie's roommate, Andy, meandered into the group home any-where between three-thirty and five in the afternoon. If I wasn't out in the main room, Andy would stand in front of the open door of the annex, never say a word, just stand there, until I acknowledged his arrival. Fifty-two years old, he moved like molasses.

Andy was a bed wetter. At six-thirty in the morning, I knocked on his bedroom door, a half an hour before I called anyone else. "Andy, time to get up."

His low, drawn out voice answered. "Oooo-kaa-aye."

I opened the bedroom door a few inches. "Are you wet this morning?"

"Someone put a hose in my bed," he explained.

"Change your bed and put your things in the washing machine before you come to breakfast." It wasn't easy to be firm with Andy, es-pecially when I knew it meant he wouldn't be joining us for breakfast.

"Morning, Jane. Sun's out," Donnie said from under the covers.

"Good morning, Don."

Evelyn, our morning aide, and I cleaned up breakfast about the time Andy wandered into the kitchen, an unlit pipe in his mouth and a collection of keys on a ring on his belt.

"We saved you some toast and orange juice," I said. "Your friend Gracie made your lunch."

"It was that soup you gave me last night," Andy said.

Going about checking the pantry, I made a grocery list while Andy took fifteen minutes to have his toast and juice. When he finished, he opened his brown lunch bag and examined the contents.

"Gracie's a nice lady," he said and closed the bag again. "I'm glad she lives in the same house with me."

I set down my pencil and list. "I'm glad, too." A grin swept over my face, meant to be tender. I took him gently by the arm and led him toward the door. "Now you better get going to the Green Garage before coffee break. They'll be looking for you." I opened the door.

"Wayne said he would try to start the John Deere today," Andy decided to tell me.

"That'll make your day. Tell Wayne I said hello."

"Bye, Jane." He started toward the sidewalk then turned around. "If it starts, I'll ask him to drive me up here on it."

"That'd be great! I'll be here. Bye, Andy."

I shut the door and went back to the pantry. When I finished my list, I glanced out the kitchen window. About a hundred feet down the sidewalk, Andy stood lighting his pipe.

At least he was headed in the right direction.

∾

During the time Walt and I lived with the residents in the group home, my mother and father decided to sell the house on London Street. There had been a number of robberies in the neighborhood—televisions, stereos, small amounts of cash stolen. The once tidy lawns, sidewalks and curbs were now home to neglected and battered cars. Layoffs at the Kelvinator factory, Treat's Drug Store closed, Sid's grocery was gone.

"Getting to be too many *sortjes*," Mother said.

Mr. VanderGoot had moved to a retirement home after Mrs. VanderGoot passed away. The DeBoers had built a new, smaller home in the suburbs. Aunt Dienke sold her house and was living just outside the city limits on a street close to Aunt Tina.

And Klikkuiken had gone to her eternal rest.

Seventy percent of the long-time members at Grandville Avenue Church had moved to the suburbs, although many still drove in on Sunday for services. As the old neighborhood changed, the newest pastor began to hold trendy worship services and hot-off-the-press education programs.

"The man's an Arminian, that's all," Father said. "Talks about evangelizing all the time and thinks God loves everybody. 'Jacob have I loved, Esau have I hated.' He forgets that."

My father had always made the claim that holding to Common Grace would undermine the doctrines of Election and Reprobation and inevitably led to Universalism. To him, the direction he saw Grandville Avenue continue in was indicative of the Christian Reformed Church as a whole. It didn't surprise me that when my parents moved from London Street to a condominium in the outskirts of the city, my father collected his theological dissatisfactions and signed with another sect of the Reformation.

"They don't believe in Common Grace," Father explained about the Protestant Reformed Church of America. "And they still understand the antithesis."

My parents made the transition from the large two-story on London Street to a small condominium, while as houseparents for a year and a half, Walt and I saved enough to make a down payment on a home of our own.

We bought a two-story handyman's special. Not in the city, not in the suburbs, but in the country.

Zes en Twintig

The eighty-year-old farmhouse sat on twenty acres. At the end of the driveway stood a full size barn that could drink a household poor on red paint. We had a corncrib where we kept field corn and mice, and a lean-to-building, the purpose of which I never understood.

We owned "livestock." A dog, two cats, and three pigs. From time to time, the neighbor's horses boarded with us. Strawberries and raspberries grew in a patch alongside a lilac bush and a cherry tree. The tree's thick branches clawed the air with a spread that called out *climb me*, and an invitation to hold a swing someday.

We planted a vegetable garden, one-third for potatoes, the rest beans, broccoli, radishes, tomatoes and squash that I harvested, canned or froze. A view from the kitchen put forth the flower garden's random mix of ruby dianthus, orange day lilies, white daisies, variegated phlox, and yellow roses.

The grassy lane behind the house separated two fields of alfalfa. I often walked the lane alone smelling fresh manure or newly cut hay. Butterflies dipped onto wildflowers. I scared up grasshoppers and baby frogs as I stepped and called Tucker, our wirehaired terrier, closer to me.

Hearing the rub of the lawn chair across wolmanized wood, Chessy the cat jumped up on the deck, rolled near my feet, and scratched at the early Saturday morning air. A neighbor's rooster crowed. I could hear Eckrich, one of our pigs, grunting. I breathed the fresh air deeply, lifted my mug and took a swallow of coffee.

Walt scraped open the screen of the sliding glass door and stuck his head out. "Morning."

"Good morning. Coffee's done."

"Be right back."

"Sure sounds great."

"What?"

"All the sounds around here."

"Oh . . . I need coffee." He scraped the screen shut again.

We had started remodeling the farmhouse after we moved in two years ago, gutting everything in the living room and bedroom on the main floor back to the studs. The three upstairs bedrooms were the next priority, the kitchen a few years after.

"Want more?" Walt asked, coming out with the pot in his hand.

I lifted my mug and he filled it.

Now that it was the end of April, we spent Saturday mornings like this, enjoying the outdoors and our coffee.

Tomorrow would be rushed. We'd get up and shower, gulp coffee and head off to church. Here in the country, I found the church people friendly, though by no means outgoing. Most were not college graduates or employed as professionals, yet they seemed wise. Many lived on small farms where their parents were raised. They nourished an inborn, hospitable kindness. The folks knew the difference between being nice and being nosy like they knew the difference between a welcomed evening thundershower and an afternoon hailstorm.

Tucker wandered over into the sun, nudging against Walt's legs. Setting his cup down on the deck, Walt scratched the coarse fur behind the dog's ears. "I called Dr. Roberts yesterday just after lunch," he said.

"Any news?"

"He said I'm mostly shooting blanks."

"Really?"

Walt kept scratching the dog and didn't answer. I got up and switched to sitting directly across from him, on the bench that substituted for a railing on the deck.

I didn't want him to have the entire burden. "It probably doesn't help much that my cycles aren't as regular as they could be," I said in a low voice, as if our nearest neighbor, a half a mile away, might hear.

Walt came and sat next to me. He put his hand on my leg, rubbing it gently. Tucker jumped up on my other side. I put an arm around the dog, burying my face in his fur.

We had our jobs. Walt in construction cutting cement, and me, a secretary and bookkeeper at a travel agency. We both liked the countryside, its gravel roads and private scenery, the neighbors, friendly, near enough yet not too near. Open spaces, gardens, pets, quiet evenings.

But I wanted a baby.

Letting out a long sigh, I looked at Walt. "Sandy at the office says her sister takes her temperature every morning to figure out when it's the best time." I got up off the bench and, shielding the sun with my hand, looked out over the alfalfa field.

"I've heard of that."

"They go to a fertility doctor."

Walt stood behind me and slipped his arms around my waist. "I really don't want to do that, Janie. Maybe we should think more on what you said about adoption."

"Maybe." I leaned against him, tipping my head on his shoulders. "We could at least do the temperature thing."

Walt ran his hand over his hair. "If you want."

We stood quietly that way for a while, in the warm early morning sun.

"It's not like that's the only time we can do it," I said.

Walt lifted my hair and kissed the back of my neck. "Wanna go back to bed?" he whispered and I nodded.

He took my hand and led me into the house, scraping the screen door between Tucker and us.

~

Walt's best friend Randy and his wife Lisa had two children. We babysat whenever Randy and Lisa went to Traverse City overnight. We often went to Randy's for cards or a movie and Lisa always made a big deal out of the kids' bedtime.

"We're going to read a story in the nursery. Want to come along?"

"I don't think so. But thank you anyway," I answered.

"Say goodnight then, boys, and give Auntie Jane a big hug and kiss."

Inevitably when we were together, Lisa would tip her head sideways, her stone earrings swinging back and forth, and haul out new pictures. Pictures of her children playing in the yard, wearing new Easter outfits, getting their hair cut.

In a restaurant one night while Walt and Randy talked business and drank Budweiser, Lisa pointed to a photo she pulled from her purse. "Last week, Billy started walking. See the little red tennis shoes in the picture? He got those from Grandma. Oh, and this one is Nick helping his dad build the swing set. And check these out," Lisa said, carefully opening an envelope. "I had the boys' pictures taken at J.C. Penny's."

"They're so sweet." Taking a long sip from my rum and coke, I smiled. "I need to visit the ladies room before our dinner comes. Excuse me."

I locked myself in one of the bathroom stalls in case Lisa had a mind to follow. I wondered how she could have such good intentions, because I knew she did, and still be so clueless. Leaning against the door, I scrunched my eyes tightly until my head started to hurt. I opened my eyes again and stood there, crying softly.

I went to wash my face at the sink. In the mirror, I saw red eyes, skin around them swollen and blotchy, all the mascara wiped away. I dug in my purse but only found a tube of lipstick. I skipped it and went back to the table.

"I was about to send Lisa in after you. Your sandwich is getting cold," Walt said. "Mind if I have a few fries?"

Keeping my head down, I took a bite of grilled chicken sandwich and pushed my plate in front of him. "Help yourself."

Later that night, home again and getting ready for bed, Walt must have heard me sniffling. He could see fresh tears on my face.

"Have a bit of a hard time tonight, dummy?" He draped his shirt over the antique chair that wasn't strong enough to sit in.

"Please don't call me that," I choked out. I hated it when he called me that.

He turned off the light and the next thing I knew he was holding me, rubbing my back. I leaned against his chest. He ran his hand back and forth on my hair.

"Don't cry, Janie. Please don't cry."

He hated it whenever I cried.

~

My hands shook as I dialed. "Hello. Umm . . . We're calling to inquire about adopting a child. Can you give us some information?"

The lady from Bethany Christian Services immediately explained. "The first thing we always ask is how long you have been married."

"Walt and I have been married for four years."

"You must be married at least five years before we allow applications to our agency. That's our policy."

She couldn't cut me off quite so quickly. "Well . . ." I persisted, "on average, after that, how long does it usually take?"

"It is impossible to predict," she said.

I felt like I'd asked a stupid question.

"Once your name is placed with us, we stretch the evaluation over one year's time."

"Well . . . Well . . . can you take down our name so you know we called?"

"If you are still interested when you have been married the required time, please feel free to call us again."

The very first day after our fifth anniversary, we called again. This time, we were permitted to give our name—name, address, phone, number of years married, interested in a Caucasian infant.

We made a get-acquainted appointment and another appointment for procedures and handling of application forms. Based on their current waiting list, the agency predicted two years before a baby would be available. Meanwhile, the evaluation process began.

We had to pass physicals. Walt and I were interviewed together and separately three different times. Scrutinized, judged, scored. At the end of twelve months, the agency did a home study. I cleaned house for weeks. And baked brown bread the day they arrived, a hint I read somewhere to create a down-home aroma.

We passed. "Approved." Put on "The List."

We had been married six years.

We kept busy working, snowmobiling in the winter, and camping in the summer. We cut, split and piled logs for our woodburning stove in the fall, planted flowers and vegetables in the spring.

The second year of the adoption process, we rode snowmobile in the winter and camped in the summer. We cut, split and piled logs for our woodburning stove in the fall, planted flowers and vegetables in the spring.

The third year, we rode snowmobile in the winter and camped in the summer. We made preparations for the woodburner in the fall and for the garden in the spring. There was no baby.

We were married nine years.

We did it all again.

But there was no baby.

So we worked at cement cutting and travel arranging and we designed a nursery. Walt played farmer, I played interior decorator. And I played the piano—a lot.

Meanwhile, Bethany Christian Services played God.

Zeven en Twintig

They call it March Madness. The local high school won the bas-ketball play-offs and headed to the state finals. Walt and Randy hadn't missed a game so far that season. After work on Friday, they left for Pontiac, Michigan, until the last game was played on Sunday.

Lisa and I made plans to go to the movies while the guys were out of town.

"We can stop for a drink at Tony's on the way home," Lisa said.

It grew dark early, a cold wind closing the clouds over the sun before it set. I stirred the ashes in the woodburner and set two more logs on the red coals. Leaving the doors of the stove open, I sat down on the carpet watching the wood catch.

My mood was gloomy and dull and I didn't feel like spending time with chatty Lisa. I considered canceling. Ever since Christmas, the frigid dimness of winter had been accumulating. Having gathered a kind of insulation around myself, I was hoping for some seclusion while Walt was gone for the weekend. I was getting tired of pretending I was fine.

I closed and latched the doors of the woodburner just as I heard Lisa's car on our gravel driveway.

"Still want to see a movie?" Lisa asked as I pulled my long wool coat out of the way and slammed the car door shut.

"Sure." I hadn't kept up on the movies lately. I hadn't kept up on anything lately. "Got any suggestions?"

"How about Mary Tyler Moore's new one?"

"What's it about?"

"I don't know—something about a family and their not being able to communicate. It's at Studio 28. Starts at 7:55. We can make that easy enough."

Sounded like she was counting on it. "Okay," I answered.

~

When *Ordinary People* ended, Lisa had to take my arm and lead me to the car. I held my body tense and stiff, trembling.

"What is it, Janie?"

"I don't know. I'm freezing."

She started the car and put the heater on full blast. I stared straight ahead, sitting on my hands trying to get warm.

Lisa turned onto the highway. "That was something else, wasn't it?"

"Really."

"Sure got to me . . . That must be what depression's like."

"Yeah."

"Whew!" She turned the heat on low and signaled to exit at 68th. "Tony's sound good?"

"I think I should go home," I said, still shivering.

"You all right?"

"Must be the flu or something."

Instead of 68th, she continued on the expressway to 100th Street. We turned on our road. Though my hands were shaking, I managed to find the keys in my purse. I held them tight so they wouldn't rattle.

"Should I come in?" Lisa asked as she steered into the driveway.

That was the last thing I wanted. "I'll be fine." Poor Lisa, she tries to be nice. She tries to understand. I should say something more. "Thanks for going out," was all I came up with.

I kept my coat on in the house, making sure no flying sparks landed on the wool while I threw kindling in the woodburner. It flamed up and I added some logs. With my hands in my pockets, I pulled the coat tighter around me and sat hunched on the floor until the fire grew large and hot. Finally, when my cheeks were burning from the heat, I pulled my hands from the lined corners and spread my fingers toward the stove. No tremor.

The time was close to midnight, yet I wasn't sleepy. The longer I sat, the less sleepy I felt. I hadn't turned on any lights. The neighbor might notice and think something was wrong with me, sitting here alone this late, my arms wrapped around myself.

I wasn't hungry. I wasn't wishing Walt would call. I wanted to be alone and wasn't missing him.

The applewood snapped.

I think I'm crazy.

I said so to myself. Not out loud, but inside so even I could hardly hear it.

I'm losing it. Just like the kid in the movie tonight. I know the hole he was talking about. I know about time and air and legs getting heavier and heavier.

My stomach tightened and pinched itself.

I don't always like my seclusion. But the more I'm with people, the more removed I am. They talk and I think they're stupid and wish they'd shut up. They laugh and I think they're shallow. They sleep and I think they don't give a shit about anything. They eat and I think they're gluttons. They sing and my stomach sinks. They move around me and I let them pass.

Honestly. I am crazy.

Then I got scared.

～

We were supposed to have an hour together.

He was especially attractive, dark hair, trimmed around his ears and down to his collar in the back. A five o'clock shadow circled his mouth although it was early afternoon. I supposed a recent southern vacation explained his tanned face, for spring had only begun the previous week. Taller than me, he was lean but not skinny. The navy sport coat gave his shoulders a broad look.

His greeting consisted of nodding his head toward a chair directly across from his desk. I sat, legs crossed, arms crossed, chewing the end of my thumb. He left the door slightly ajar.

He was handsome and I wished he wasn't.

Loosening the black band of his wristwatch, he placed it on the desk. From where he sat, he could see the face of the watch, but I could not.

I wished the hour was already over.

We said nothing. I watched the foot of my crossed leg bounce up and down, assuming it made me appear bored instead of jittery. Each time I sneaked a glance at him, I saw him watching me. Not staring, but watching me closely.

Minutes passed.

A cigarette would have helped, but there was no ashtray.

So now what.

This is so new to me.

More minutes passed.

Maybe I'm supposed to start.

I stopped biting my thumb, letting my arm drop to my lap. With a loud sigh, I lifted my head. He was studying the watch. I decided to look around.

The office was smaller than I had expected, more like a cubicle, except all the walls were closed in to the ceiling. The one painting in the office was done in pastels—a view of a harbor at sunset with a sailboat slipping into the peaceful, deserted bay.

I glanced over at him again, but quickly focused on the floor when he lifted his eyes.

I wished he would say something.

Through the window, I could see the earth unfold its promise of spring. The afternoon was delivering anticipated sunshine. The few traces of winter remaining were disappearing into puddles. I counted four robins on the lawn. I knew my tulips at home were piercing through the soil. My daffodils held thick buds and the crocuses were blooming.

But I continued my hibernation.

Alternating the tips of my thumbs, I resumed bouncing my foot up and down, contemplating what to say and how I would say it, if I would say anything at all.

I was scared to death but thought it important not to look shaken.

It occurred to me I must appear quite nervous.

"When can I leave?" I blurted, still turned away.

He didn't seem at all startled and his answer sounded stony. "I can call someone to accompany you back whenever you say."

"I mean the hospital."

"The average stay is four to six weeks," he said like a programmed appliance.

I'm not average. I'll be out sooner than that.

I eyed the watch with a new scary ache in my gut.

Unless they never let me leave.

I noticed a photograph on his desk. "Your family?" I finally looked straight at him. I was trying so hard.

"Yes. My wife and daughter." He didn't look back at me.

"They're lovely."

He didn't reply but looked at the wristwatch and blinked slowly.

Nice guy, I thought.

"What about visiting home?" I asked.

"What about visiting home?" he repeated back to me.

We spoke face to face now. "I mean, when can I go home for a visit?"

"Do you feel you should?" he asked.

I don't *feel* anything, jerk head.

I didn't bother to answer and instead looked out the window.

"Can I go home this weekend?" I asked, still turned away.

"Normally, we don't give passes the first weekend."

More silence.

I fidgeted in the chair.

"I can't sleep here. My roommate snores." I faced him again.

"The nurse offers you a sleeping pill each night, which I understand you refuse."

"I don't do drugs."

From my chair, I began to browse the titles of his books, expecting to see self-help collections, maybe some twelve-step booklets. I didn't recognize any names.

I wondered if he knew any theology. I wondered what he believed about election and reprobation and if he understood the difference between common grace and special grace. I wondered what he knew about the antithesis. I wondered where emotions belong on his modal scale and what their objective and subjective relatives would be. I wondered how the hell he could help me.

He was looking at me again. I wished I dared to look at my own watch, but thought it would count against me.

Once more, silence.

"I should let Bethany know where I am," I said.

"I wouldn't advise rushing into it."

"I'm supposed to contact them the first of each month."

"April first isn't until Tuesday," he said.

This asshole is never going to work.

"Don't you think they should know?"

"I don't advise rushing into it," he repeated.

I scowled. "What if they try to call me with some news in the meantime?"

"Your husband can talk to them."

"That would not be a fair conversation."

With a long, soft sigh, he lifted his hands off his lap and folded them on his desk. His voice was very quiet when he spoke.

"Jane." He paused before going on. "Why don't you let them worry about you for a while?"

I took it as a reprimand. Yet he spoke so kindly . . . Blinking away tears, I looked down.

My foot tapped silently in space and I bit on the end of my thumb, not intending to answer.

I realized I had spent all my practiced guises of nonchalance.

I hate this. I hate this so much. He will never understand how much I hate this.

When I finally spoke again, it came out a whisper. "Would you call the attendant for me now?"

He lifted the receiver and dialed the extension.

Time moved so slowly here. Three endless nights without sleep. The flashlight in my face every fifteen minutes.

Neither of us spoke while waiting for my escort, the one with thick rubber soles on his silent feet. But I heard the jangling keys rattle loudly as the heavy door with the big brass knob and windows of wire mesh slammed closed.

And I wished I were dead.

Acht en Twintig

Ginny's mom, from Grandville Avenue Church, worked in the admitting office and had been there the day I came in. If she wasn't a Do-It-Nothing Gang mother, I probably would have turned around and fled for home—seeing someone from Grandville Avenue there.

"It's a little awkward for both of us," she had said with honesty. She looked from me to Walt to me again. I handed her the clipboard with all seven pages filled out. "You know, of course, I won't say a word to anyone," she explained. "But, Janie, how should we handle this with Ginny? Do you want me to tell her?"

"Whatever you think is best. I don't care who knows." I appreciated her *verstond*. "It can't really matter at this point."

Walt looked confused. "But this morning you made me promise not to tell anybody."

"That's right. I don't want *you* to tell anyone," I said. "You already told your brother."

He shrugged, twisted his hands and mouth, raised his eyebrows. He ran his hand over his hair.

Ginny's mom didn't hug me or anything. She told Walt, "We'll let Janie tell who she wants, and when she wants."

I loved her for that.

$\sim$

I was sure dead was better than crazy and I was convinced crazy was what I really was.

Fear overcame everything else. Fear of insanity. Fear to die. Fear not to die. Fear of fear. It would suffocate me. There were wide empty gaps where I fell endlessly and dark narrow shafts where I hardly fit.

I wished to God someone would help me. I wished to God I knew where God was.

~

My room has two beds, two nightstands. My roommate snores, but that's about all I hear from her, except when she stands facing the corner and talks to the beige painted block wall.

I stay dressed morning and night. Scared as I am, I come off quite collected anyway whenever the staff peeks through the wired windows or when they unlock the door to ask if we need the restroom.

They let me take a shower the second day. An aide stays in the bathroom with me the whole time, but I may draw the curtain and the warm water running over my body feels divine.

The third day, one of the attendants walks me down to my therapist appointment again. The attendant calls me Janie. Says his name is Martin.

It's my second session with Dr. Owens.

We don't say anything. Then he surprises me when he talks, making statements that seem like questions.

"Your roommate annoys you."

"Yes."

"You're not sleeping."

"Yes."

"You don't eat."

How the hell does he know. "Yes."

He seems to stare right through my skull.

"You're scared."

"Yes."

He's reading my mind.

"You wish you were dead."

Damn.

He's trying to tell me he can read my mind. Oh damn. People can read each other's minds.

He adds things I hadn't thought of.

"Wishing you were dead is not the same as doing it."

"Of course."

"You don't have to kill yourself just because you wish you were dead."

"Of course." Good to know.

"Once you've thought of it, there's no obligation."

"Of course."

Two important things. I might not do myself in. He could read my mind.

That's enough for now, so I ask "Can we call it short today?" Before he answers, I'm out the door. I stop, trying to remember which way back to the ward.

A pay phone hangs on the wall. I pick up and dial "O."

"Please give me 555–333."

My brother Arie J answers, and after telling him where I am, I convince him I'll be okay because I just finally caught on to the secret that people could read other people's minds as long as the person had figured out on their own that it was possible. I explain that I'm sad and pissed-off that for twenty-nine years no one had ever told me, but that it must be it was important for someone to learn this for himself, or they would have told me. Arie J can tell that I am exuberant at having figured it out, and now that I know, I tell him I'll soon be going home again.

All Arie J says is, "Whose idea was it for you to go there?"

"Mine," I tell him.

"I'll come," Arie J says.

"That's not necessary. Now that I know, I know I won't be here long. I'll call you."

I hang up and notice Martin standing a few feet from me. I set out down the hall, but weave from one side to the other until he takes me by the arm and walks me to the ward.

"When's the last time you ate anything?" Martin asks.

"I don't know. Some when they brought dinner trays last night. Didn't taste good."

"Did you have breakfast today?"

I shrug.

We pass the small kitchen near the nurses' station. He opens the refrigerator and pulls out a foil ball. "Here's a hard-boiled egg."

I shake my head. "How do you know somebody didn't shoot dope in it or something?"

He rolls his eyes. "I brought it from home. Here."

"No. It's yours."

"Eat it." He grabs a carton of milk and a box of Corn Flakes. "I'm going to sit here and watch you until all of it's gone." He sets down a bowl and spoon, and pulls out a chair, so I sit.

I stare at the egg and remember the set of china eggcups Deannie and Ronald Lee gave my mother one year on her birthday. Instead of storing the cups in the buffet for *bizonder,* Mother kept them with everyday dishes and proudly set them along side our cereal bowls like they were polished silver or real crystal.

"Janie. Eat the egg." Martin's voice bumps me back to the present.

I pick up the egg and tap it a few times on the bowl. The shell comes off easily. "How do you know I like this stuff?" I mumble.

"I don't."

I sigh and look at the bare egg. "Any salt around this god-awful place?"

Martin rummages through a drawer and comes up with salt and pepper. He puts the packets on the table and sits down to monitor me.

I examine the egg again. I lick the top of it, sprinkle some salt, take a deep breath and a small bite, chewing slowly, trying to prepare my system. Finally I swallow. Martin winks at me and nods.

~

Security was discontinued the fourth day.

I could still hear the jangling keys rattle. I could still see the heavy doors with wire mesh in the window. They no longer confined me, but their presence had another kind of restraint. On this side of the locked barriers were fewer limitations, less deterrence, and none of the verifications at fifteen-minute intervals.

But with less confinement comes less protection.

Negen en Twintig

J oanne, my new roommate in my new room, was in class this
morning. I had asked Walt to bring me one of the braided throw
rugs from the farmhouse. I stood, showered and dressed, on my rug
in front of our dorm-like window, watching snow melt.

Martin knocked on my door that was opened the required 12
inches. "We're going to take a little walk, Janie. Show you around."

"You're awfully bossy," I said.

Martin's oversized shirt, with baggy corduroys, gave him a casual
look. His reddish, wavy hair flattered his many freckles. I wasn't afraid
of him but let him walk ahead of me. He turned around to speak.
"Here are essentials. Soap, towels, bed linens."

"I know. I used to work here," I said at the storage closet.

Martin smiled. "Really?" He shut the closet door and walked on.
"Here's the . . ."

". . . cafeteria. I know."

"When you're off ward restriction, you can eat your meals here.
They have great coffee and desserts, too."

"Yeah, they do. I know. I was the housemother at Westwood
once. After that, I worked on call—pharmacy, transcription pool, that
kind of stuff."

"Hmmm."

He showed me the classrooms. "Schedules are passed out on
Sunday night. You'll start Monday."

We left classroom 14A. He locked the door behind us and grinned
at me like he was my mother. "Ate all your breakfast this morning,
huh?"

"Yeah." Put it in the damn chart, I thought.

"This is the music room," he said.

"Uh-huh." Most of the room was taken up by an old upright Steinway and a two-manual electric organ. In an impulse, I ran my fingers up a chromatic scale on the piano.

"You play?" Martin asked. "Go ahead."

"Not in front of anybody." I scooted past him, back into the hallway, wondering if they let people practice on the organ. It must have been at least three years since I played one.

We went left, down a wide corridor of block and windows that reminded me of a Red Roof Inn. Martin pointed to an entrance. "Here's the gym."

"Yes. I remember."

Stopping short, he crossed his arms, his smile gone. "And that's about it for orientation."

I followed Martin back to the ward, supposedly oriented. At the nurses' station, the girl with a nametag "Linda" asked me, "How was the tour?"

"I used to work here."

Martin gave me a disgusted look. I went to my room and left the door open one inch. I stood on the rug, staring out the window.

Quit telling them you worked here, I told myself. You scare them. They don't want your camaraderie.

That's the thing about isolation. It is not eliminated by unlocking doors.

~

My surrender was slow and it remained incomplete. The staff misdiagnosed my inability to trust them as uncooperative, and considered my refusal to "share" as being difficult. As head of my team, Dr. Owens must have had the same impressions. Mondays, Wednesdays, and Fridays when we met one-to-one, I kept myself holed up as much as possible.

Until the end of my third week.

Maybe he finally realized I was more terrified than disagreeable. After I stared out the window, bounced my foot up and down, and chewed the end of my thumb without saying anything for a while, Dr. Owens sighed. "I want to be clear about something, Jane," he said.

I faced his way, but kept my eyes down. He rolled his chair several inches away from his desk, until it bumped the wall, and crossed his legs. "Sometimes my clients think I can read their mind."

"They do?"

"Yes. In fact, many clients think so at first."

"Well," I said. "That's dumb."

"No, it's not dumb." No condescension in his voice. "But it's not true."

"Of course not." I whipped my head sideways and stared out the window some more.

These long stretches of dead air hadn't seemed to bother Owens in previous sessions. Yet today, he interrupted my reticence a second time.

"Tell me what you are most afraid of."

No way, I thought.

I was no longer afraid to check my watch. There was over a half an hour left.

The second hand circled twice.

I sighed.

Finally I asked. "You mean usually or while I'm here?"

"Either."

I faced the ceiling and closed my eyes, breathing like blowing up an air mattress. There was so much to fear. I rubbed the sides of my neck with my hands, looked at the floor, then at the ceiling, then at the floor again.

"It's okay," he said. "Go ahead."

Focusing out the window, I took more deep breaths, my open hands in front of my mouth, hesitating.

"Shock Treatment."

I turned in time to see Owens tip his head back, nodding at the air as if he just recognized the concept of *substantia* in the Nicene Creed or something.

His face remained somber. He spoke slowly and carefully, but without patronizing in his tone. "Electroconvulsive therapy. Electroshock. Shock Treatment as you say, is extremely rare in this day and age." He studied his hands for a moment, folded loosely on his lap, before looking up, his eyebrows crimped. "I'm curious to know why you think of it."

I waited, indecisive.

"Perhaps you worried you were a candidate?"

Tipping my head down I massaged my neck with both hands—sides, back, sides, back.

"They did it to my sister here," I said at last.

"I see."

I chewed the end of my thumb and blinked fast.

"When?"

"Back in '67. Didn't you know?" While I was at it, I said, "Maybe even my mom, too, before that. Don't you check these things out in the records?"

"It's best when you tell me."

We were both quiet.

Everything I did in this place, everything I said or didn't say, I thought hard about first. For over three weeks, every little move I'd made or wouldn't make, if I scratched myself or didn't scratch myself, if I ran my hand through my hair or let it fall in my face, if I put on lipstick or went without, how I walked, how I breathed, every single thing they scrutinized. That was how they judged who was crazy or not.

I didn't stare out the window now. It didn't matter anymore.

"That must be very frightening to think about," Dr. Owens said.

I didn't answer and kept wiping off my face with the tips of my fingers.

"Tell me about the tears."

I shook my head.

"Tell me what you're feeling."

"I don't know," I whispered.

"Try," he answered softly.

I shook my head again.

Then I said, "Embarrassed."

~

Whether or not my roommate appreciated my solitude, she respected it. With her gregarious personality, Joanne spent most of her free time in the main commons area where we could smoke.

The nurse Susan instructed positive thinking and personal growth classes where I always got an "F" in participation. Her class was mandatory and full of trash I didn't believe in and didn't want to hear about, especially from her. She was eight months pregnant. On Saturdays and Sundays, Susan worked the floor. I could tell her fanny had been wide for years and I hated the way she flaunted her bulging, pregnant stomach all over the ward. Whenever she got up or sat down, she groaned and exhaled with exaggeration. If Susan happened to be in the commons after dinner, I forfeited my cigarette.

Phys Ed class, also mandatory. Martin was always there, but Linda was in charge. There were eleven of us today, including staff. I did the stretches and jumping jacks and jogged around the freezing gym with the others.

"Let's form a circle now, everyone," Linda called.

Shit. Here we go. I changed my pace to slow walking, pretending to be out of breath.

"You too, Jane." Linda waved her arm, signaling in that direction.

"Come on. Over here by me," Robert yelled. He was an "A" ward person with me.

I went and stood next to him, Martin directly across from us.

"OK," Linda instructed, "everybody take hands."

I gave Martin a disgusted look before I walked over near the exit and sat on the floor.

"I want you to think of a color that matches the way you're feeling today," Linda said, ignoring me.

What color is puke, I thought.

～

We slid our orange plastic dinner trays onto a cafeteria table.

"I've gained three pounds," I told Walt while I opened Saltines and crushed them into my vegetable soup. "How's the potatoes and gravy?"

"Institutionalized."

Robert approached our table, dressed in a flannel shirt, jeans, cowboy boots, and holding his dinner tray.

"Hey," I said. "Walt, this is Robert. Robert, my husband, Walt."

"Please'ta meetcha," Robert said.

"Likewise." Walt stood and they shook hands.

"Robert's on the same ward with me."

"This girl's amazing. Nobody around here like it. Nothing but cold cash."

Walt looked at me, puzzled.

"No drugs. No medication, day or night," I explained.

Robert headed for Joanne's table on the other side of the cafe.

"Is that old man a redneck or what?" Walt asked.

"Yeah. But he's sweet."

"I brought your mail." Walt handed me envelopes and my monthly theological journal. He moved his apple pie onto his empty plate. "I have to leave in a few minutes."

He didn't see my face fall all over the cafeteria floor.

"They're showing *Fiddler on the Roof* in the gym tonight," I said. "I thought maybe you'd stay."

"Sorry, Janie. You know how uncomfortable I am around here. I hate hospitals."

I stirred some sugar into fresh coffee and took a sip. My cup clinked louder than I intended when I set it on the saucer.

"Things going okay?" he asked between bites. "Anything new?"

"I'm getting pretty sick of it."

"Now, don't get discouraged."

I remembered the night he came home from the basketball play-offs and I told him I wanted to come here. "Oh, Janie, no," he had said. "Let's take a vacation." He kept trying to convince me. "We can go to Florida. Spend time on the beach. Lots of sun. You'll love it. You'll feel better."

Walt continued his pep talk now while he ate dessert. "The sooner you get better, the sooner you can come home."

I wondered what better meant. His not having to come here anymore?

"What is it you're sick of?" Walt asked.

"All of it."

Lips pressed together, he twisted his mouth to one side.

"Sentiment decides everything," I went on. "Truth according to Fromm or Rogers. Or Art Linkletter." I wasn't sure Walt knew the difference.

He rolled his eyes. "What's so bad about that?"

"Well, you know . . ." My face flushed and I shrugged. "It's so subjective."

He took another bite. "What about Reverend Visser? Didn't you say you kind of liked him?"

"He's not so bad," I had to agree. "Know what? He's the guy that married Deannie. The other day for devotions, he read Psalm 42. But the other chaplains talk down to us. They read a little meditation and tell us God wants us to grow and that we should trust Him and stuff." The flush worked its way down my neck.

Walt dabbed his moustache with a napkin and pushed his chair away from the table. He looked across the cafeteria. "Maybe they're right. Maybe you should have a little more faith."

I considered what blessed faith he'd have, how cocksure he'd be in this hellhole.

All I said was, "You don't get it."

One of these days I won't be able to wait to cry until Walt leaves. That night, we kissed inside the door and I watched him walk to his car. I headed to the ward and arrived in tears. Martin stepped from behind the nurse's desk.

"Walt just leave, Janie?" I only nodded and kept walking.

Martin caught up. "You really care about him, don't you."

I stopped in front of the door to my room. "Stupid, huh? . . . He pisses me off so much . . ."

"No, not stupid," Martin said. "Not stupid at all."

"I'm exhausted." I went inside and closed the door all the way.

Whenever it was Joanne got back, I didn't know. I just stood in the dark for a long time at the window on the throw rug. Like the rug was a kitchen register.

Dertig

A downpour of chilly rain was only one distortion of the winter day, the first of February, 1940. The bakery was especially busy on Saturday. Customers came to buy fresh cinnamon rolls and bread. Some wanted the crispy windmill cookies. Others bought *banket* or raisin bread with almond paste.

Mr. Wiersma kept her busy all through the morning and into the afternoon. She worked with him behind the counter and waited tables set to one side of the small store for those who bought a donut or *ollie bollen* and loitered with their coffee and smokes.

"*Hoe laat het is, Pietje?*" Mr. Wiersma asked when she finished wiping the counter.

"It's quarter to four," she answered.

"*Je meekomen voet nu,*" he urged.

Tired from the extra hours she had worked, she gladly exchanged the stiff white apron for her blue woolen coat on the hook.

"*Dag!*" she called as she waved to her boss.

"*Wel te rusten!*" he said.

Tulip Street was nine blocks away. She met the raw drizzle outdoors and braced herself for the walk home with an extra layer of scarf and thoughts of Saturday night's hot *erwt soep*. Soon the drizzle turned to heavy rain and before she walked a second block, the gloomy sky opened wide again. She began to run.

An automobile pulled slowly along the curb, the whitewall tires splashing the puddle. The auto stopped and the passenger-side door opened. Someone called her name.

"Pearl! Pearl!"

She recognized him. From church? From school? From the neighborhood? From somewhere. With a gesture of his hand, he summoned her into the car. A grand shiny model, new, trimmed with chrome, warm and dry inside.

He gave her a ride. Rescued the shivering, immigrant teenage girl from the savage weather.

And did not bring her home until he took full advantage of her.

∾

"Mama?"

"Mama?"

A panic flashed through me. I sat up in bed, clutching the pin-striped sheet in my fists. I looked around, drenched in sweat. Joanne was sound asleep. The Baby Ben read two fifteen. Lowering my feet to the floor, I aligned them with the terry cloth slippers. I put on my robe and closed it tight with the fabric belt. In the hall, passing the desk, I squinted for a moment in the bright fluorescent lighting then silently nodded at the nurse. I entered the lounge, sat at the table, and lit a cigarette, running the story through my head.

She would never dare tell. My mother would never tell her protective brothers. She certainly would never tell her father.

But the man had written a note and instructed her to bring it to the pharmacy.

"Who told you to get this, Pietje?" the pharmacist had asked my mother.

"Nobody," she insisted. "Nobody."

"You don't need this, my child."

The pharmacist returned the paper. My mother never threw it away.

I lit another cigarette.

The nurse came in. "Are you all right?"

"Yes," I answered. "Thank you."

"Do you need a sleeping pill?"

"Yes. But no. No thanks."

My hands were trembling when I took out a third cigarette. I could hardly light it. I smoked a half dozen more after that.

My mother should have explained it before. Before we'd gone out today. I had earned my car keys and a three-hour pass. I picked up my mother. We went shopping and stopped for coffee and pie afterward.

She never said anything about it. Not for all my twenty-nine years. The only thing I had noticed today was that Mother hadn't let go of her white lacy handkerchief the entire time we were away, even during coffee. She had a second cup and finished her cherry pie without ever bringing up the story.

We drove back and sat in the car in the driveway.

"You want to come in yet?" she asked.

I left the car running. "No. I better not. They're pretty strict about the time," I answered.

I could tell my mother was stalling. "Are you sure you're okay?" she finally asked, twisting her handkerchief. "In that place."

"I'm okay, Mom. I'm going to be fine. I'll be going home soon. I don't want you to worry." I hated it when I made her worry.

"Of course I'm worried." Her voice was hoarse, as if she hadn't used it in a long, long time.

Then, she told me the story. That is, she told the dashboard of my car the whole story.

I shut off the car and watched her as she struggled with the words, facing forward, wanting to tell me, not wanting to tell me. The bakery, the car, the man and the rain.

I believe she had never told it before to anyone. Not in full. I doubted that even Gracia knew. But today my mother sat there in my car telling the whole story aloud, turning and twisting her white handkerchief over and over in her thin hands, vulnerable in a way she had never been again since the time she sat in his car.

When she finished, Mother continued staring at the dashboard. I didn't know what to say. I chewed on the end of my thumb while my stomach pinched.

"I don't know what people from the hospital tell you," she said. "I don't know what you think. I don't know what everyone else thinks. But you need to know that I didn't understand. I didn't know. I didn't want what happened."

I wished I had said something, but I didn't. I only nodded.

I think Mother saw me nod. I hope she saw me nod.

"My brothers wanted to kill him." She placed her hand on the door handle and then hesitated. "It's in the Bible, you know, about courts and judges. Opa said, *'Niet to court te brengen'* and so that was that."

I walked her up to the back door. "Maybe I should come in."

"No. No, you better not be late."

I pursed my lips, nodded again, and left without saying anything more, without embracing her. Damn it all—without even clutching Mama's hand.

～

The rest I figured out myself.

Opa believed in God's Sovereignty and God's Providence. Opa understood his responsibility. There would be no eliminating life through the pharmacy, or any other way. There would be no adoption alternatives. He would love his granddaughter as his own. Maybe more.

But my mother, she got in trouble.

Or so they would say.

She should have told me the story a long time ago.

～

I'm cold a lot. A draft comes through the window. My room-mate's in class. I stand on the rug in my room and stare and remember. I remember an old cardigan sweater, the variegated knitted slippers, the warm register air.

Opa, my mother's father. Just like my own father. Holding God's Sovereign Will the starting point of everything. God is in control of everything. Omnipotent, omniscient, immutable and impassable. God is beyond our understanding, but we know nothing happens against his Sovereign Will. We accept suffering, for somehow God intends it for our good. God "will avert all evil or turn it to our profit." It's right there in the form for Holy Baptism.

It didn't work for me.

I stood on the rug—stuck. Between a transcendent, sovereign God, unable to be affected, or an immanent God, present, open, movable—to me, an even more frightening prospect.

I shivered and re-wrapped my robe more securely around my body.

I gave up the Sovereignty part. Laid it aside. Something like God must have done when he decided about man and freedom and love.

Een en Dertig

During the next few days, I spent most of my time on the rug at the window, turning the story over and over in my head. Outdoors, strong spring thunderstorms drenched the grass and winds hunched the evergreens.

I knew Mother chose to tell me because I was in this hospital where more than once she had been through her own realms of hell. She feared for me. She wanted to help me. She loves me more than herself.

I wasn't going to disclose what I had learned to the hospital staff. Mother had reasons for the silence she chose and I would not betray her. Nor would I tell Walt. He can't keep a secret. He would think poorly of my mother, poorly of me. I would not disclose her story.

That decision, or maybe the story itself, marked an essential shift in my hospital stay.

On some days, I slept in. I started skipping classes. I took walks instead of keeping appointments. When the instructors talked about our "journeys" or "personal growth," instead of frustrated, I rolled my eyes and considered it bullshit.

Dr. Owens gave me permission to visit home over the weekend. My pass ran from Friday afternoon until Sunday evening. When I first walked in the house, the room jumped for a fraction of a second right in front of my eyes because an unexpected sweep of recognition surged through me. I hadn't realized how far removed my own kitchen had become.

Walt and I acted like things were pretty much back to normal. We raked the yard and washed the Fiat in the spring sunshine. He started up the antique Farmall tractor. I climbed up behind the seat and hung on to him, arms around his waist while we putzed around through the field corn. After dinner, we read by the woodburning stove and sipped Brandy Manhattans.

Then we made love.

∾

On Monday, I downed a quick breakfast of cold cereal in the hospital lounge, slipped on my jean jacket, and went out for a walk around the grounds. Rumor had it that temperatures on this last day of April would reach the upper sixties before noon. I found the fresh air and sunshine more therapeutic than any of those self-esteem exercises.

That evening while Joanne was off playing volleyball, Martin knocked on our door.

"Janie, a bunch is going to the Windemolen Restaurant for coffee and we thought you might want to come."

"Nah. Thanks anyway. I'm going to stay put and read tonight," I answered.

Susan waddled over and stuck her whole fat self in the doorway. She sighed much deeper than any pregnancy warranted.

"What?" I asked her.

"You really ought to stop hiding and get out in the real world."

I half snorted through my nose and chuckled. "By going to Windemolen's?"

"It'd be a start for you. Broader community and experience than in here," she said.

"Look lady. That *is* my community out there," I said. "That *is* my experience. I know the people who own the Windemolen. I know the people who work at the Windemolen and I know the people who eat there and I'm not dealing with that crap."

"I'll get you a carrot cake to go," Martin said, taking Susan by the arm and steering her down the hallway.

∾

It seemed the entire hospital knew about the appointment.

"Hey! Janie! Good luck this afternoon!" Martin caught up to us. "Knock 'em dead."

"Thanks, Martin," I said.

Walt and I walked down the corridor to 178C, the Lilac Room, where we found the door spread open. Armchairs arranged like a three-quarter circle took up most of the room. In the corner, an oak-finished pedestal table held a tray of coffee and tea. Draperies had been pushed to the edges of the windows, letting in full daylight.

The perpetually handsome Dr. Owens shook our hands. "Good afternoon, Jane. Walt. Please help yourself to a warm drink and have a seat." He straightened his tie. "An assistant from Bethany called to say Ms. Walma is running a few minutes late."

"I'll pass on the coffee," Walt said. "Just finished a big lunch." He unzipped his windbreaker and spread it on the back of his chair.

It was just after two o'clock. I made myself a cup of tea to appear relaxed. As I stirred in sugar with a plastic stick, Beth Walma appeared in the doorway.

"Come in, come in," Dr. Owens said.

Beth had a natural, no-makeup look with a wide, pretty smile. Her long hair was pulled up in a silver barrette. She set her briefcase on the floor while Dr. Owens took her coat. We shook hands. "Jane. Good to see you. You're looking good."

"Thanks. Thank you." I let my arm relax, and she let go of her grip. "Beth, this is my therapist, Dr. Owens. Dr. Owens, this is our social worker, Beth Walma."

"Ms. Walma. Glad you could come."

"Of course. And please, it's Beth." She turned and with her sunny expression, nodded. "Hello, Walt."

"How's it going," he answered.

"Well. Let's sit down and get started." Dr. Owens took the chair directly across from me, and once everyone was seated, said "Ms. Walma. Beth. Why don't you go first."

She uncrossed her legs, placed her arms on her lap, palms up, and leaned forward. "I don't have a whole lot. As you know, we've been concerned about Jane since she called in April and told us she had entered the program here." She cleared her throat and spoke directly to me. "It's important that you realize Bethany appreciates your openness. Their attitude is that you have nothing to be ashamed of, Jane. They admire your willingness to admit your situation."

My eyes shot to my therapist. He looked at me at the same time. Admit. As if I'd failed at something and now was due credit for confessing and owning up to it. Dr. Owens sneaked a wink across to me. We had gone over this a hundred times in our one-to-one sessions. It helped to know he was thinking what I was thinking.

Looking at Walt, I wondered if he caught Beth's reference. She might only be paraphrasing Bethany's ideas without catching the insinuation herself. That would be consistent with her smiling freshness, which I realized had helped me balance some of my cynicism. Now, I suspected her just plain credulous.

"As Bethany's representative," Beth continued, "I've been asked to visit you and Walt this month in this environment, note what Dr. Owens has to say, and report back to the agency's directors."

My tea was cold, but I sipped it anyway.

"Jane? Questions or comments?" Dr. Owens asked.

"Ummm, nope."

"Walt?"

"Yes." Walt addressed Beth. "How does Bethany know what Jane's worked on here, what she's done, what she's learned?"

"That's where I come in," Dr. Owens jumped in on my behalf. "Allow me to address your question, Walt, because the answer pertains to one of two reasons for my participation in this meeting this afternoon."

"All right," Walt said.

"When Jane came to the hospital, it was voluntarily." Dr. Owens looked at Beth. "In fact, she had to persuade Walt that it was appropriate. She wasn't sleeping well, had lost her appetite altogether. She was afraid. Unaware of what was happening to her, how her body was reacting to the stress she was undergoing."

He went back to addressing Walt. "What Jane has said or done while in our program, what difficulties she might have encountered, whatever she's learned—everything takes place within a strict professional and confidential trust. Jane has the right to tell who she wants, when and if she wants, or choose not to disclose any of it to anyone."

Owens stopped. "Any questions so far?"

Walt shuffled his feet under the chair and shook his head.

"Ms. Walma?"

"No. I understand," Beth answered.

"Jane, care to add anything?"

"No." I wanted him to get on with it since I knew what was coming.

"Okay. The second reason I've been included today is to answer Bethany's request of Jane's prognosis. I have an official written report from our team to pass on to you, Beth." He handed her a manila envelope. "Jane's circumstance and her state is not, and has not been, such that would interfere with or jeopardize her ability to be a parent. *And* . . ." he cleared his throat, "we are recommending placement of a child with Jane and Walt as soon as possible."

Everyone was grinning.

Twee en Dertig

F at Susan called from behind a table supplied with scissors, glue, and at least thirty stacks of different colored felt. "Welcome, Jane." Her maternity sweatshirt displayed a flying stork of felt holding a diaper in its beak. An infant painted with pastel glitter peeked out.

Boredom was a luxury I appreciated compared to my early days at the hospital when living with only ongoing fear. Boredom brought me to the craft room for the first time that Thursday. I swallowed my pride. Okay, I told myself. Here I was in the nuthouse craft room. Put it on my chart under so-called progress.

Parts of a ceramic wind chime were spread on a table in front of Joanne. Two other girls at the table wrapped thin wire around orange and yellow fiberglass, making floral designs while advising Joanne about her color choices. Robert sat on a stool along the counter, concentrating on his needlepoint. The supposed cowboy had been teased originally, but as the splendid image of a quarter-horse emerged from the yarns he poked in and out, the razzing ended.

I moseyed past the shelves of materials. Pencils and chalks, knitting needles, crochet hooks, stained glass tools, wood blocks meant for carving. I sighed heavily and finally made a selection from a bin of pre-packaged kits. Spreading the directions out on the counter next to Robert's work area, I laid out the tiny rawhide scraps. He looked at me and nodded his approval like a proud sibling. We worked silently side by side as I sent the large needle in and out, in and out, drawing the edges together with the tan cord until one of the little moccasins took shape.

The chatter at Joanne's table continued while Susan paraded around the room, checking people's projects and progress. I didn't look up when her bulky outline approached the counter but quickly wiped my eyes with the back of my hand before any tears got too far down my face. I heard her take a quick breath behind me. She stood there for a moment without any comment at all. Then she patted my back twice and moved on.

∼

I wanted to go home for good that next week, but Dr. Owens advised I wait until after Mother's Day. "It's only one more week. Mother's Day will be hard. Make it easier on yourself."

When the day for me to leave arrived, Joanne plunked down on the bed next to my laundry bag and suitcase. "So, you're set to go, huh?" The usual lilt in her voice was missing.

"Yup," I said. "No more crappy coffee. No more involuntary volleyball. No more 'my turn to share' junk."

"Seems like it wasn't that long ago you came."

"Seven weeks. Longer than I thought it'd be." I tossed the laundry bag on the chair, pushed the suitcase over. "And what about you, Joanne? When you leaving?" I sat on top of the orange cotton bedspread with my feet under me, Indian style.

"I don't know. Owens says I'm getting too comfortable here. He's right. I don't want to leave." Joanne pulled up her knees and wrapped her arms in a circle around them. "So, I'll miss ya, Jane."

"I had to promise to come back for out-patient. Maybe I'll drop in the ward and see you."

"You don't wanna do that. You leave here, don't come back, Jane. It's not good to come back."

"Yeah." I thought a moment. "You're probably right."

Joanne jumped up. "Well, I'm goin' to class."

"I'll walk that way with you. Got Owens at eleven and I need to pick up my craft."

When I knocked on Dr. Owens' open door and walked in, I set the leather moccasins on his desk. A tiny left foot and a tiny right foot, like booties.

"Aren't they great?" I laughed and relaxed into the chair.

"Amazing how small a baby's foot is."

"Hard to imagine . . ." I didn't finish but exhaled, blinked hard, and looked up at the ceiling. Funny how quickly I teared up these days.

Owens waited, probably thinking he was giving me a chance to "feel."

There was a magical tone in his voice when he started to speak. "But do you let yourself imagine, Jane? The adoption. A baby. When you're home, it's important you let yourself imagine. Anticipate."

I looked out the window. "Yeah. I can do that." My fingers caught a tear before it reached my cheek. "It will happen." Shit. I grinned and sniffed. How positive of me. Setting my mouth in a one-sided smile, I nodded slowly. "So," I finally said.

"So," Owens answered. "You're going home."

"Sure am."

"How are you feeling about this?"

"I'm looking forward to not having to tell people how I feel."

He laughed and, after a pause, turned serious. "And scared? Is there any fear about going home for you, Jane?"

I didn't answer right away. Instead, I crossed my legs and jiggled my foot a while.

The hell with it. "Yeah, I'm afraid," I said, holding my foot still.

"To be expected. Not unusual when you're first released."

I think his comment was supposed to be reassuring.

"Jane. Tell me more about your fear. Can you say what that's about?"

Judas, man. More?

We had over a half-hour left. I looked past his wall sculpture, the sailboat, and out through the window. I'd be home in time to put on my suit and lie out in the sun. On the deck in my lounge chair with a glass of iced tea.

There was a lot to be afraid of. I kept looking outside. "For one thing, I'm afraid I'll be like Joanne and end up here again in a few months."

"But you're not Joanne," Owens said. "You're Jane, of course."

"I know." I tipped my head far back and spoke to the ceiling. "I'm afraid I won't sleep."

"You'll call me if you go more than two nights without sleep, right?"

I looked down only long enough to answer. "Yeah."

"And you know your limits. The signs. Not eating, for example."

"Uh-huh."

"Keep your out-patient appointments," he said.

I nodded, still looking up. Think I'll make some peanut butter cookies.

I looked at my watch. "There's still twenty minutes . . . Maybe I can get out early—last day and all."

"Not a good idea," Dr. Owens said and we looked at each other for at least thirty seconds.

"I'm not afraid like when I came," I volunteered. "Not scared the way I first was here."

Owens nodded and I did not look away. The tip of my thumb went between my front teeth.

"I was so scare . . ." My foot bounced up and down again. I made an effort to hold it still. "I don't . . ." I heard the tremor in my voice. "I don't ever want to let myself get that bad again . . . I promise I'll tell someone. Call someone."

My breath was short and I put my fingers over my mouth. Taking a full, deep breath, I shifted in my chair. "I don't know the words . . ." I swallowed before saying more. "Do you know how afraid I was?" Now I was whispering. "I mean . . . the idea of . . ."

I didn't wipe the tears this time. I just let them cover my face. They dripped down my nose and chin, on to my ears and neck when I looked up. Owens started handing me tissues.

"God, I hate this place." Both my hands were in tight fists on my lap.

He kept nodding, ever so slightly.

"My sisters . . ." I hesitated, worried that later I'd feel manipulated again.

Then words ran off my tongue. "I hate this place. I always thought this place ruined my mom. And hurt her bad. I didn't think anything or anyone here helped her one bit. I thought if she hadn't been here, she wouldn't have had to put up with all the talk from everybody. All that gossip and crap and . . . stigma . . . the unbelievable stigma." My throat swelled and it took a moment to get my voice back. "Do you have any idea . . . how much I hate this place?"

Maybe this was some sort of break-through a therapist waits for because Owens smiled. Not a smart-ass, ah-ha, know-it-all smile. Just a little, kind one.

"I figured it out," he said. "Just like you."

"Damn." I tossed the tissues basketball style into the wastebasket at the side of his desk, one at a time.

My voice was hoarse. "My mother . . . she's . . . she's . . .

He leaned back, nodded slowly and spoke quietly. "Your mother is a very courageous woman."

I sat a few minutes, quietly weeping right in front of Dr. Owens and using up most of the tissues. I stood to leave.

Owens picked up the tiny moccasins and passed them to me like bequeathing a token. We shook hands and didn't do one of those hug things.

By noon, I signed my release, walked outside resolute and spotted the Fiat in the parking lot under one of the many evergreens.

I drove away. I had learned enough for now. It's okay. It's fine, I told myself as I turned down our gravel road toward home.

Drie en Dertig

They didn't come to the house. They didn't request a meeting or send a letter in the mail. The second week I was home from the hospital, the agency called and cancelled the adoption over the telephone.

Eleven days later, Walt and I met face to face with Bethany's director, appealing to the agency to reconsider. We were told the decision was not negotiable. That was when Beth agreed to make one last attempt on her own to persuade the agency on our behalf.

I parked my car in the restaurant lot the following Tuesday. I weighed ninety-eight pounds when I entered the hospital. Since then I gained six pounds. So this morning I'd chosen a navy polo shirt, sandals, and light khaki pants that drindled at the waist with side pockets that gapped slightly open. The pants gave the illusion I was heavier, and the pockets were convenient when I didn't know what to do with my hands.

Swinging my bag over my shoulder, I walked into the restaurant, hands pocketed.

I spotted Beth immediately and joined her in the booth.

"I thought I'd go ahead and get a place," Beth greeted me. "I only get an hour for lunch."

"This is fine," I answered.

"How have you been?"

"I've been good, thanks."

"Walt too?"

"Yeah. He's cool."

Beth never did look like a social worker to me—not like an old maid wearing a navy-blue suit with her hair in a tight bun, marching to a gray car parked on London Street. Beth's hair curled to the middle of her back and perhaps her large brown eyes were naïve, but they were kind. Sometimes she came off as prudish, but that could have been the agency's conditioning. It was her job to come off that way.

The waitress took our order. I fidgeted with my purse handles under the table. My coffee came. I took a sip and lit a cigarette.

"You probably didn't know I smoke."

Her smile had vanished. "I guess there's a lot I don't know about you."

"Well, anyway, I'm quitting soon," I said, flippant with a wave of my hand. I slowed myself down. "You know, the adoption people ask an awful lot of questions and, seems to me, not always the right ones." I sighed, deep and loud. "I've always answered honestly, Beth, and . . ." I took a full breath and bit my tongue.

Beth's salad came.

"Go ahead," I said, stubbing out a half-smoked cigarette. "I know you're short on time."

She bowed her head and prayed silently while my hands fidgeted under the table.

My sandwich came. I took a bite, set it down, chewed slowly and swallowed. I looked at Beth and then procrastinated with a sip of water.

"So what's the verdict?" I finally asked.

Beth set her fork down. Her eyebrows wrinkled above her nose, her shoulders rose and tightened slightly as she inhaled. "They won't give in." Frowning, she looked me straight in the eye as she told me. "Because of your hospitalization, they won't place a baby with you."

It dug pretty deep. Like a pick-axe whacked through my ribs.

She cleared her throat. "They are willing to do a re-evaluation at the end of six months."

She looked down and quietly added, "I'm so sorry, Jane."

The waitress came with more ice water and left again before I said anything.

"They still don't get it, do they." I paused, shaking my head the way people do when they don't believe the awfulness right in front of them. "They don't seem to have a clue what it's like waiting days, weeks, month after month, year after year." My voice broke. I didn't want to cry. I calmed myself by thinking not this time, not this time.

"So," I continued, "four years ago they said it would be two years. And last October you said, 'I think you're going to have a very happy holiday.' That's exactly what you said. Then you asked if our nursery was ready. In November you told me 'Any day!' In December, nothing. In January, nothing. February. Nothing. Damn it, it was March before I went in the hospital. And then you still wouldn't tell us what was going on."

"All that information is confidential," Beth said for the hundredth time since I've known her.

"Fuck confidential." The crimp in my stomach grew while I sat and stared at my hardly eaten sandwich. I swallowed hard twice before looking up at Beth again. "I'm pregnant."

Her eyes blinked back at me. For a moment, I felt wickedly superior.

"My gosh." Beth reached for her water with lemon. "Oh my gosh!" Her wide smile spread further. "Congratulations!" She set her glass down and leaned back in the booth. "Well, well, well! I am so happy for you, Jane. Walt, too." Her chin dipped in a quick nod, like when speaking confidentially. "This happens sometimes, you know."

Here we go, I thought.

"When are you due?"

"In an eternity, it seems. But February, actually. I did one of those home pregnancy tests the first of last week and this Monday my doctor verified it."

"I'm so excited. This is wonderful news." Beth picked up her fork and rummaged through her salad before she put the utensil back on the table without taking a bite. "You know what?" She went right on talking before I could answer. "Maybe this explains why you had to go through all this. All your waiting, the postponements, everything. I mean, you know. God had His reasons."

I could feel my anger burn across my face. Her summary sickened me and I spit words out in a loud whisper. "I don't believe it. I don't believe any of it. How can you say that?" I put an elbow up on the table and dropped my forehead on my hand as I stared at her. "How can you excuse them? 'God has His reasons' my ass."

I had a strong urge to leave the restaurant. Just walk out. Who needs them? Screw 'em.

But I didn't want to give them the satisfaction. I lifted my head and stayed put.

"Okay, Beth. Wait a second," I said. "I know you stuck your neck out for us. And I do appreciate it." I hesitated only briefly, remembering I had nothing to lose this time. "The truth is . . . well, the truth is . . ." I switched to a stronger, yet quiet voice. "God didn't put me through this hell. You guys did."

First, she stared at me. Then wiggling in the restaurant booth, she looked down, fussing with the back of her hair and running her fingers through it.

"I'm really sorry you feel this way," she finally said. "You're really angry, Jane." Still fingering her hair, she sipped some water, gave me a quick glance and checked her watch. "I'm going to have to get back to the office." She wiped her wide, pretty mouth. "My hour's already over."

"You certainly don't want to break any rules or anything."

She gathered up her purse. "Maybe we should talk again sometime."

"Yeah. Probably. I'll call you . . . after six months or so." I picked up the check. "Hey, my treat."

I followed Beth out and watched her car exit the parking lot before I rested my head on the steering wheel of my Fiat and wept.

~

Walt went out to play cards with his guy friends that evening. In the twilight, the summer air was still warm. Through the screen, a breeze moved the lace bedroom curtains. I could smell manure in the neighbor's field.

As I undressed, I looked down at my middle, like ladies with babies in their tummy do. I could see a thickening in my waist, a slight protruding of my stomach, definite swelling in my breast.

I wasn't fooling myself. I carried something bitter as well.

You think you know so well, Bethany. You act like you're certain God is on your side. Or even that you know better than him. You thought you knew better than Deannie. You thought you knew better than Mother and Father.

I slipped my nightie over my head and covered myself, shivering in spite of the warmth.

Tell me. Explain it, Bethany. Explain it to me, to Gracia, to Mom and Dad, to Ronald Lee.

Ask Ronald Lee if it was all worth it. Look at the flowers he sends Deannie. Look at the card he signed: "Thank you for being my mother."

Explain to me how a child learns that kind of love in an environment you consider undesirable. An illegitimate child—born in sin.

He remembers his mother's struggle, that's how. Remembers Opa. Remembers Gracia.

Remembers someone standing silent on the kitchen register.

Vier en Dertig

"I can tell. Maybe your face is filled out a little," Dr. Owens said. "Or just that glow women get when they're carrying a child."

"Really?" I sat back and indulged in a moment of pride. He might be exaggerating but I liked hearing it anyway.

"And how are you doing?"

"Pretty good." After a pause, I sighed. "February's a long time away, though," I said, my voice wistful. "A lot can happen between now and then."

"You're worried something will happen to the baby."

"Right." Of course, I thought. Who wouldn't worry?

I folded my arms "I find it strange," I told him.

"What is it you find strange?"

"That people expect so much now. I mean I'm thrilled. And thankful. And all that. But . . . it's not that simple. And I'm just not the sparkly type, you know?"

"I've noticed that."

"So now that I'm pregnant, people expect me to be all cheery. They think everything's all fine and dandy."

"What people?"

"Oh, a lot of people. Even Walt," I admitted.

"And the adoption people? How did it go with Beth the other day?"

With my elbow on the arm of the chair, I rested my cheek on a fist and looked away, out the window. "They said no." Whatever glow might have been on my face disappeared. I let my fist drop. My hands opened and lay still on my lap. "Then I told Beth I was pregnant."

"And how did that feel?' he asked.

I pulled one side of my mouth into a half-ass smile. "Wonderful . . . Fantastic . . . Deliciously mean . . . Satisfying. Well, not entirely."

"What did Beth say?"

"She seemed relieved. Let off the hook or something. She started to play Monday morning quarterback with me. Then the platitudes—good endings, stuff about God's Providence, that kind of thing."

"Very difficult for you."

"I almost lost it in the restaurant."

"Understandable." Owens paused before continuing. "What else?"

I shifted in my chair and hesitated for a long moment.

"I hate them."

Owens nodded.

We sat without saying anything. I surprised myself, settling relatively comfortably in a chair across from my therapist.

Then his eyes narrowed and he cleared his throat. "I need to ask you something."

"Okay," I said, nonchalant.

"Jane, there's been a buzz."

"What kind of buzz?"

"I have to ask you . . ." His eyes scrutinized me. He shifted in his chair and cleared his throat again. "Is Walt the father of your child?"

"You're kidding. Are you kidding?"

"Please, answer my question."

"What the heck? Of course he is. What are you saying, exactly?"

"Well," he uncrossed his legs. "You were an in-patient here three months ago." He leaned forward, grabbing his knees with his hands. "People were asking."

"I went home those last three weekends."

"You told me yourself the doctors said Walt's sperm count is too low."

My chin drew an invisible circle in the air as I rolled my eyes. "For crying out loud."

The probing didn't deserve explanation. Maybe he owed me an explanation. "Who the hell's talking?"

"It was brought up at our staff meeting."

"The staff?" My hands balled up. I tapped a fist against my mouth. My gaze searched the office as if the entire team encroached the space. I inhaled deeply then let my breath out slowly. "What is it with all of you? It's that same old, everlasting . . ." I crossed my legs, one foot on the floor, one foot dangling. I bounced the back of my sandal up and down with my toes and it made a fast, snappy sound.

"I'm sorry, Jane. I had to ask."

"Had to?" I lowered my foot, both on the floor now. "Bullshit. And this trust we've been talking about all these weeks?"

Tapping both feet on the carpet, I thought for a moment. "Fuck 'em." I whispered.

"Tell me more about that."

"I'll tell you what . . ." I lifted my purse from the back of the chair and stood. "I'm not doing this."

I closed the door firmly all the way as I left.

Vijf en Dertig

Over the years, twelve grandchildren and four great-grandchildren have been born. Even so, my parents were genuinely moved to hear of my pregnancy. Already, Mother had knit a hat and booties in pastel yellow and crocheted a baby blanket in soft white yarn.

One early September morning, visiting at the kitchen table of our farmhouse, my father asked, "You'll have the baby baptized?"

"Yes, Dad. Of course we will."

"Not that we're Roman Catholic . . . Still . . ."

"Baptism's important, Dad. I've always believed that."

Through the sliding door, we could see my mother in the garden. She had just placed a small basket of ripe red tomatoes along the edge of the grass and began to cut some remaining daisies. Morning sun through the screen warmed us as my father and I sat at the table.

"My first son died after six weeks, you know." He looked out into the yard. "The baby with my first wife. Jackie's mother."

I did know, from Arie, who mentioned it once soon after Walt and I were married. Not details, though, until last summer, over a few brandies Arie and I shared when I visited him in Milwaukee. "The death certificate says crib death," my brother had told me. "What happened is they left a Teddy Bear in the crib and the baby suffocated on the plastic bag." We finished the entire bottle of brandy that night.

When I consider our family secrets, I think my father sometimes forgot to whom he opened his heart and where and when. He continued talking at my kitchen table as if it were all old news, while my mother gathered flowers.

"We were in the PR church back then, too. Reverend Veenstra told me I could never be sure our baby went to heaven."

"Why in the world would he say that?"

He turned to me. "The baby never grew up to prove he was God's Elect. If you carry the doctrine through . . . how do you know for certain?"

"The Church told you that?"

My father nodded. "They were wrong, of course."

~

Tip-toeing through the door, I lifted my long terrycloth robe with one hand so as not to stumble. The nursery had the scent of baby powder. The night-light spread a soft amber glow through the room and cast a faint shadow of the miniature carousel on the window shade.

I peeked into the crib, smiling at our son. He lay on his tummy, his double-bundled bottom protruding in the air. His dimpled hand was wrapped around a pacifier, as if he'd anticipated needing it desperately sometime later during the night. I carefully lifted the handmade quilt of pastel solids and calico print squares and gently tucked it around him. In the corner of the crib sat Saakel Dog, the button eyes of the stuffed animal gazing down like a guardian angel. Warmth spread through me like the first taste of steaming oatmeal on a snowy winter morning.

A tear slipped down my face. I kissed his forehead, his cheek. "Night-night."

On the dressing table lay the gown I wore when I was baptized. Although my mother had stored it in tissue paper and a cardboard box, thirty years had yellowed the dress.

"Soak it in dishwasher soap and dry it in the sun," Mother had told me.

The gown had whitened significantly. A satin ribbon, nearly thin as thread, gathered the bodice and dangled the length of the dress. Three tiny roses embroidered at the neck were as small as the nail on Mark's littlest finger.

~

I took Walt's arm as we approached the baptismal font in front of the church.

"John Mark Weber, I baptize you in the name of the Father, and of the Son, and of the Holy Spirit. Amen."

The water. The promise. Sprinkled on his forehead. The baby. The real.

~

Every day I believed a little more. Touching his face, his arms, his little legs, one finger stroking his chubby knee, wrist, dimpled hands. When I nursed him, when he nestled against me, when I held him on my shoulder, when our faces touched, when I felt his breath, smelled his powdery skin. All verified. Every day in the rocking chair, slow movement, soft creaking, quiet singing.

> *Jesus loves me, this I know; for the Bible tells me so.*
> *Yes. Jesus loves me. Yes. Jesus loves me.*

~

Three weeks before Mark's first birthday, we learned I was pregnant again.

A beautiful never-dared-ask-for wonder. Born in July. A dark-eyed, five-pound flawless gift. A little girl we named Katherine.

A full night's sleep lived only in my imagination. I quit nursing Kate when she turned six weeks. Maybe she had colic. We switched to formula and used a dairy sensitive brand. It seemed to help.

Kate's tummy wasn't our only issue. During those first weeks she wouldn't cuddle on my shoulder. She wouldn't let me sooth her to sleep in the rocking chair with songs of Jesus' love. I put her to bed awake. She fussed and fell asleep. I wondered how a little baby could have such a strong mind of her own.

And then, when Kate reached nine weeks, we melded.

Double loads of cloth diapers in the laundry were not a bother. My days filled with our children, the gardens, the farm, fresh air. Contentment.

The children took their first steps among dandelions. We took walks in the buggy on unoccupied gravel roads. We visited ponds and

horses, played peek-a-boo behind the barn door, giggled at the kittens, warmed ourselves near the woodburning stove.

~

On a cloudless, quiet spring morning, I heard my father's Olds 88
pull into the gravel driveway. Tuesday morning. Ten o'clock. The same
day and the exact time my parents always came for coffee.

With Katie in one arm and my hand on Mark's shoulder, we
stood in the grass waiting for their grandpa to shut off the motor.

"Hey there, big fella!" My father lifted Mark up in the air easily,
his arms still muscular from years lifting sides of beef.

My mother and Katie reached for each other, Katie bending
forward and Mom taking her in both arms. "Didn't your Mother put
your sweater on this morning?" Mom rubbed her hands over Katie's
little elbows. "I'll bet she's chilly," she said to me. "It's a lot cooler . . ."
Katie's tiny fingers went into my mother's mouth, so she kissed them
instead of finishing her sentence.

Dad set Mark on the gravel driveway and fumbled back in his
pocket for his car keys. "There's a surprise in here," he said, opening
the trunk. I could live in that trunk, it was so big. "Under here." He let
Mark pull the bright plaid car blanket. Underneath, a spanking new
Radio Flyer.

"Big wheels, Grandpa!" Mark said, stepping away.

"You bet." My father flushed. He picked up the wagon and turned
it back and around, making sure to clear the trunk opening. He set
it down in the driveway, four large rubber tires on spotless white
hubcaps proud and ready to roll. Like our Farmall tractor, the wagon
shone bright red. It had a box framed in wooden slats on the front,
back, and each side.

"It's for you and your sister," Father said.

Mark stood gleaming, his hands inside the bib of his little overalls. My father boosted Mark over the wooden slats and set Katie in
front between his legs. Mark scooted up and intuitively wrapped his
arms around his little sister. Taking up the handle, my father pushed
backwards at first, moving the wagon over the drive. He faced straight
ahead and pulled out onto the gravel road.

In all the excitement, my mother and I followed.

~

The summer before Mark was born, Walt and I had started our own cement cutting business. Walt spent long, hard-working days cutting concrete with core drills and diamond blades. The business grew, making it necessary to spend our evenings working on billing, bookkeeping and tax forms after the children were in bed.

By the time Kate was a year and a half, we realized the challenge of self-employment more fully. There was the work of maintaining hay fields, gardens, yard, the woodpile, the barn and farmhouse. All while spending the time I wanted with Mark and Kate.

Walt was eager to continue the business. I remained hesitant.

We sold the farm the first month it was on the market.

If there had been a snow or if it were cold and raining that day, the farewell might have been easier. But it was late April and the weather mild. I indulged in a final ramble along the lane, the sounds of the insects and frogs, birds, and distant horses amplified, the smells of grasses and clover exaggerated.

The children's attention stayed with Walt and the big moving truck with a lift. I locked the door and crossed the stone driveway to the barn. Picking up Chessy and her furry kittens, I lifted them to my cheek and whispered good wishes in their ear. "You'll get to know them soon. They'll take good care of you."

I started the Fiat and followed the orange and white U-haul out of the yard, out of the country and into the burbs. Pseudo country décor houses. Women who didn't leave home without their makeup, earrings, minivans. I wondered if I'd ever feel at home again.

Zes en Dertig

Families and other folks carrying Bibles walked across the parking lot toward the church entrance. I could hear the organ's robust prelude. The women and the girls carried their Bibles covered in quilted print material with heart-patterned covers and handles for convenient toting. The men just carried theirs bare.

"Each individual should bring his own Bible to church," Reverend Nyhoff had said. "What better way to make your relationship with Jesus more personal, alive, and real."

These things should have been a sign to me.

We entered the church, one of Katie's little hands in mine, her other wrapped around a roll of Smarties candy. Walt and Mark helped themselves to the church bulletins on the table. I waved to Ginny and her husband across the vestibule.

"Good morning, everyone!" Reverend Nyhoff greeted when the organ quit blaring.

"Good morning!" The congregation replied in unison. Not me.

"Couldn't you be a little more obliging?" Walt asked on our way home.

"I'm not an enthusiast." Trying to soften my edge, I added, "It's so casual."

"Is casual so awful?"

"As a matter of fact, yes." And off I went. "Church is a one-of-a-kind thing. People gather to meet God. Sacred time in a sacred place. Not a breakfast club or a golf outing or potluck, for cryin' out loud." I sighed, leaned over and pulled off one of my high heels. "Whatever happened to 'The Lord is in His holy temple, let all the earth keep silence before Him'?"

"What the heck's that?" Walt asked.

"You know. The way they used to start church in the morning."

"You sound like your dad."

"So what?"

"There are a lot of people who don't understand that stuff. Who does besides you?"

He turned on the radio.

Symbols, ceremony, liturgy, I thought. They weren't puzzles or obstacles. They weren't that hard to understand. They *take on* meaning.

Besides, I wanted to know what gave them the right to worship any way they wanted. Precedent was on my side . . . church order . . . tradition . . .

And so it festered.

～

The potatoes were peeled and placed in a pot of cold water on top of the stove. I ironed my dress. "*Op Zondag?*" my mother would protest about doing these chores on Sunday, if she knew. The children got up and paraded silently with their *kussie* blankets, through the kitchen, into the basement family room for cartoons. Walt came out of the bathroom, poured his coffee, and settled into reading the newspaper.

"Remember. I have to get to church early this morning for choir warm-ups," I said, joining him at the kitchen table.

"Oh. You sure? I thought you were singing tonight." Walt bit into his cinnamon roll.

"Yep. I'm sure. Ginny's picking me up. I'll meet you in the back before church starts."

He dug the sports section out from under a pile of ads. "Make sure the kids are ready before you leave."

The roast was in the oven. I fixed Mark and Kate's breakfast. After I dressed, I helped the kids get dressed. There was time to braid Kate's hair before Ginny arrived.

～

When Walt and the children entered the vestibule, I took Katie's hand. Mark walked next to his dad, following the usher while the organist and pianist played "Majesty."

"Let us begin with a song of praise."

We began with a song of praise. We filled in with songs of praise. We finished with a song of praise.

After the opening hymn, everyone turned to greet the people nearby with a handshake and a smile. Then we sang a song about the Lord's presence, glory on people's faces, and an audible brush of angel wings.

And people thought *I* was crazy.

The choir filed up to the front of the church. We arranged ourselves on three steps in front of the pulpit. The director motioned us to smile and we sang, "Magnify the Lord." When finished, we haphazardly made our way back to our families amid a round of applause.

I passed peppermints to Mark and Walt. Katie opened her roll of Smarties quietly and spread them out on top of a *Psalter Hymnal*.

Reverend Nyhoff read five verses of the Scripture. Then he read Lord's Day 44 from the catechism, including the part about the longer we live the more we may look to Christ for righteousness.

He was a heavy man. His round, bald head looked like a basketball, turning left and right as he rolled out the points of his sermon. The Evils of Coveting. David coveted Bathsheba. He talked about coveting homes, jobs, cars, spouses. He said we ought not to be busy with the things of this world. Forget depth. Forget contextual exegesis. He gave a typical topical sermon.

He finished with an "Amen." Amen with a long "a."

The deacons brought our offerings forward. We rose for the benediction and doxology.

A doxology is *supposed* to be a hymn of praise.

～

At five o'clock we returned for the evening service. Impromptu prayer, an extended sequence of special music by a men's trio followed by enthusiastic clapping.

I don't clap during a church service.

That evening, after Mark and Kate were in bed and Walt fell asleep on the couch, I began to nod while reading and went upstairs to brush and floss my teeth. Waiting for the cold cream to soften my eye makeup, I wondered why we even bothered attending the evening worship service. "Well," I told myself, wiping off the mascara with a tissue. "It's Sunday. That's why."

I thought back to the morning sermon. Reverend Nyhoff stressed how we should be striving to become more and more renewed. He hadn't said anything about King David's child dying. Or the king's repentance. Or the part that says the longer we live the more we may look to Christ for forgiveness and righteousness. Only the striving, striving, striving.

Zeven en Dertig

Father retired after my parents moved from London Street. They came to our house at the end of the cul-de-sac every Tuesday for coffee, just like when we lived on the farm. Saturday mornings, I went to their place while Walt and the kids stayed home and watched cartoons.

My father and I were debating Common Grace/Special Grace again. He still loved a good debate and our Saturday *koffie kletsen* became our amateur theology hour. He still claimed the problems in our churches pivoted on "so-called Common Grace." I granted him the idea of one grace, but disagreed it was neither common nor special. "It's on-going and over-all. Like a blanket covering creation. Spread over everything. But only some recognize it. Ta-daah! Election."

"What will it lead to?" he asked.

"You always say that," Mother chimed in as she poured more coffee.

"It doesn't have to lead to anything. I'm agreeing with you, Dad." I reached for an almond cookie.

"Well, don't forget the Hoeksema-DeWolf case. DeWolf's sermon 'Suffer the Little Children to Come Unto Me.'" He had told me the story a hundred times.

"DeWolf preached an Offer of Salvation," I said.

"Absolutely. A Conditional Salvation sermon. Maybe it was. Maybe it wasn't. But what did it lead to?"

I didn't have to answer. My father still liked his theological postulates to have the same conclusion—the slippery slope to Universalism. The door was open for the Arminian and the discussion was finished.

He relaxed his pointed index finger. Those stubby fingers played Psalms on the piano without a flaw. I watched him from across the table—his Jimmy Durante nose, eyes that bulged almost to the point of being homely, receding hair accentuating the widow's peak. His sense of humor had grown over the years, sometimes substituting for absent-mindedness.

"You get the same thing when it comes to hymns." Father's finger popped up. "They're not satisfied with singing the Psalms. 'What will it lead to?' I asked them. Now they have hymns and songs of the Arminians and choirs and special music and programs, the whole business."

He stopped for air.

"They don't know the Catechism any more. They don't know the Canons of Dort any more." His index finger pounded the tablecloth near his saucer. "They want to be part of the world . . . They forget the antithesis, that's all."

He dunked the end of a windmill cookie in his coffee.

Instead of a rebuttal, I paused and told them, "I'm going to teach catechism."

Mother set her coffee cup down on her saucer with a clang. "Don't tell me."

"I just don't know any more." Father shook his head and pursed his lips. "The Church now days. All this business about women. It's just a bunch of humanism."

"I'm only teaching catechism, Dad. High school kids. It's not like an office or anything."

"The minister or an elder should teach the catechism." He kept shaking his head slowly. "Besides, what will it lead to?"

His rebuke had hurt, but as I got ready to leave, my father hugged me. "Bye, little girl," he said and handed me three large hardcover books. "Here. Take these."

I opened the first volume—*The Triple Knowledge: An Exposition of the Heidelberg Catechism.* "Hey, thanks, Dad."

We really didn't know what it would lead to.

∾

The catechism class met each Sunday after morning services in the back of church in a room too small for fifteen teenagers. My hope was the students would learn an appreciation for the Heidelberg Catechism, learn its intent—a comfort they could refer to over and over.

We began in September and studied God's faithfulness. He doesn't change his promises, doesn't change his Word. By Christmas, the students knew the baby in the manger as the same Word of creation and the same Word of Scripture, this time in human form.

We talked about the Ten Commandments. I said that even though the Law is a teacher of sin, the Law is good and not at odds with the Gospel. We compared John Calvin's doctrine of the Law with Martin Luther's.

Around the middle of January, some of the parents invited me to meet with them one evening at the Windemolen Restaurant.

There were seven couples around an oval table. I knew the ladies best, from a Bible study group I led. They eyeballed my worn jeans as I sat down and after we said hello, chatted among themselves while I observed.

When the men noticed my quietness, Mr. Terbeek spoke up. "I'm glad you were willing to come," he said. The waitress brought his coconut cream pie.

I smiled and sipped coffee while the others tasted their brownies and carrot cake.

"No dessert for you, Jane?" Rhonda's mother asked.

"Too full. Just finished dinner," I said, smiling and patting my tummy.

Mr. Terbeek managed a bite of pie on his fork. Smacking his lips, he let me know what was on his mind. "About catechism. You know, Jane, our children aren't very happy."

I let out a short laugh. "Mr. Terbeek. Were you ever happy about catechism when you were a kid?"

"Well, no," he answered and chuckled. "No, I wasn't. And please, call me Jim." He slipped in another bite. "Today's kids have a lot of pressure. Sports, schoolwork, Young People Society . . ."

The others at the table nodded.

And I had thought we were just having coffee.

"Memory work is Reverend Nyhoff's requirement," I said. "I agree with him on that. But he wants the tests."

"My son's schedule's pretty heavy," Mr. Aardema said. "He's a good student, but he didn't do very well on the test you gave."

"I don't think I could pass that test," Mr. Nylon laughed. "And I'm an elder!"

I cleared my throat and smiled. "If you'd been in the class and paying attention, you'd pass."

"We have to be careful with these kids." It was Rhonda's mother. "They're getting their driver's licenses this year. They'll want to use the car, visit other churches. We want them to like it here at Providence. We don't want to lose them."

Setting my coffee down, I glanced around the table. I thought a moment and summoned my nerve. "Listen. I think I understand what you're saying." I sat up straighter, pulled my feet underneath my chair. "You really can't lay all that responsibility on me. I just teach catechism. If they're required to learn catechism then that's what I teach."

Mr. Aardema jumped in. "We know it's not easy having those fifteen kids in that small room every Sunday. Don't think we don't appreciate you."

An objection that I was female wouldn't have surprised me. It had not occurred to me they would confirm my father's grumblings.

My hands would tremble if I lifted my coffee cup. I wiped my sweaty palms on my jeans. Mr. Aardema went on to say memory work wasn't necessary these days. Mr. Barons would appreciate it if the class would dismiss promptly at 12:15 so Sunday dinner wouldn't be late. Rhonda's mother continued to whine . . .

This is bullshit. I politely excused myself, paid my tab at the register and went home.

~

In catechism that March, we studied Christ's suffering and death. Then came Easter.

"The resurrection is our hope," I said. "But here's the thing. People preoccupied with heaven tend to have their heads in the sand."

Doug's hand shot up. "Don't you believe in the resurrection?"

"Yes. I do believe in the resurrection," I explained. "But what about now?"

The students looked blank.

"We need to love our neighbor. That takes a lot of time." I paused and glanced around the room. "There's a lot of suffering out there." No comments, so I asked, "Anybody know the word 'mortification'?"

"Like mortician?" Rhonda asked.

Amy covered her mouth and giggled. Doug laughed right out loud.

I grinned and tapped the toe of my high-heel on the linoleum. "That's not far off." I wrote on the chalkboard: Theology of the Cross.

"Here's what I'm saying. We're still on this side of the resurrection. The Bible says, 'do justice, love mercy, walk humbly.' I'm telling you, heaven is for later."

In the final weeks of class, we covered Profession of Faith. It's like First Communion. It's expected when the student finishes catechism. I repeated our main theme. "Our faith is based on Christ's righteousness, not our own. So, don't wait to make Profession of Faith until you've earned the right. That's the whole idea. We are justified by faith alone."

I erased the board and set the yellow chalk on the ledge. "Okay. If you get this right, no test next week. Here is *the* question . . . Where does one find God?"

They looked around, each waiting for the other. Then Chris answered. "In the Church."

"Very good. That's where The Word and Sacraments are. The Means of Grace. *Depositum fidei.*" I said. "The strength of the Church is not its building, or its budget, or its numbers . . . or its piety. The strength of His Church is in the blood of Jesus."

Tossing my coffee cup into the wastebasket, I reached for my purse. "That's it. You guys did great. Don't forget, party at the cottage Saturday. Bring your swim suits."

We dismissed at 12:20 instead of 12:15.

Acht en Dertig

Minerva and I ordered a pitcher of beer in the pub a few blocks from Grandville Avenue Church. Minerva is Bobo's wife and also one of my best friends.

"I put your name down for the reunion," Merv said.

"What does that do?"

"Signs you up for the picnic and a copy of the centennial celebration booklet."

I took a sip of the cold, reddish beer. "This happens in September?"

"Yep. Weekend of the twentieth. The picnic is Saturday and the services Sunday."

Bobo and Merv lived in a two-story house with original woodwork and hardwood floors in the city less than a mile from London Street. They were the only ones in our family that still belonged to Grandville Avenue Church.

"How's it been, working on the anniversary committee?" I asked Merv.

"I've enjoyed it. Bobo's been in the planning, too, being an elder and all."

"Yeah. Ha! Bobo an elder at Grandville Avenue." I wasn't mocking, only teasing. "Man, just like Dad."

"Think Mom and Dad will come to the anniversary?"

"Did you put their name down?"

"Yup."

"Do they know that?"

"Uh-huh." Merv opened her purse and dug out a pack of cigarettes. "Janie, the strangest thing happened." She lit up. "They ask for
people's maiden names, you know."

"Yeah. So?"

She exhaled slowly. "Actually, I'm not sure I should tell you this."

When Merv acted apprehensive, I worried. "Come on, say it," I
said.

"Well, I could hear them talking from the other room."

"And?"

"Mrs. Feenstra, she said, 'Who's this on the list?' Albert Meyer
answered, 'You know Pearl Ritsema.' Then Mrs. Feenstra said, 'Oh yes,
Don's wife.' Albert Meyer said, 'Not that Pearl.'" Merv shifted sideways
in the booth, facing the aisle of the restaurant. She blew her cigarette
smoke straight up in the air with a whistling sound. "He said, 'You
know Pearl, Orie's wife. The one who got in trouble.'"

I uncrossed my legs. Both feet slapped the floor. "What the
world?" I stared at Merv.

"He said Mom's name and called her 'The one who got in trouble.'"

"He said that?"

She crushed her cigarette out in the ashtray. "He did."

My mug slammed on the heavy wooden table more than I intended. The beer foamed. Elbows on the table, I tapped my chin with
my fist and squinted. "Holy Shit." I leaned back and took a couple of
deep, long and loud breaths. "Did you say anything?"

"Janie, they didn't know I was listening."

The aroma of someone's hamburger repelled me.

Merv shook her head, frowning. "Maybe I shouldn't have told
you."

Scanning the bar, I lit a cigarette. Merv watched me, patiently.
With my free hand, I started to pound my fist on my mouth like a
silent gavel against my face could clear my brain. I watched the foam
bubble in my mug. "You did right. I can't stand not being told stuff."

We passed the cigarette back and forth.

"Judas, I can't believe it. What idiots." I looked around the bar as
if one of the patrons could explain. "Fools."

I inhaled deeply, took a swallow of beer, looked long and hard at
Merv before I spoke.

"Won't they ever get it? Or at least shut up . . . Can't keep their mouth shut . . . Damn it, that's the least they could do." I spoke softly now. "Why don't they just shut the hell up?"

~

If Merv hadn't been on the anniversary committee at Grandville Avenue, I might never have grasped the full extent of the offense. Or how the entire distortion still gnawed inside me.

When I arrived home that night, I peeked in on Mark and Kate, both sleeping soundly. Once in bed, I squirmed, stretched out on my back, turned on my left side, then my right.

"When did you get home?" Walt asked, half awake.

"About an hour ago."

"Hmmm. Go to sleep," he mumbled.

I wiggled around some more. Then I got up and settled into the stuffed chair in the den, lights out.

I thought of my mother.

I thought about Deannie and the time she took Ronald Lee away. Maybe not in anger. Maybe not in revenge. Maybe not to avoid my parents. Maybe just to escape the whole damn community. The arrogance, the scorn. Their same old story.

That old, old story.

And it wasn't of Jesus and His love.

In the dark in the middle of the night in the stuffed chair, I drew connections. Deannie leaving, coming back, leaving, coming back. Leaving again, finally taking Ronald Lee with her.

Finally allowed to love him.

Not that his grandparents didn't love him. Deannie knew they loved him. Ronald Lee knew. Everyone knew that. But Deannie couldn't love him while people continued their gossip. And so the abduction. So his grandparents were not allowed his love in the same way again.

Didn't I hear someplace that the relinquishing of one love brought to expression another, more perfect love?

And my mother.

She had to love Gracia secretly. While people gossiped and scorned.

Her grandparents loved her openly. Mother knew they loved Gracia. Gracia knew. Everyone knew that. *Ogenappel,* Opa would say—apple of his eye.

But Opa died when Gracia was four. He stepped off the curb without looking, into the path of an automobile and was killed.

Mama?

Mama?

Could you finally hold Gracia that day? Were you finally allowed to openly love her?

Didn't I hear someplace that the relinquishing of one love brought to expression another, more perfect love?

Negen en Dertig

Mom had the mugs set out on the placemats when I got there, red silk begonias in the middle of the table replaced with the tin of windmill cookies.

I put a bakery bag next to Dad's mug. "I stopped at Ida's on the way."

"Your father's in the den. Tuned out to everything but his puzzle."

Only the top of his head showed from the back of the Sleepy Hollow chair. "Hey, Dad."

"Hi there, Skeezix." A square of cardboard balanced on a wooden TV tray stood in front of my father. He had linked the edge pieces together first. Inside the frame, a trillion other pieces were spread out, all shades of blue.

"What are you working on?"

"It's Lake Superior." He showed me the photo on the box.

"Three thousand pieces. Well, that'll last you about a week."

"*Koffie drinken!*" Mom called.

We came to the kitchen table where my father picked up the bakery bag and peeked inside. "What do we have here?"

"Sweet rolls. I got you one with raisins."

While I arranged them on a platter, Mom poured coffee. Unabashed and eager, she announced, "Piersma's preaching at the anniversary."

"How do you know that?" I asked.

"Bobo told us. Merv is on the committee, you know."

I caught a short breath and held it, seized by my conversation with Merv at the bar last week. Mother passed the sweet rolls.

"What else did he say about the anniversary?"

"Not much. Just that Piersma will be there."

"Cool." I passed the butter to my father.

"Bobo and Merv are singing in some sort of alumni choir," Dad said.

"Maybe I should join. You know I quit the choir at our church."

"Why would you do that?" mother asked.

"Sandy always chooses praise songs or Gnostic junk." I sang a line from "Lord Lift Me Up to Higher Ground" as an example. Dad grinned at my phony vibrato, so I sang from "Fix Your Eyes Upon Jesus." In that hymn, things of earth grow dim.

Dad shook his head. "That's what it leads to. Shouldn't be a choir during church."

Mom veered from his comment right away. "You still lead the Bible Study group?"

"I'm ready to quit that too—they're really into personal piety and growth garbage."

"It's humanism, that's all," Dad said.

"The study book asks what is it that God says to you individually. So I said that God speaks collectively in the Bible and they looked at me like, Huh?"

Now my mother began to sing. "I come to the garden alone . . . and He walks with me and He talks with me . . ."

"You got it." I went to the stove and turned on the burner under the coffee pot. "But the long-range planning committee is just about over." I straightened the country-quilt pad on my chair before sitting again. "You'd go crazy, Dad. They discuss church growth. Tear into the service. Mr. Let-the-Spirit-be-his-guide, that's what I call the chairman, he says we should be more spontaneous." I popped a bite of cinnamon roll in my mouth. "Forget God's saving acts in *history*."

Father scraped the frosting off his plate with his fork. "They got no business messing around with Church Order."

"It's like they think they're Synod or Vatican II or something," I said.

"They forget the Catechism." He pushed his index finger on his placemat. "The Means of Grace. Preaching. Baptism. The Lord's Supper."

"Nyhoff wants grape juice instead of wine at communion. He says it's really not that big a deal. He said what's important is our personal relationship with Jesus. I told him that was an oxymoron."

"Oh oh oh!" Mother said. "You shouldn't talk to the minister that way, young lady." She handed my father a napkin. "Why don't you go in the living room and play the organ for a while, Janie?"

"No, not today." I pushed my chair a little farther away, resting my elbows on the table. "Nyhoff wants the children to have their own church in a different room down the hall. Can you believe the nerve?" I set my chin on my fist. "Well, Walt and I've been going to St. John's Lutheran some of the time."

"Don't tell me," my mother said. "I thought Walt knew better."

"Problem with the Lutherans is they think they're free from the Law," my father said. "They don't believe in sin."

"Oh, come on, Dad. Yes they do. Just because they emphasize Gospel instead of Law? If you believe in sin, you have to believe in forgiveness."

"Well, what does it lead to? Give me one of those windmill cookies, will you Mom?"

I sat up and crossed my legs under the table. "Maybe I'll become Catholic."

"That's not funny," Mother said.

"Bunch of idolatry, that's all," Dad said. "Salvation by good works."

Tipping my chair on its back legs, I crossed my arms in front of me. "But what's the difference, Dad? Justification by works, or all this duty and moral stuff to verify how right we are with God?"

My father dunked his cookie.

I let the chair come to rest and leaned forward. "Spiritual growth, sanctification—whatever you want to call it. There's no such thing." I waved my hand in the air and knocked over my mug, spilling the rest of my coffee.

"Aach. So worked up," Mom laughed. She reached for the *schijndoek* and wiped up.

"You're right, though," Dad said. "The Catechism, Lord's Day 44."
We both took a deep breath.

My father drained his mug. "It's like with the antithesis . . ."

The last thing I needed was more coffee, but let Mom pour me some anyway.

~

I got up to head home and put my coffee mug in the sink. "Going to the pool hall, Dad?"

"You bet. I'll grab my stick and walk you to the car." He went in the den to retrieve his cue case.

"See you later, Mom," I said and followed my father outdoors.

When we reached the carport, he stopped behind his Olds. He opened the trunk and dug out a pack of Camels stashed in a towel wrapped around the end of a garden shovel. He lit one up.

"One for me, please," I said.

He shook his head, handed me the cigarette and lit another for himself.

We smoked quietly for a moment on the pavement.

"I want to say this," he said in a serious tone, holding his cigarette between his fingers European style.

I waited. We each took a pull from our cigarettes, blew the smoke in the sky.

"Make sure you kids include Gracia. You know. When I'm gone." He turned and faced me, solemn as ever. Before I said anything, he continued. "I've always thought of her like my own. I've always treated her the same." His eyes welled up. He swallowed hard. "I love her the same like the rest of you. You kids make sure Gracia knows that."

He hadn't pulled his reference out of the blue. I was wise to him and his anxieties. He might be a prisoner to his theology, but he hadn't locked his heart away.

I dropped my cigarette on the pavement and put it out with my shoe. "Don't worry, Dad. She knows."

~

With Kate's hand in mine, I followed Walt and Mark past the bell tower and into St. John's Church. We slipped into the row second from the back.

An acolyte lit three candles. As a processional began, the congregation stood. Someone carried a towering, wooden crucifix down the aisle. Clergy followed in long vestments and stoles.

"In the name of the Father and of the Son and of the Holy Spirit. Aah-men."

Everything proceeded without explanation.

Near the end of the service, parents left momentarily and returned from the nursery with their little ones for Holy Communion. Parishioners formed a line along the altar, first bowing and then kneeling. We watched as the elements were given. Pastors blessed the young children and announced the Peace.

Walt knew how I felt. Being a son of a preacher and all, he was fine with our old church, fine with the denomination in general. On the way home that morning he said, "Maybe we should try that new church on 44th Street."

"People carry coffee and bagels into the pews with them."

He turned onto the cul-de-sac. "The chapel by the lake would be okay with me."

"With the roller skating music? I don't think so."

We parked in the driveway. Mark and Kate unfastened their seat belts, jumped out and ran to their bikes. I rolled the window down. "You need to change your Sunday clothes first." Walt stayed put and pushed in the lighter.

He lit his smoke, tipped his head back and stretched his arm out on the top of the car seat between us. "I suppose you'd like to go back to Grandville Avenue."

"No way. Not there. Got one for me?"

He handed me his Marlboro and lit another.

"What is it you don't like about St. John's?"

"I don't know," he said, looking out the window on his side.

"They have Confession and Reconciliation first off," I said. "They refer to the Trinity a lot. They read the Old and the New Testament. They even stand for the Gospel reading."

"Yeah, yeah. I know."

I thought for a minute. "You know the best part? They have Holy Communion almost every week. And everybody gets to come."

"But here's the thing," Walt said, turning and staring straight at me. "You know Mel Verstraat goes there. I won't go to the same church as my competitor."

So I went alone.

Different branch, same Reformation. No big deal. I attended St. John's at eight in the morning, arrived home on time every Sunday to go to Providence with Walt and the children at ten.

It was a big deal. Walt hated it. The people at Providence just didn't get it. My father would kill me.

Lutherans didn't talk about the antithesis—they didn't even call it the antithesis.

But they knew its place. Right through the middle of us, cutting our hearts the same.

~

"I am the Good Shepherd. I know my sheep and my sheep know me . . . The Lord is my shepherd, I shall lack nothing . . ."

From the loft in St. John's Church, a choral group sang slowly, reverently. They wore blue robes and flaxen shawls.

> *How . . . [lovely] are Thy Tabernacles, O Lord of hosts!*
> *My soul longeth, yea, even fainteth for the courts of the Lord:*
> *my heart and my flesh crieth out for the living God.*
> *Yea, the sparrow hath found an house,*
> *And the swallow a nest for herself, where she may lay her young,*
> *even thine altars.*

The Reverend prayed, "O God, whose Son Jesus is the Good Shepherd . . ."

Even from the back pew, I had an excellent view of the Shepherd. Though not on stained glass, he was there and he was stained.

I watched. The affluent, the poor, the healthy, some with canes, some in wheelchairs, all the children, mothers and fathers with babies in their arms—bowing and kneeling at the altar. All in the same boat. None more righteous than the other. Not one.

"Take, eat; this is the true body of our Lord and Savior Jesus Christ, given into death for your sins," the Reverend announced, presenting the wafer.

"Take, drink; this is the very blood of Christ, shed for you." A common chalice filled with wine.

The physical. The sacred. The earthy and the holy.

Here was what I craved. What Grandville Avenue didn't give. What Providence didn't need. Here was forgiveness and here I approached.

"Given to you for the forgiveness of sins."

Seeing him, smelling him, I knelt. Touching him. Tasting him.

Him. The Savior I had always known.

Veertig

A chill hung in the September air and the rain beginning to fall made it worse. Walt dropped me off with Mark and Kate at the front entrance of Grandville Avenue Church. He parked the car and joined us in the third row from the front with the rest of my family.

Mr. Bachuizen began the prelude, "*Alle Roem is Uitgesloten.*" A few years ago I had purchased my own copy of the sheet music and now the song was one of my own favorites.

Reverend Piersma led the anniversary service. I never doubted my parents would be there.

Everyone stood to sing a Dutch celebration anthem. "*Ere zij God.*" Many of us knew the song from memory in de Nederlands. I glanced down the row and winked at Kate and Mark. Their teacher had taught the Dutch version of the song to all the first, second, and third-graders. I looked further, watching Arie J sing it, watching Bobo watching us sing it, and at the other end of the pew, hearing my parents' native rendition.

I faced forward, smiling how my mother sang with brazen composure in this church. Her sanctuary and her slap in the face at the same time.

Reverend Piersma read the story of Rahab from the book of Joshua. Rahab hid the spies that were sent into Jericho. Rahab saved their lives. When Reverend Piersma finished reading Scripture, the lights in the sanctuary were dimmed. He stood in his black robe with his hands behind his back, bouncing up and down on his toes before he began.

"I have entitled the sermon this morning, 'The Scarlet Cord.'"

He bounced up and down on his toes again. "There are three points: Rahab the Harlot, The Scarlet Cord, Jehovah the Covenant God."

I put the first peppermint in my mouth.

"Rahab the Harlot. The prostitute. Rahab is not an Israelite."

I recognized Mrs. Kamps across the aisle, sitting with one of her sons. Mr. Kamps had joined the saints of all ages.

"The second point is The Scarlet Cord."

The second peppermint went in my mouth.

"In Hebrew, the word 'cord' means 'hope.' The two spies are in Jericho. There, a scarlet cord hangs from a house, indicating a house of ill repute.

"While hiding the spies, Rahab moved the cord to the back of the house and the spies made their escape by it. This is where the cord remained."

Bouncing on his toes, Reverend Piersma pulled his chin down and formed an "O" with his mouth before going on. He reminded us that Rahab acknowledged her sin and showed repentance by moving the cord from the front to the back of the house, assisting the spies.

"Let us look at the third point—Jehovah, the Covenant God."

Time for the third and final peppermint.

"Rahab heard about Jehovah God, how He gave Israel the land before them. She heard the Word of God and all His deeds. And when she heard Jehovah's word, her 'heart did melt' it says in verse eleven."

His hands were behind his back as he began his bounce once more. He stuck out his lower lip like a pouting child. But when he spoke again, a slight smile crossed his mouth and his words were gentle and calm. "Rahab, you see, heard the Word of God and this woman of ill repute—this harlot—had faith and she had hope. She believed God and His promises.

"Brothers and sisters, Rahab is included in the genealogy of Christ. Rahab was the mother of Boaz, who married Ruth and begat Obed, who begat Jesse, who begat David the King."

As he finished, each sentence diminished in volume. "The Harlot. The Scarlet Cord. The hope for the Christ, who is the hope for the harlot, the hope of the sinner. The hope of you. The hope of me."

"Aaa-men."

After the Benediction and Doxology, there was cake, coffee and ham on buns in the basement.

~

Once we were in the church basement, Mark and Kate made a dash for their grandpa and grandma. My father crouched down to meet Mark. "Hi, big fella! My lands, you're getting big!" As if he hadn't seen Mark just this Tuesday. Mark put his arm around his grandpa's neck and they squeezed tightly.

"Hi Babies!" my mother said. She let Kate grab her around the leg and press her little head against her dress in a way my sisters and I were never allowed to do.

The children switched places and Father lifted Kate. Her black patent shoes reached just to his knees. "Grandpa's little girl," he called her. "Don't you look pretty!" He smooched her face. Kate must have thought she'd be tickled. She scrunched her shoulders and giggled.

Folding chairs and rows of tables were set up in the assembly room. Aunt Dienke and other women from the Ladies Aid Society were serving from behind one of the tables. We got in line behind Gracia and John, who had sat in the balcony during the service this morning with Babe. We weren't expecting Deannie.

The rainy weather prevented any outdoor activities planned from taking place, but an adjacent room had been designated as a game area for children.

"Can we go to the game room?" Mark and Kate wanted to know when we finished our lunch.

"We'll take them there a little while," my mother said.

Kate walked holding her grandpa's hand on one side and her grandma's hand on the other. Mark and his cousins followed.

Walt visited at the table with Gracia and John, enjoying a second piece of cake while I began my meandering through the church building.

First, I visited the highest area of the edifice. I climbed up the third stairway into a small, roughed-in space where Mr. Kamps faithfully rang the church bell precisely at nine o'clock and again at nine-thirty every Sunday morning. I wondered if anyone had thought to sound the bell when Mr. Kamps passed on to Glory.

Next, I went down to the second floor and stepped into one of the Sunday School rooms used for primary grades. Little wooden folding chairs, fifty or sixty of them, were lined up in their rows facing the podium, exactly as I remembered. Maybe they still hand out the little cards with pictures of Bible characters and verses on them when the children say their memory text word for word.

Stepping back into the hall, I recognized Bobby Garrison, my old alphabetical partner, talking with Florenze DeGraaf.

"Janie! How are you? This is so cool. I've run into so many people. Florenze, you remember Janie, don't you? She always knew her catechism, remember?"

"Sure I remember." Florenze smiled. "But we liked you anyway."

A group of couples that looked to be retired and only vaguely familiar to me entered the balcony. I followed them. They chatted in Dutch, keeping their voices hushed as they stopped to look out over the sanctuary. When they moved on, back to the hallway, I pushed down the bottom half of the wooden chair and took a seat in the balcony's front row.

The sanctuary was empty. I took in the view of the pulpit, the communion table, the baptism font, the organ and its pipes and I imagined the sound of Mr. Bachuizen playing Psalm 42. Along the east side and the west side of the church, each stained-glass window from my childhood.

And in center-front, the Good Shepherd.

I turned to confirm no one lingered. I faced the Shepherd and brought the tip of my fingers to my forehead, my chest, my left shoulder, my right.

∾

Back on the main floor of the church, the display of commemorative items in the vestibule held my attention—old catechism books, photographs of a church picnic the year I won a beach towel, a Sunday School pin with a wreath and fine gold chains connecting eight honor strips, one for each year of attendance.

A rare sense of attachment to Grandville Avenue Church came over me along with a seldom-acknowledged connection to the very people celebrating there today.

Inside the fireside room, a group of elderly people unable to manage the basement steps had gathered. I went in and said hello to Mrs. Hoekstra, the aged little lady whose driveway I used to shovel on London Street. When she realized who I was, her eyes turned watery and she clung to my arm.

Klikkuiken had died many years ago. But in that room I recognized her follower, Rena Grasman, dressed in a fussy, gray tailored suit and whispering to her sister.

I returned to the main hallway, passed the library and headed toward the basement corridor. Bertha Feenstra passed me on the right, one of the ladies Merv had overheard at the committee meeting. I froze right there on the first step and grabbed the handrail for support.

"Excuse me," the person behind me said, maneuvering around me. I continued down the stairs and headed for the ladies' room.

That's when I bumped into Albert Meyer, the ringmaster of distortion himself.

I stiffened and stared at him from the bottom step. In his old age, Mr. Meyer seemed oblivious to my scrutiny. My legs, rigid and tense, began to tremble. My hands went cold. I could feel sweat under my arms.

I took a breath but didn't say it. Didn't say the words that had seethed inside my head for a long time now. I didn't say, "Listen up mister and listen close. She didn't get into trouble. That is rape. She was raped. That man raped my mother."

I didn't say a thing.

Instead, I turned away. I pushed the heavy wooden door and slipped into the ladies' room. With a wet paper towel, I patted my forehead, imagining Opa's words and hearing them in my ear.

Niet voor het hof brengen. No bringing the matter to court.

It's in the Bible.

Damn it.

I tossed the towel into the trash.

The church hid it. Perverted the whole thing. Stripped her of her dignity and her reputation in a community where survival without good standing just didn't happen.

∾

I hurried the children through the crowded church basement and up to the main floor. Seeing the downpour, Walt volunteered to get the car and pick us up at the door. My parents caught up with us in the foyer.

"Good-bye, Grandpa. Good-bye, Grandma."

They held Mark and Kate close. I wiped my eyes, hiding tears as my mother and father hugged them, loving them openly here.

My parents returned to the basement to find Aunt Dienke. While I waited for Walt with Mark and Kate, Mrs. Feenstra approached, clucking like her mentor used to do.

"Oh, Janie, your children. How lovely, dear. Let's see—they're adopted, right? But they look so much like you. Who would ever know? My, my, my."

I shrugged instead of speaking, instead of spitting in her face. Yes, Mrs. Feenstra. Our children. The loving kindness of our Lord in living color.

They will hear the old, old story. They will hear the story and picture the kitchen register and the woman who stood there shivering, not so easily warmed, regardless of slippers and housecoats and forced furnace air.

Mother. Her child. Born in sin.

Only not her sin. Your sin.

∼

It was raining Noah-style by now. We dashed out of the church and into the car.

"Let's go down Mom's old street!" Mark said when we were in our seat belts.

"Yeah!" his sister joined in. "Let's go down Mom's old street!"

"It's raining so hard, we won't be able to see much," Walt answered.

"Let's go anyway!"

"Yeah, let's go anyway," Kate said.

I must have looked unsettled. "You okay?" Walt asked.

"Yeah," I said.

"Want to take that way?"

"I guess. Sure."

He turned up the blower to defog the windows.

We drove through the alley, past the entrance of the tunnel beneath the intersection, onto the avenue along the four blocks I once so frequently walked.

Croften Street, Hogan Street, Lynch. The wipers scarcely kept up.

There it is. London Street.

He turned left onto the narrow street.

"That's the house. Look, Mark and Kate. That's it. See it through the rain?"

The front porch and steps. The painted bricks along the driveway. The garage my father built himself, piece by piece, week by week. The white picket fence and the gate that latched.

There it is—without the precisely trimmed bushes. Without the marigolds and hostas or swept sidewalk and curb. Without the windmill or tulips.

Rook, canasta, and Catechism. The house of casseroles, pancakes, and pea soup. The place where Reformation was a requirement. Where depravity was recognized and well known. Where election was elevated and people persevered in limited but irresistible grace. Where good and evil were too quickly defined. Where God was as predictable as pork chops. Where God played Hide and Seek.

The place of so many reconsiderations on a heated kitchen register.

All on the north side of London Street.

And where was the line? That line once as thick as my jump rope, as visible as the clothesline my mother filled on Monday mornings.

The line was no longer clear. So close. Inside us. The line was all the more blurred. Not because of the steadfast rain on the windshield was the antithesis hardly distinguishable.

We looked out from the automobile, watching the rain as it splashed the sidewalks, the downpour flowing along the pavement, the tears flooding my eyes. Sewers were not keeping up.

Someone was running along the sidewalk as the rain continued.

A young girl was running along the sidewalk in the rain.

Mama?

Mama?

edgments

go, you read the very first rough draft
me of the story's worth. Rough draft
t you have given me all along the way
you.

membering time in Marcia's home,
en we discussed music, painting, lit-
and these pages, makes me smile.

ofessor Basney critiqued my early
d revisions. Now and then he would
met each week to review a chapter
ave had his guidance.

ish professor and advisor at Calvin
ofessor Basney's death. You volun-
ed time each week to discuss them.
story regarding my father's antith-

ot: Many thanks for your reading,

k: Especially my editor, Matthew

omplun. I appreciate all your good
w   for any "Dutchisms."

To the Monday night writers' group: Sylvia Cooper, Edie Bajema,
Barbara Carvill, Kristy Quist, Carol Rottman, Mary VanderGoot. Thank
you. Special thanks, Sylvia, for the early reading, support and friendship.

To West Michigan Writers' Workshop—Extra credit to Steve Beck-
with. Special love and thanks to Sheila Shotwell, Lisa Mcallister, Nathan

TerMolen. A big thank you to my friend Pat Cook. Also, thank you Albert Bell, Vic Foerster, Dan Johnson, Fred Johnson, Sarah Kaake, Norma Lewis, Laura Rheame, Paul Robinson, Lisa Sokolwski, Bill Wheintzelman, John Wolohan, Brandon, Stephanie, Nicci, Jo—all of you.

To Bobo and Merv—For your trust and support even before reading the manuscript. And then more after. Thank you.

To my sisters:

Jackie—Sending warm wishes your way. Don't forget me.

Gracia—Thank you for always being my sister and for being dear.

Deannie—Before I was twelve, I recognized your independence and courage.

Babe—(d. 2012) We shared so much. I miss you.

To Mom and Dad: (d. 2010, d. 1997) Your devotion I admire and appreciate. Your love I have never doubted.

To Mark and Kate: My children. Welcome to the family. You've given me so much joy, so much joy, so much joy. Thank you.

To that guy: Tom. My husband and gem. He gets it. Endless love to you. Thank you for your ever-present encouragement. Let's dance.